# Punishment in International Society

# Perspectives on Justice and Morality

*Carolyn Hafer and Mario Gollwitzer*

Series Editor

## Books In The Series

*Unequal Foundations: Inequality, Morality, and Emotions Across Cultures*

Steven Hitlin and Sarah K. Harkness

*The Moral Punishment Instinct*

Jan-Willem van Prooijen

*Why People Radicalize: How Unfairness Judgments are Used to Fuel Radical Beliefs, Extremist Behaviors, and Terrorism*

Kees van den Bos

*Socializing Justice: The Role of Formal, Nonformal, and Family Education Spheres*

Clara Sabbagh

*Punishment in International Society: Norms, Justice, and Punitive Practices*

Wolfgang Wagner, Linet R. Durmuşoğlu, Barbora Holá, Ronald Kroeze, Jan-Willem van Prooijen, and Wouter Werner

# Punishment in International Society

*Norms, Justice, and Punitive Practices*

EDITED BY

**WOLFGANG WAGNER,
LINET R. DURMUŞOĞLU,
BARBORA HOLÁ, RONALD KROEZE,
JAN-WILLEM VAN PROOIJEN,
AND WOUTER WERNER**

**UNIVERSITY PRESS**

Oxford University Press is a department of the University of Oxford. It furthers the University's objective of excellence in research, scholarship, and education by publishing worldwide. Oxford is a registered trade mark of Oxford University Press in the UK and certain other countries.

Published in the United States of America by Oxford University Press
198 Madison Avenue, New York, NY 10016, United States of America.

© Oxford University Press 2024

All rights reserved. No part of this publication may be reproduced, stored in a retrieval system, or transmitted, in any form or by any means, without the prior permission in writing of Oxford University Press, or as expressly permitted by law, by license, or under terms agreed with the appropriate reproduction rights organization. Inquiries concerning reproduction outside the scope of the above should be sent to the Rights Department, Oxford University Press, at the address above.

You must not circulate this work in any other form
and you must impose this same condition on any acquirer.

Library of Congress Cataloging-in-Publication Data
Names: Wagner, Wolfgang, editor.
Title: Punishment in international society : norms, justice, and
punitive practices / [edited by] Wolfgang Wagner, Linet R. Durmuşoğlu,
Barbora Holá, Ronald Kroeze, Jan-Willem van Prooijen, and Wouter Werner.
Description: New York, NY : Oxford University Press, [2024] |
Series: Perspectives on justice and morality |
Includes bibliographical references and index. |
Identifiers: LCCN 2023032657 (print) | LCCN 2023032658 (ebook) |
ISBN 9780197693483 (hardback) | ISBN 9780197693506 (epub) | ISBN 9780197693513
Subjects: LCSH: Punishment. | Imprisonment. | Criminal justice, Administration of.
Classification: LCC HV8693 .P86 2024 (print) | LCC HV8693 (ebook) |
DDC 364.6—dc23/eng/20231031
LC record available at https://lccn.loc.gov/2023032657
LC ebook record available at https://lccn.loc.gov/2023032658

DOI: 10.1093/oso/9780197693483.001.0001

Printed by Integrated Books International, United States of America

# CONTENTS

Acknowledgments vii
Contributors ix

1. Norm Violations and Punishment Beyond the Nation-State: Normative Orders, Authority, and Conflict in International Society 1
   *Wolfgang Wagner, Linet R. Durmuşoğlu, Barbora Holá, Ronald Kroeze, Jan-Willem van Prooijen, and Wouter Werner*

2. A Social Psychological Approach to Punishment 17
   *Mario Gollwitzer, Melissa de Vel-Palumbo, Moritz Fischer, and Mathias Twardawski*

3. The Fruits of Wrongdoing in International Law: What Does (and Does Not) Happen When Laws Are Broken 44
   *Stephen C. Neff*

4. Penal Logics in International Politics: Nordic Foreign Policy on International Justice 73
   *Kjersti Lohne*

5. Punishment Beyond Borders: Attitudes Toward Punishment in Interpersonal and International Contexts 99
   *Linet R. Durmuşoğlu, Jan-Willem van Prooijen, and Wolfgang Wagner*

6. Why Sanctioning? The Rise and Purpose of Sanctions in
   International Politics  118
   *Michal Onderco*

7. Supporting the Punishment of Atrocity Crimes: A Broad Coalition
   Among a Narrow Elite  141
   *Mikkel Jarle Christensen*

8. International Sanctions and Contested Normative Authority  167
   *Elin Hellquist*

9. Deciphering International Punishments: A Perspective from the
   Global South  187
   *Siddharth Mallavarapu*

10. Punitivity and Norm-Setting in the History of Colonial and
    Postcolonial Relations: The End of the Inter-Governmental Group on
    Indonesia in 1992  209
    *Farabi Fakih and Ronald Kroeze*

Index  241

## ACKNOWLEDGMENTS

This book would not have been possible without the VUvereniging, a network of supporters with a link to Vrije Universiteit Amsterdam. The VUvereniging brought us together and provided generous funding for this interdisciplinary project. We are grateful to Willem Schoonen and Duco Stadig in particular for their support. We are also grateful to Lourdes Melese, who did a wonderful job in helping us edit, format, and index this volume.

# CONTRIBUTORS

**Mikkel Jarle Christensen** is a Professor WSR in iCourts at the Faculty of Law at the University of Copenhagen.

**Melissa de Vel-Palumbo** is a Senior Lecturer at the College of Business, Government, and Law, Flinders University, Adelaide.

**Linet R. Durmuşoğlu** is a PhD candidate in Political Science at the Amsterdam Institute for Social Science Research (AISSR) of the University of Amsterdam.

**Farabi Fakih** is a Lecturer and Senior Researcher at Universitas Gadjah Mada Yogyakarta and a Senior Researcher at Vrije Universiteit Amsterdam.

**Moritz Fischer** is a PhD student at the Department of Psychology at Ludwig-Maximilians-Universität München.

**Mario Gollwitzer** is a Professor of Social Psychology at the Department of Psychology at Ludwig-Maximilians-Universität München.

**Elin Hellquist** is a Researcher at the Department of Political Science at Stockholm University.

**Barbora Holá** is Senior Researcher at the Netherlands Institute for the Study of Crime and Law Enforcement and Associate Professor at the Department of Criminal Law and Criminology at Vrije Universiteit Amsterdam.

**Ronald Kroeze** is Professor of Parliamentary History and Director of the Centre for Parliamentary History, Radboud University Nijmegen.

**Kjersti Lohne** is a Professor at the Department of Criminology and Sociology at University of Oslo.

**Siddharth Mallavarapu** is a Professor and Head of Department at the Department of International Relations and Governance Studies at Shiv Nadar University.

**Stephen C. Neff** is a Professor of War and Peace at the University of Edinburgh.

**Michal Onderco** is a Professor of International Relations at the Department of Administration and Sociology at Erasmus University Rotterdam.

**Mathias Twardawski** is a Research Associate at the Department of Psychology at Ludwig-Maximilians-Universität München.

**Jan-Willem van Prooijen** is an Associate Professor of Psychology at Vrije Universiteit Amsterdam and Senior Researcher at the Netherlands Institute for the Study of Crime and Law Enforcement.

**Wolfgang Wagner** is a Professor of International Security at Vrije Universiteit Amsterdam.

**Wouter Werner** is Professor of International Law at Vrije Universiteit Amsterdam.

# 1

# Norm Violations and Punishment Beyond the Nation-State

*Normative Orders, Authority, and Conflict in International Society*

WOLFGANG WAGNER, LINET R. DURMUŞOĞLU,
BARBORA HOLÁ, RONALD KROEZE, JAN-WILLEM
VAN PROOIJEN, AND WOUTER G. WERNER

Throughout history, the punishment of norm violators has fostered cooperation and, in fact, helped small groups of early human hunters and gatherers survive (Greene, 2014). The "moral punishment instinct" (van Prooijen, 2018) is a part of human nature, and punitive practices can be found in every society. At the same time, punitive practices vary enormously between societies and over time. In his social history of prison reform in the late 18th century and early 19th century, Ignatieff (1978) traced how punishments directed at the body, such as whipping or public hanging, were replaced by solitary confinement as a new form of punishment directed at the mind. Although the "birth of the prison" (Foucault, 1975/1977) has been copied throughout the world, major differences in its use remain. Whereas growing prison populations in the United

Wolfgang Wagner, Linet R. Durmuşoğlu, Barbora Holá, Ronald Kroeze, Jan-Willem van Prooijen, and Wouter Werner, *Norm Violations and Punishment Beyond the Nation-State* In: *Punishment in International Society*. Edited by: Wolfgang Wagner, Linet R. Durmuşoğlu, Barbora Holá, Ronald Kroeze, Jan-Willem van Prooijen, and Wouter Werner, Oxford University Press. © Oxford University Press 2024. DOI: 10.1093/oso/9780197693483.003.0001

States, the United Kingdom, and other liberal democracies point to more retributionist penal philosophies since the late 1960s (Garland, 2012), Japan has emphasized reintegrative shaming and restorative justice (Braithwaite, 1989) in its response to norm violations.

Punitive practices are highly revealing of a society's social fabric, normative order, and power structure. In his classic *The Division of Labour in Society*, Emile Durkheim (1984) argued that criminal law is a perfect indicator of the norms and values of a society. In fact, the main function of criminal law to him was not to prevent harm in society and to deter potential wrongdoers but, rather, to express a society's norms and values and to make it aware of them. Similarly, Michel Foucault (1975/1977) examined changing punitive practices to demonstrate the emergence of new technologies of exercising power.

However, the social sciences and humanities have hitherto studied punishment mostly in the context of the nation-state by examining how people, organizations, and legal institutions punish individual offenders within national boundaries. This book examines punitive practices of a society that has barely been approached from such a perspective: international society.

The absence of a punitive lens on international politics is surprising because states and non-state actors invest enormous amounts of time and resources into the negotiation of international norms. Moreover, violations of international norms are regularly followed by the very moral outcry and indignation that characterize the response to the violation of norms in domestic society. In addition, states have responded to international norm violations with the imposition of sanctions that are also costly for themselves. The sanctions imposed on Russia after the full-scale invasion of Ukraine in 2022, for example, have driven up energy prices and further fueled inflation in the sanctioning countries in Europe and elsewhere.

However, we find several reasons for the reluctance to study punishment beyond the nation-state: First, the modern state system revolves around the principle of sovereign equality of states, which has also been firmly enshrined in modern international law. Although this system allows for arbitration in cases of disputes over the precise nature of commitments and obligations, it finds the notion that a sovereign would be judged and punished by a peer detrimental to its core principle of sovereign equality. This is not without irony because the moral punishment instinct evolved in the nonhierarchical context of small egalitarian groups. If anything, anarchy—that is, the absence of a central authority—should be particularly conducive to the emergence of punitive practices (Rathbun & Pomeroy, 2022).

This brings us to a second reason, namely that punishment in the absence of an established criminal law system comes with the stench of uncivilized, "wild justice" (Jacoby, 1983), vigilantism, and "rough justice" (Ballard & Douglas, 2017) that characterizes frontier societies and other areas of weak statehood. Such self-help or second-party punishment lacks impartiality and objectivity because avengers are likely to be acting out of self-interest and motivated by moral emotions such as anger. People generally prefer the delegation of punishment to a third party due to concerns about fairness. One core precondition to enable fair punishment is the impartiality and objectivity of the "punisher" (see procedural justice theory; Leventhal, 1980; Thibaut & Walker, 1975)—that is, the absence of a personal stake in the outcome for the punisher (e.g., there should be no personal relationship with either the victim or the perpetrator) along with an objective, emotionally detached assessment of the evidence. In the civilizational discourse of the late 19th century and the 20th century, the depersonalization and institutionalization of punishment have therefore been viewed as a marker of civilized, in contrast to "primitive," societies (Liszt, 1883/1948; Mauss, 1896/2012). Because international punishment has been institutionalized to a much lower extent, punitive practices are often justified under different headings, including self-defense or humanitarian intervention (Wagner & Werner, 2018).

Third and finally, punishment beyond the state becomes a form of *collective* punishment because international politics is made by corporate actors, first and foremost states. Holding entire societies accountable for norm violations that occurred in their name, however, is difficult to justify in an era that highly values individual human rights. The discomfort with collective punishment explains efforts to design targeted economic sanctions and use military force "surgically" and, of course, to have individuals tried in international tribunals. Notwithstanding these efforts, however, ordinary (and innocent) citizens remain affected by international punishment.

The reasons just mentioned explain why practitioners and observers of international politics have been uncomfortable with the notion of international punishment. The avoidance of the vocabulary of punishment, however, does not take away international punishment as an established practice in international politics.

## 1.1. PUNITIVE PRACTICES IN INTERNATIONAL POLITICS

In international society, punitive practices have assumed three main forms: sanctions, international(ized) courts and tribunals (ICTs), and the punitive use of armed force. First, growing interdependence since the late 19th century has made sanctions a popular instrument of deterrence, coercion, and punishment (Mulder, 2022). Although successful in some cases against minor powers, their record in targeting major powers has been poor, if not counterproductive (Mulder, 2022). Nevertheless, sanctions have remained frequently used instruments of economic statecraft. The Global Sanctions Data Base records more than 700 cases of economic sanctions since 1950—that is, binding restrictive measures applied by individual nations, country groups, the United Nations, and other international organizations to address different types of violations of international norms by inducing target countries to change their behavior or to constrain their actions (Felbermayr et al., 2020). Some of these sanctions have lasted for decades and severely crippled entire economies.

Second, ICTs have punished individuals, such as former heads of states and other governmental officials, army generals, rebel leaders, or ordinary foot soldiers, for international crimes.[1] Since the

---

1. International crimes are considered "the most serious crimes of international concern" and include genocide, crimes against humanity, and war crimes. See ICC Statute, Preamble, Arts 6, 7, and 8. We use the terms "international crimes" and "mass atrocities" interchangeably.

1990s,[2] several ad hoc ICTs dealing with specific situations of mass atrocities have been established by the international community, such as the International Criminal Tribunal for former Yugoslavia (ICTY),[3] the International Criminal Tribunal for Rwanda (ICTR),[4] and the Special Court for Sierra Leone (SCSL).[5] In 2002, the permanent International Criminal Court with a potentially universal reach and global jurisdiction was set up. In this form, international punitive practices resemble "ordinary" penal practices as we know them from nation states. Individuals are tried in front of a court of law, which is, however, representing not a single state or a national society but, rather, the international society and "humanity." If found guilty beyond any reasonable doubt, convicted individuals are sent to prison. In contrast to punishment in domestic criminal justice systems, the ICTs are not only courts of law but also important global political actors.[6] International punishment of individuals is highly selective (in a sense of what situations of mass atrocities end up within the purview of ICTs and in a sense of which individuals ultimately end up prosecuted by the ICTs within such situations) and dependent on the political will and cooperation of nation-states (Cryer, 2005; Levi et al., 2016). In addition, the ICTs' ambitions seem to be much "higher" and "broader" compared to domestic courts. The ICTs seek not only to respond to mass atrocity violence by holding individuals accountable and punishing them but also to transform the legal, political, and societal landscapes on global, regional, and national levels. They strive to establish international peace, to write history, to send messages about international normative order, to

2. The tribunals in Nuremberg, Germany, and Tokyo, Japan, are of course predecessors of the modern ICTs.

3. Statute of the International Criminal Tribunal for the Former Yugoslavia (adopted May 25, 1995) UNSC Res 827(1993), as amended (ICTY Statute).

4. Statute of the International Criminal Tribunal for Rwanda (adopted November 8, 1994) UNSC Res 955(1994), as amended (ICTR Statute).

5. Statute of the Special Court for Sierra Leone (adopted January 16, 2002) pursuant to UNSC Res 1315(2000) (SCSL Statute).

6. Of course, as the high-profile cases of Eichmann or Barbie illustrate, this can be different when a domestic court deals with international crimes.

promote rule of law, and to reconcile societies, among others. Whether and how punishment of selected individuals does and could achieve these ambitious goals have been hotly debated in the scholarship (Clark, 2014; Drumbl, 2007; Hola, 2012; Stahn, 2020; Wilson, 2011). In this context, one may also wonder about the extent to which international criminal trials are indeed only about the responsibility and punishment of individuals. The individuals—often prominent politicians or (para)military leaders—who stand trial invariably are part of a larger organization, a wider policy, and a criminal form of conducting politics. This wider context also stands trial, and thus so do the collectivities that enabled or supported the crimes.

Third and finally, military force has been used in response to norm violations in punitive ways. According to Lang (2009), "Punitive interventions are increasing in frequency since the end of the Cold War" (p. 77). In contrast to courts, tribunals, and sanctions, however, the punitive character of military force has almost always been downplayed and relegated to an undercurrent (Wagner & Werner, 2018). Typically, the language used to justify military intervention takes into account that punishment is not a legitimate reason for the use of force under international law. At the same time, it is meant to be deciphered as punitive by audiences at home as well as in the target state. Studies of U.S. public opinion have found that support for the use of force was driven, among other factors, by retributiveness and revenge motives. This has been shown for the 1991 and 2003 wars against Iraq (Liberman, 2006; Liberman & Skitka, 2017), for a hypothetical invasion of Syria (Washburn & Skitka, 2015), and for the hypothetical use of nuclear weapons against Iran (Rathbun & Stein, 2020; Sagan & Valentino, 2017). On the level of state policies, Rachel Stein (2019) finds that "democracies with more vengeful citizens tend to behave more belligerently" (p. 166). Onderco and Wagner find that large prison populations are a good predictor for democracies' confrontational response to a violation of nonproliferation norms by Iran and North Korea (Onderco & Wagner, 2017; Wagner & Onderco, 2014). Taken together, and notwithstanding official justifications as self-defense or humanitarian intervention, military force has frequently been used for purposes of international punishment.

## 1.2. THE VALUE-ADDED OF A PUNITIVE LENS ON INTERNATIONAL POLITICS

A punitive lens on international affairs contributes to our understanding of international society in three ways: It identifies which norms and values are at the core of the international order and its conception of justice, it helps identify structures of power and authority in international society, and an analysis of the penal philosophies that buttress the punitive enforcement of norms points to the potential for conflict and cooperation in international society.

First, as Durkheim and others emphasize, punishment has an expressive function in reinforcing support for community values and norms by expressing contempt for their violation. An examination of the punitive responses to international norm violations thus contributes to our understanding of the fundamental norms, core values, and concepts of justice in international society. As historian Nicolas Mulder (2022) shows, sanctions in the inter-war years "focused narrowly on stopping inter-state war" (p. 294) and addressed human rights violations only after 1945. During the Cold War, sanctions against the racist regimes in Rhodesia and South Africa reflected the minimalist normative consensus between the two antagonistic blocs. The proliferation of sanctions in response to violations of human rights, minority rights, and democratic standards and the establishment of courts and tribunals reflect the dominance of liberal values in the international normative order after the end of the Cold War.

Second, the analysis of punitive practices helps identify structures of power and authority in international society. As critical criminologists and sociologists have shown, punitive practices are embedded in a society's often unequal power relations, which might manifest in criminalization and harsh punishment for some conducts and/or groups of individuals and no repercussions or very lenient sanctions for others. As Garland (2002) argues, governments "quickly turn to penal solutions to deal with the behaviour of marginal[ized] populations rather than attempt to address the social and economic sources of their marginalization" (p. 200). Penal solutions "allow controls and condemnation to be focused on low-status outcast groups, leaving the behaviour of markets, corporations and the more affluent social classes relatively free of regulations and censure" (p. 201). Similarly, Rothe and Kauzlarich (2016) emphasize how "crimes of the powerful" often elude penal sanction and are "reframed as a 'bad decision' or a 'rare mistake'" despite an enormity of the harms such conduct ordinarily entails. Similarly, in international society, punitive practices reveal not only changing power differentials between particular (groups of) states but also the rising influence of non-state actors such as international organizations and nongovernmental organizations.

With a view to international relations, double standards in response to norm violations have often been lamented: Violations of the prohibition to use military force against the territorial integrity of another sovereign state have been met with military action in 1991 (Gulf War) and with sanctions in 2022 (Russia's invasion of Ukraine) but not in 2003 (U.S.-led invasion of Iraq). Similarly, defendants at the International Criminal Court in The Hague have come mostly from African countries, although Western countries have been accused of war crimes, too (Lough, 2011). Anthony F. Lang (2009) concludes that current punitive practices "designed to promote justice and peace produce unjust and violent outcomes" because "they do not exist within a just political order" (p. 3). And yet, even powerful states cannot escape the application of norms. The Iraq War led to parliamentary enquiries in the United Kingdom and the Netherlands, and the diplomatic damage of the illegal war was considerable (Börzel & Zürn, 2021, p. 295).

Third and finally, an analysis of the penal philosophies that buttress the punitive enforcement of international norms points to the potential for conflict and cooperation in international society. When retributivism guides public opinion and state behavior, conflicts are more likely to escalate because the use of force is viewed as an instrument to inflict the damage and pain that a norm violator deserves. In contrast, a rehabilitative penal philosophy that aims at the reintegration of wrongdoers into international society is much less likely to resort to coercion or the use of force.

Several authors have noted that the United States has been the main driver behind the proliferation of punitive practices in international politics (Lang, 2009; Mulder, 2022), and several military interventions, including in Afghanistan and Iraq, have been attributed to the idiosyncrasies of American counter-humiliation policy (Saurette, 2006).

## 1.3. CONTRIBUTIONS TO THIS VOLUME

The study of punitive practices is inherently interdisciplinary, and this certainly applies to international punishment as well. This book thus brings together scholars from the social and behavioral sciences, law, and the humanities. Building on the rich literature on punishment in social psychology, in Chapter 2, Mario Gollwitzer, Melissa de Vel-Palumbo, Moritz Fischer, and Mathias Twardawski introduce key concepts and definitions that are also highly useful for the study of *international* punishment. They emphasize that punishment is intentional, not incidental, and it is a sanction in response to a norm violation. In contrast to revenge, punishment is always embedded in a normative, often legal framework and is thus rule-based. Furthermore, they distinguish between punishment by the victim of a transgression (second-party punishment) and that by a third party who has not been directly involved in the original offense (third-party punishment). Gollwitzer et al. also discuss restorative justice as an alternative paradigm, which aims at the reparation of the relationship between victim and offender, typically involving both in a process of dialogue and healing. Taking the example of the U.S.-led war on terror, they discuss the challenges of applying a conceptual framework developed for interpersonal relations to the international realm in which the main actors are collectives.

In Chapter 3, Stephen C. Neff traces the evolution of responses to violations of international norms in the realm of international law. Reviewing a wide range of practices, including just wars, reprisals, self-defense, collective security, and humanitarian intervention, Neff concludes that the prime focus in international law has been on compensation rather than punishment. Although the system of international law has obviously undergone major changes since the Middle Ages, the shadowy existence of international punishment as a legal remedy for violations of the law has remained remarkably constant. This, Neff argues, reveals a major shortcoming of the international order, namely the absence of a community that is glued together by a thick web of shared norms. Emphasizing the contrast to nation-states, Neff views the fragmentation of international society as an obstacle to give punitive action a more prominent place in international law.

Similarly, in Chapter 4, Kjersti Lohne shows that the sociology of punishment has by and large assumed that penal power rests with the nation-state because there is neither a monopoly of force nor a public constituency of voters in international politics. Nevertheless, a transnational penality has been emerging, which is driven by the penal values and discourses of states and societies. To illustrate how domestic practices work as bridges to international punitive practices, Lohne analyzes the discourses about international criminal justice and about the prosecution of foreign fighters in Norway and Sweden. She identifies two main discourses that drive Nordic penal policies in international politics: A humanitarian discourse to "do something" about the suffering of distant others has been driving policy on international criminal justice. In contrast, security considerations have been at the forefront in the discourse about foreign fighters and their prosecution. In both countries, a penal humanitarianism has been used as a status-seeking device, asserting moral authority in international politics.

In Chapter 5, Linet Durmuşoğlu, Jan-Willem van Prooijen, and Wolfgang Wagner use experimental studies to explore whether and how support for international punishment is informed by penal philosophies in domestic society. They show that transgressions of international norms trigger similar punitive responses as violations of norms within a society. In addition, citizens' support for the use of punitive force corresponds closely to their support for punishment of individual offenders. At both levels of analysis, citizens consider the delegation of punishment to a third party more legitimate than second-party punishment. This gives the United Nations Security Council as the most obvious third party in international politics a prominent role in responding to norm violations. However, because the United Nations falls far short of an international monopoly of force, second-party punishment still enjoys a high level of support in the international context.

In Chapter 6, Michal Onderco examines a form of international punishment that has been distinct from, yet complementary to, the punitive use of force: the imposition of mostly economic sanctions. Their proliferation is puzzling because there is a broad consensus that sanctions rarely make targets change their behavior. Drawing on insights in sociology, criminology, and psychology, however, Onderco highlights the communicative function of sanctions as a signaling device. Imposing sanctions, then, is a way of expressing contempt for a norm violation and of confirming continued commitment to the validity of the norm that was violated. The shift to tailored, targeted sanctions reveals another key characteristic of the normative order: the appreciation of the individual and subsequent efforts to spare civilians from any harm inflicted by sanctions. In contrast to domestic society, however, the individualization of punishment is difficult to fully realize in international politics. This has made sanctions contested domestically as well as internationally and has motivated the search for alternative responses to norm violations, such as restorative justice.

The chapters by Mikkel Jarle Christensen (Chapter 7) and Elin Hellquist (Chapter 8) show how punitive practices are inextricably linked to questions of authority and power structure in international society. Christensen demonstrates that the emerging "cosmopolitan penality" for atrocity crimes—that is, international criminal justice—is driven by a predominantly well-educated male elite from or linked to the Global North. Although they claim to speak on behalf of the victims of international norm violation and international society more broadly, their vision of international justice remains tied to liberal internationalism and takes the legal systems of the Global North as unquestioned standards. This affects the ways in which international punishment is understood and implemented, as well as where its institutions and organizations, including international criminal courts and tribunals, focus their attention.

Hellquist shows how regional organizations have been claiming a place in the international sanctions landscape, reflecting the trend to regionalization since the end of the Cold War. Hellquist introduces a relational understanding of sanctions and punishment. From this perspective, the identity of the sanctioner matters for the target. Hellquist argues that the legitimacy of both unilateral and United Nations sanctions is tainted by their association with external interference. In contrast, regional sanctions are ingroup measures that draw their legitimacy from being imposed within a normative community. As the example of the African Union shows, they also resonate with ideas of restorative justice.

In Chapter 9, Siddharth Mallavarapu takes the perspective of the Global South, and of Third World Approaches to International Law in particular, to show how punitive practices have been inextricably linked to (post)colonial structures of power and inequality. For a long period of colonialism, punishment was done in defense of an unjust order that revolved around the exploitation of the South by the North. Mallavarapu also points to the question of reparations which has been conspicuously absent from the punitive discourse and practice in international society, probably because its focus on relations between collectives does not square well with the individualization of punishment that has characterized the Global North approach to norm violations.

In their case study of postcolonial relations between Indonesia and the Netherlands, Farabi Fakih and Ronald Kroeze show in Chapter 10 the close links between normative orders, power relations, and punitive practices. The colonial period stands out for an open, undisguised use of punishment in enforcing the unequal hierarchical relationship between colonizer and colonized. Fakih and Kroeze zoom in on the failed attempt of the Netherlands in 1992 to discipline the former colony of Indonesia by withholding development aid in response to the "Dili massacre" on East Timor in November 1991—a huge human rights violation conducted by the Suharto regime. Their detailed case study demonstrates how changes in power, status, and prestige have reversed the roles between the sender and target of punitive measures.

Taken together, the contributions to this volume show the added value of a punitive lens to international politics in at least three ways. First, punitive practices reveal the contours of the international normative order. Of course, international norms and normative orders can and have been studied without attention to punitive practices, focusing instead on the thick web of international treaties and agreements. Zooming in on the response to norm violations, however, a punitive lens can distinguish between norms whose violations trigger anger, disgust, and penal heat and those whose violations are understood in much milder terms or ignored. A punitive lens thus helps detect structures and hierarchies within the normative order. Such a perspective highlights the prominent position of individuals in the current normative order. Violations of individual rights are a recurrent trigger to impose sanctions or even initiate a procedure in a criminal court or tribunal. Individual rights also shape punitive practices by relying on targeted individualized sanctions whenever possible.

As several contributions to this volume remind us, however, support for the normative order is far from uniform. A punitive lens reveals a major cleavage in the international normative order between a Global North that emphasizes individualized, retributive punishment for atrocity crimes, even if implemented highly selectively, and a Global South that puts reparations for past colonial wrongs on the agenda. This cleavage is visible in the Northern elite consensus on punishing atrocity crimes and in many of the sanctions imposed on actors in the Global South.

Second, in contrast to a nation-state, the authority to sanction and thus to act in defense of the normative order is far more dispersed and contested in international society. Although limited to citizens from the Global North, survey experiments reveal that states taking justice into their own hands is the least legitimate and desired punitive practice in international society, analogous to domestic forms of self-help and vigilantism. Although there is a demand to embed punitive practices in procedures and institutions, the most legitimate site of such authority remains contested. Mirroring the trend toward regionalization that has characterized international politics since the end of the Cold War, regional organizations such as the African Union compete with the United Nations for the authority to sanction and act in defense of the normative order. Interestingly, this competition is associated with different penal philosophies: Whereas the United Nations Security Council and the international courts and tribunals subscribe to an often retributive logic, restorative justice seems to resonate more strongly in the African Union and the Global South more broadly.

Third, the contributions to this volume discuss two main competing penal philosophies. A restorative justice paradigm aims at the reparation of the relation between victim and offender and emphasizes compensation and reparations. It has a firm basis in international law, and it resonates particularly in the Global South. In contrast, a retributionist paradigm revolves around the principle of "just deserts." It projects penal practices that are firmly established in the nation-states of the Global North into the international realm.

## 1.4. OUTLOOK

This book cannot provide an exhaustive treatment of international punishment. The contributions to this volume are inroads into the understudied field of international punishment, but they can do little more than illustrate the added value of a punitive lens on international relations. Notwithstanding ever better data collections on sanctions, our knowledge of punitive practices in international politics remains incomplete. With the partial exception of the African Union (see Chapter 8), we know very little about punitive responses to norm violations below the level of the United Nations system and outside the Global North. In addition, we have only limited insights into the generalizability of findings on citizen attitudes toward appropriate punitive practices and procedures. The contributions to this volume give us reason to believe that a focus on atrocity crimes, on international courts and tribunals, and on a retributive penal philosophy that tends to claim our attention eclipses a plethora of alternative punitive practices with, among other things, stronger emphasis on restorative justice.

Because punitive practices are inextricably linked to structures of power and inequality, future research should study them also in the broader context of the crisis of the liberal international order. To the extent that the proliferation of international courts and tribunals and the individualization of punishment were driven by a Northern and Western elite, their future in a post-liberal international order appears uncertain at best. Rising powers may want to project alternative penal philosophies onto the international system, which raises interesting questions about the penal discourses in China, India, Brazil, and other countries.

Notwithstanding the differences between the criminal justice systems of nation-states and punitive practices in international politics, the penal heat triggered by the violation of fundamental norms does not differ fundamentally across the two domains. Whether it will be channeled through the current system of international courts and tribunals or whether states will fall back on practices of self-help has obvious consequences for international politics.

### References

Ballard, C., & Douglas, B. (2017). "Rough justice": Punitive expeditions in Oceania. *Journal of Colonialism and Colonial History*, 18(1), 1–11.

Börzel, T. A., & Zürn, M. (2021). Contestations of the liberal international order: From liberal multilateralism to postnational liberalism. *International Organization*, 75(2), 282–305.

Braithwaite, J. (1989). *Crime, shame and reintegration*. Cambridge University Press.

Clark, J. (2014). *International trials and reconciliation: Assessing the impact of the International Criminal Tribunal for the Former Yugoslavia*. Routledge.

Cryer, R. (2005). *Prosecuting international crimes: Selectivity and the international criminal law regime* (Cambridge Studies in International and Comparative Law Vol. 41). Cambridge University Press.

Drumbl, M. A. (2007). *Atrocity, punishment, and international law*. Cambridge University Press.

Durkheim, É. (1984). *The division of labour in society*. Palgrave Macmillan.

Felbermayr, G., Kirilakha, A., Syropoulos, C., Yalcin, E., & Yotov, Y. V. (2020). The Global Sanctions Data Base. *European Economic Review*, 129, Article 103561.

Foucault, M. (1977). *Discipline and punish: The birth of the prison*. Pantheon. (Original work published 1975)

Garland, D. (2012). *The culture of control: Crime and social order in contemporary society*. University of Chicago Press.

Greene, J. (2014). *Moral tribes: Emotion, reason, and the gap between us and them*. Penguin.

Hola, B. (2012). International sentencing: A game of Russian roulette or consistent practice? [PhD thesis]. Vrije Universiteit Amsterdam.

Ignatieff, M. (1978). *A just measure of pain: The penitentiary in the industrial revolution, 1750–1850*. Macmillan.

Jacoby, S. (1983). *Wild justice: The evolution of revenge*. Harper & Row.

Lang, A. F., Jr. (2009). *Punishment, justice and international relations: Ethics and order after the Cold War*. Routledge.

Leventhal, G. S. (1980). What should be done with equity theory? In K. J. Gergen, M. S. Greenberg, & R. H. Willis (Eds.), *Social exchange* (pp. 27–55). Springer.

Levi, R., Hagan, J., & Dezalay, S. (2016). International courts in atypical political environments: The interplay of prosecutorial strategy, evidence, and court authority in international criminal law. *Law and Contemporary Problems, 79*, 289–314.

Liberman, P. (2006). An eye for an eye: Public support for war against evildoers. *International Organization, 60*(3), 687–722.

Liberman, P., & Skitka, L. J. (2017). Revenge in US public support for war against Iraq. *Public Opinion Quarterly, 81*(3), 636–660.

Liszt, F. v. (1948). *Der Zweckgedanke Im Strafrecht*. Vittorio Klostermann. (Original work published 1883)

Lough, R. (2011). African Union accuses ICC prosecutor of bias. Reuters. https://www.reuters.com/article/ozatp-africa-icc-20110130-idAFJOE70T01R20110130

Mauss, M. (2012). *Schriften Zur Religionssoziologie*. Suhrkamp. (Original work published 1896)

Mulder, N. (2022). *The economic weapon: The rise of sanctions as a tool of modern war*. Yale University Press.

Onderco, M., & Wagner, W. (2017). The ideational foundations of coercion: Political culture and policies towards North Korea. *European Political Science Review, 9*(2), 279–302.

Rathbun, B. C., & Pomeroy, C. (2022). See no evil, speak no evil? Morality, evolutionary psychology, and the nature of international relations. *International Organization, 76*(3), 656–689.

Rathbun, B. C., & Stein, R. (2020). Greater goods: Morality and attitudes toward the use of nuclear weapons. *Journal of Conflict Resolution, 64*(5), 787–816.

Sagan, S. D., & Valentino, B. A. (2017). Revisiting Hiroshima in Iran: What Americans really think about using nuclear weapons and killing noncombatants. *International Security, 42*(1), 41–79.

Saurette, P. (2006). You dissin me? Humiliation and post 9/11 global politics. *Review of International Studies, 32*(3), 495–522.

Stahn, C. (2020). *Justice as message: Expressivist foundations of international criminal justice*. Oxford University Press.

Stein, R. M. (2019). *Vengeful citizens, violent states*. Cambridge University Press.

Thibaut, J. W., & Walker, L. (1975). *Procedural justice: A psychological analysis*. Erlbaum.

van Prooijen, J.-W. (2018). *The moral punishment instinct*. Oxford University Press.

Wagner, W., & Onderco, M. (2014). Accommodation or confrontation? Explaining differences in policies toward Iran. *International Studies Quarterly, 58*(4), 717–728.

Wagner, W., & Werner, W. (2018). War and punitivity under anarchy. *European Journal of International Security, 3*(3), 310–325.

Washburn, A. N., & Skitka, L. J. (2015). Motivated and displaced revenge: Remembering 9/11 suppresses opposition to military intervention in Syria (for some). *Analyses of Social Issues and Public Policy, 15*(1), 89–104.

Wilson, R. A. (2011). *Writing history in international criminal trials*. Cambridge University Press.

# 2

# A Social Psychological Approach to Punishment

MARIO GOLLWITZER, MELISSA DE VEL-PALUMBO, MORITZ FISCHER, AND MATHIAS TWARDAWSKI

> Our grief has turned to anger and anger to resolution. Whether we bring our enemies to justice or bring justice to our enemies, justice will be done.
> —George W. Bush (September 20, *2001*)

## 2.1. INTRODUCTION

On September 20, 2001, nine days after the terrorist attacks on the United States, in which almost 3,000 individuals lost their lives, U.S. President George W. Bush gave a speech to Congress. In this address, he revealed that the ringleaders behind the attacks were a "collection of loosely affiliated terrorist organizations known as al Qaeda,"[1] led by a person named Osama bin Laden. President Bush also declared that the United States would start a coordinated, large-scale, long-term military operation referred to as the

---

1. https://www.washingtonpost.com/wp-srv/nation/specials/attacked/transcripts/bushaddress_092001.html.

Mario Gollwitzer, Melissa de Vel-Palumbo, Moritz Fischer, and Mathias Twardawski, *A Social Psychological Approach to Punishment* In: *Punishment in International Society*. Edited by: Wolfgang Wagner, Linet R. Durmuşoğlu, Barbora Holá, Ronald Kroeze, Jan-Willem van Prooijen, and Wouter Werner, Oxford University Press. © Oxford University Press 2024. DOI: 10.1093/oso/9780197693483.003.0002 "war on terror" with the ultimate goal to stop and defeat "every terrorist group of global reach," starting with the al Qaeda network.

It is interesting to note that President Bush avoided words such as "punishment" or "revenge" in his speech. In fact, he used the word "retaliation" only once ("Our response involves far more than instant retaliation and isolated strikes"). In retrospect, however, many would agree that the war on terror was indeed a punitive, retaliatory, vengeful act against a fuzzy social category of violent (or violent-prone) radical Islamists, as the quote at the beginning of this chapter testifies (see also Liberman & Skitka, 2019; Washburn & Skitka, 2015). Thus, America's war on terror represents a viable example for punishment in politics. In this chapter, we use this example to discuss whether and to what extent theory and research on punishment from the area of social psychology can be applied to punitive acts in international politics.

We admit up-front that this is a risky endeavor: After all, the context in which punishment has been investigated in social psychology is typically restricted to post-transgression interactions (a) between one victim and one offender (i.e., without any group context; *interpersonal punishment*), (b) between victim(s) and offender(s) who belong to the same group (e.g., organization, team, or classroom; *intragroup punishment*), or (c) between victim(s) and offender(s) who belong to different groups (e.g., sports teams, religious, or ethnic categories; *intergroup punishment*). Punishment between *states*, however, is different from these contexts in that it is typically commanded by an authority (e.g., the U.S. President), exercised by a specialized force (e.g., the military), approved by an executive or a legislative institution (e.g., the parliament), and often (more or less) indirectly accepted by the citizens of the respective nation. Empirically, we do know something about the latter perspective—that is, the level of public support for specific (punitive) policies (e.g., public endorsement of harsh interrogations, torture, or capital punishment; Carlsmith & Sood, 2009; Ellsworth & Ross, 1983; Lindén et al., 2016).[2] But these data do not

---

2. Note that these data are typically collected in democratic countries.

necessarily allow us to test a comprehensive conceptual framework for understanding punishment in politics.

So, despite the higher level of complexity with regard to punishment between states, we think it is worthwhile to examine the social psychological literature on punishment and to cautiously reflect on whether any of the findings from that literature can be used to understand and explain at least some phenomena in the international politics arena, such as America's war on terror.

## 2.2. CONCEPTS AND DEFINITIONS

### 2.2.1. Punishment, Retaliation, and Revenge

In social psychology, punishment is defined as "a negative sanction intentionally applied to someone perceived to have violated a law, rule, norm, or expectation" (Vidmar & Miller, 1980, p. 568). The crucial elements of this definition are (a) punishment is an intentional behavior (not an incidental one), (b) it is a negative response toward a negative act (i.e., a violation of some kind of norm), and (c) it is the subjective perception that this negative act represents a norm violation—the existence of some objective standard for evaluating the act is not necessary. The latter point may sound trivial at first glance, but it is important: Even in the absence of a codified law or a commonsense justice rule, acts may be subjectively interpreted as a norm violation. This points to an axiom that is fundamental for the social psychology of justice and morality: What is "just" is always in the eye of the beholder (e.g., Walster et al., 1978), and, thus, different people will always give different answers to the question whether a punishment is "fair," "deserved," or "appropriate" (Gollwitzer & Sjöström, 2017).

Legal scholars and philosophers typically argue that punishment is something conceptually different than revenge. Their point is that punishment requires a normative frame, a law (i.e., penal code), in order to be considered legitimate and fair. Francis Bacon (1601/1985), for instance, talked about revenge as "a kind of wild justice, which the more man's nature runs to, the more ought law to weed it out" (p. 11), and Sir James Fitzjames Stephen (1863/1985)—historian, legal scholar, and philosopher (and uncle of Virginia Woolf)—noted that "the criminal law stands to the passion of revenge in much the same relation as marriage to the sexual appetite" (p. 99). In social psychology, the terms "punishment" and "revenge" are used differently, and the conceptual distinction between these terms is less sharp as in legal philosophy (e.g., Nozick, 1981). This is because the sentiments that underlie people's judgments regarding the appropriateness of a legal sanction are largely the same as the sentiments that guide vengeful inclinations (Gollwitzer, 2009). However, also in the social psychological literature, the term revenge carries more semantic baggage than the term punishment: In its prototypical form, revenge is often considered as a highly emotional (i.e., anger-driven) response enacted by the victim outside a legal/normative structure, whereas punishment is often considered to be more rule-based and, thus, normatively appropriate.

### 2.2.2. Second-Party and Third-Party Punishment

When a victim (i.e., an individual who feels unjustly treated by another individual) punishes the offender in response to what they did to them, we call this *second-party punishment*. Another form of interpersonal punishment occurs when another person, who has not been directly involved in the original offense, exercises the punitive act. This is referred to as *third-party punishment* (Fehr & Fischbacher, 2004; Lieberman & Linke, 2007; Pfattheicher et al., 2019). Third-party punishment, which is sometimes also labeled "altruistic" punishment (because punishers do not necessarily benefit directly from investing their resources into punishing the offender; e.g., Leibbrandt & López-Pérez, 2011), has attracted ample attention from evolutionary psychologists and behavioral economists—probably because this behavior is so apparently inconsistent with the "rational choice" axiom. From a social psychological perspective, there is not much to be surprised about third-party punishment: It reflects humans' genuine concern for justice (e.g., Miller, 2001; van Prooijen, 2018).

Social psychological research has elucidated the conditions under which third-party punishment is more versus less likely to occur and when third-party punishment is more versus less severe than second-party punishment. A quite large body of research has examined the role of inter- and intragroup dynamics: Research shows, for instance, that offenders from a social group to which the punisher does *not* belong (an "out-group") are punished more harshly than offenders who belong to the same social group as the offender ("in-group")—even though the transgression was the same (e.g., Lieberman & Linke, 2007; Yudkin et al., 2016).[3] Similarly, third-party punishment is typically harsher when the victim belongs to the punisher's in-group versus an out-group ("parochial altruism"; Bernhard et al., 2006). In addition, individuals experience more anger and moral outrage—emotions that strongly predict punishment—when the victim is an in-group compared to an out-group member (Lickel et al., 2006; Stenstrom et al., 2008). Based on the assumption that people's identity partly depends on their memberships in social groups—a core tenet of social identity theory (Tajfel, 1981; Tajfel & Turner, 1986)—harming an in-group member threatens one's social identity by reducing collective self-esteem (e.g., Luhtanen & Crocker, 1992). Therefore, attacks on one's group increase group members' motivation to prosecute offenders partly for self-protective purposes. Thus, the magnitude of third-party punishment heavily depends on the extent to which a punisher identifies with the victimized group (Lickel et al., 2006; Yzerbyt et al., 2003). We discuss this in more detail later, when we introduce the concept of vicarious retribution.

---

3. Note, however, that in some situations, in-group offenders are punished *more* harshly than out-group offenders—a phenomenon that has been referred to as the *black sheep effect* (Marques et al., 1988). Interestingly, in-group favoritism in punishment and the black sheep effect are rooted in basically the same motive: to derive a positive social identity (either by perceiving the in-group members' misbehavior as less severe or by derogating unlikable in-group members). Whether people are more or less tolerant with in-group members' misbehavior depends on context characteristics, such as intergroup status differences (van Prooijen & Lam, 2007), the salience of intergroup stereotypes (Sommers & Ellsworth, 2000), the probability that the offender is actually guilty (Kerr et al., 1995; Taylor & Hosch, 2004), or the offender's record of prior transgressions (Gollwitzer & Keller, 2010).

## 2.2.3. Displaced, Collective, and Vicarious Punishment

Three more concepts from the social psychological literature are relevant for punishment in international politics: displaced, collective, and vicarious punishment. Punishment is *displaced* to the extent that the target of a punitive reaction is not the same person who committed the original offense (Gollwitzer & Sjöström, 2017). *Collective* punishment means that an entire group is being punished for an offense committed by a member of that group (Pereira et al., 2015). In addition, displaced or collective punishment that is exercised by a third party (instead of the victim themself) is referred to as *vicarious* punishment (Lickel et al., 2006).

The term "displaced" is borrowed from the literature on displaced aggression: It denotes aggressive responses toward provocations where the target of the aggressive act is not the same person as the original provocateur (Bushman et al., 2005; Marcus-Newhall et al., 2000). Research shows that displaced punishment is more likely to occur when the displaced target and the original offender share some similarities or can be categorized into the same social group. The degree to which a target and the original offender are perceived as interchangeable—even if they merely share some superficial commonalities—makes displaced punishment more likely to occur (Lickel et al., 2006; Stenstrom et al., 2008). Furthermore, the perception of interchangeability (or "entitativity"; see Campbell, 1958) increases a victim's perception that displaced revenge is deserved and appropriate (Sjöström et al., 2018; Sjöström & Gollwitzer, 2015). And because scapegoating often functions as a way for victims to re-establish control in response to highly threatening or inexplicable events (Rothschild et al., 2012), perceptions of entitativity might also be formed post hoc, as a justification to satisfy victims' need for revenge. In line with these findings, survey studies among U.S. Americans showed that hate crimes in the United States against Arab Americans, Muslims, and similar targets increased dramatically after the September 11, 2001 (9/11), attacks (Skitka et al., 2009); probably because these targets were perceived as an entitative social category. Also, public support for the

Iraq invasion in March 2003, on which the G. W. Bush administration insisted even though evidence for an active involvement of the Iraqi government in the 9/11 attacks had always been weak (and partly false), can be explained by the American public's desire for displaced punishment and perceptions of entitativity (Liberman & Skitka, 2019; Washburn & Skitka, 2015).

Collective punishment—aggressive responses against an entire group to which the offender belongs—can be explained along those lines, too (Gaertner et al., 2008; Newheiser et al., 2012). Just as displaced punishment (against single individuals), collective punishment is positively related to the perceived entitativity of the offender group. One important factor in this regard is the extent to which other group members, including those who have not been involved in the original offense, are held responsible for the offense (Denson et al., 2006; Lickel et al., 2003): The more the offender group is perceived as entitative, the more likely victims think that each and every group member carries some responsibility for what happened because they (a) indirectly contributed or (b) could (and should have) prevented the offense (Newheiser et al., 2012). Thus, Americans' public support for a war against Iraq as a response to 9/11 may have been motivated by a desire for collective punishment against 'them' (Skitka et al., 2006).

Last, the concept of vicarious punishment may be vital for the topic of this book and the purposes of this chapter. This concept describes the combination of third-party punishment and displaced punishment. In a vicarious punishment episode, "neither the agent of retaliation nor the target of retribution were directly involved in the original event that precipitated the intergroup conflict" (Lickel et al., 2006, p. 373). After all, when a state punishes another state (or some other social entity) for some unjust action, neither the immediate victims of that initial injustice are identical to those who command or exercise the punishment nor are the offenders facing the punishment. The war on terror that George W. Bush declared in response to the 9/11 attacks is, thus, a form of vicarious punishment (Huddy & Feldman, 2011; Morgan et al., 2011).

## 2.3. PUNISHMENT GOALS AND MOTIVES

Punishment is a response toward a perceived norm violation. But what exactly does punishment aim at? In other words, what do punishers hope to achieve by investing their own resources into harming others? The philosophical literature has distinguished two different purposes of punishment (which may be represented as goals or motives in the punisher's mind): retribution and utilitarianism. *Retribution* is based on the normative argument that punishment should rebalance the scales of justice or close the "injustice gap." According to this view, punishment should "fit" a norm violation in terms of its moral reprehensibility—psychologically speaking, it should be proportional to the amount of anger and moral outrage it produces (Darley & Pittman, 2003). *Utilitarianism*, by contrast, is based on the normative argument that punishment is only morally justifiable if the benefits outweigh the costs, including the damage done to the offender. Thus, punishment should be effective in reducing recidivism (specific deterrence), deterring others from committing similar wrongdoings in the future (general deterrence), or protecting society by incapacitating the offender (Carlsmith & Darley, 2008).

The social psychological literature has been heavily inspired by this philosophical dichotomy. Early work in this area has asked whether people think, feel, and act more like a "retributivist" (i.e., according to the motto "an eye for an eye") or rather like a "utilitarianist" (i.e., according to the motto "the end justifies the means"). Many empirical findings suggest that the intuitive conceptualization of punishment in people's minds is a retributive one: Punishment should "fit the crime," rebalance the scales of justice, and be proportional to the offender's responsibility for the wrongdoing. Moreover, punishment is strongly associated with anger about the offense. The extent to which a punitive response deters the offender or others from engaging in future misbehavior, by contrast, appears to be less of an issue when thinking about punishment (e.g., Carlsmith & Darley, 2008; see also Twardawski et al., 2022).

More recent research has moved beyond the retribution/deterrence dichotomy and started examining the proximal goals that people pursue when considering (or exercising) punishment. This work suggests that what victims care about is to send a moral message to the offender—a message that implies both a moral condemnation of the offense and a lesson to be learned for the future (French, 2001; Heider, 1958). Experimental and survey studies consistently show that exercising punishment leads to more positive affect, a stronger sense of justice achieved, and more psychological closure on the side of the victim if this message is received and understood by the offender (Gollwitzer & Sjöström, 2017; Miller, 2001). Thus, the crucial feature of punishment is that it is a communicative act (Cushman et al., 2022; Sarin et al., 2021), which contains retributive as well as deterrent elements.

### 2.3.1. Punitive Messages in Interpersonal Contexts

A punitive message can come in different flavors and emphasize different aspects (at the cost of other aspects). Research suggests that the variability in messages can at least partly be accounted for by the context in which the punishment occurs. In many interpersonal contexts, victims seem to be concerned with sending a "moral change" message to the offender: They want to make the offender understand that the offender's behavior was morally wrong and that it is not to be repeated (Aharoni et al., 2022; Fischer et al., 2022; Funk et al., 2014). The goal of effecting a moral change in the offender is more important than other goals, such as regaining a sense of power and status vis-à-vis the offender (Fischer et al., 2022; Twardawski et al., 2021) or achieving a balance in suffering (Gollwitzer et al., 2011).

The conceptual difference between moral condemnation (as part of a punitive message) and retribution is crucial in that regard. In its purest sense, retribution is about rebalancing the scales of justice: the proverbial "eye for an eye." So, if punishment was all about retribution, *anything* that brings the scales into balance should be hedonically beneficial for the victim—including fateful harm befalling the offender. Research shows, however, that this is not the case: Seeing the offender suffer from fate is typically less satisfying for a victim than punishing the offender and delivering a message (Gollwitzer & Denzler, 2009; Gollwitzer et al., 2011; Gollwitzer & Sjöström, 2017). Recent findings suggest that offender suffering does indeed impact retributive reactions, but more so when delivering a message is not possible (Aharoni et al., 2022).

### 2.3.2. Punitive Messages in Intragroup Contexts

When a punitive episode involves more individuals than just the victim and the offender (e.g., *within* a sports team, an organization, or a group of friends), the message delivered via punishment often has a slightly different flavor: It is still a message of moral condemnation (i.e., retributive), but its "utility" lies in reinforcing consensus about the validity of the norm that the transgression has (symbolically) violated (Duff, 2001; Feinberg, 1965; Vidmar, 2001). That is, in such situations, punishing misbehavior (publicly) aims at reaffirming value consensus both within the in-group and against other out-groups (Okimoto & Wenzel, 2009). Importantly, such value concerns play a major role in intragroup as opposed to intergroup conflicts (Wenzel et al., 2008).

### 2.3.3. Punitive Messages in Intergroup Contexts

When a punitive episode involves an intergroup context—that is, when victim and offender belong to different social categories and the group context is salient (e.g., conflicts *between* sports teams, organizations, peer groups etc.)—the punitive message is different. It still contains a moral condemnation of the offense, but a core element of that message is the display of power, strength, and vigilantism toward the offender group (Okimoto & Wenzel, 2009; Wenzel et al., 2008). The message to be delivered in that case is more "Don't mess with us!" instead of "I want you to become a better person." Again, it is important to note that sending this message is more than simply rebalancing the scales of justice (i.e., retribution). For instance, research shows that displaced revenge—punitive acts addressing an uninvolved member of the offender's group—is most satisfying when both the original offender and the displaced target understand why the punishment occurred (Sjöström et al., 2018). Without such understanding, displaced revenge fails to reach its goal and is less satisfying for the punisher. This finding suggests that delivering a message ("Don't mess with us!") is more than just harming the offender or the group to which the offender belongs.

More direct evidence for this theorizing comes from two studies (Gollwitzer et al., 2014) that examined people's hedonic reactions toward the death of Osama bin Laden, who was assassinated by U.S. Navy Seals on May 2, 2011, in a secret hideout in Pakistan. In a first study, Gollwitzer et al. (2014) measured the extent to which Americans experienced (a) a sense of justice achieved and (b) psychological closure after bin Laden's death. The data from this study, which were collected in June and July 2011, were matched with data from a survey from early 2003, in which the same respondents were asked about their support for the U.S. invasion in Iraq, commanded by President G. W. Bush. Specifically, participants were asked how much the Iraq War would help resolve "a sense of moral outrage about the 9/11 terrorist attacks," "a desire to hurt those responsible for the 9/11 attacks," and "a compelling need for vengeance for the 9/11 attacks"—in other words, a desire for vicarious retribution for the 9/11 attacks. Despite the time interval of more than 8 years between these two measurement occasions, retributive desires in 2003 reliably predicted a sense of justice achieved after bin Laden's death in 2011—above and beyond general attitudes toward retribution, political ideology, and demographics. This speaks to the idea that Americans' support for the Iraq War in 2003 was motivated not only by deterring a potential attack by former Iraqi leader Saddam Hussein, as the Bush administration liked to frame it at that time, but also by a desire for retribution (Liberman & Skitka, 2019; Washburn & Skitka, 2015). A second important finding from that study is that retributive desires in 2003 predicted a sense of justice achieved in 2011 uniquely via perceptions that killing bin Laden had sent a message to the world not to mess with the United States—over and above expectations of the deterrent effects of the assassination or feelings of safety. In other words, the main driving force underlying Americans' hedonic reactions to the death of Osama bin Laden was the perception that his assassination had delivered the message "Don't mess with us!" which, as we have argued, has both retributive and utilitarian flavor to it.

In a second study, Gollwitzer et al. (2014) scrutinized whether the communicative feature of punishment can be empirically separated from mere retribution. First, participants were given a brief report about the actual circumstances of bin Laden's death and reported their degree of justice-related satisfaction (i.e., the feeling that justice has been done and psychological closure is possible). Next, participants were presented with five different counterfactual scenarios, according to which bin Laden had been (a) killed by the Pakistani Secret Service, (b) killed by the British military, (c) killed during an air strike led by U.S. military forces, (d) killed during an accidental airplane crash, or (e) captured alive and taken to court. If punishment was merely about rebalancing the scales of justice, then all of these scenarios should be satisfying. However, results showed that Americans experienced a stronger degree of satisfaction about the killing as it actually happened compared to the scenario in which Osama bin Laden would have been killed in an airplane crash. Again, this shows that delivering a message via punishment is more than just "comparative suffering."

The communicative aspects of intergroup conflict (both in appraising the initial threat and its punishment) also play a key role in the vicarious retribution model (Lickel et al., 2006). First, intergroup threats carry a symbolic meaning and, thus, elicit a strong motivation for retribution among those being attacked. This symbolic meaning is emphasized if the provocation targets people or symbols that are of particular relevance for the defining nature of the group. This is particularly apparent in the case of the 9/11 attacks, which deliberately targeted national symbols of the United States: the World Trade Center, the Pentagon, and the White House. This communicative aspect of intergroup threat strongly fuels people's demands for vicarious retribution.

So far, we have extensively discussed the communicative aspects of (vicarious) retribution between groups—the message that the victim group aims to send to the offender group. In addition, it is worth examining the communicative aspects of vicarious punishment within the victim group: After all, such punishment is often commanded and enforced by political authorities (e.g., President G. W. Bush in the case of the 9/11 attacks). It is plausible to assume that commanding vicarious punishment as a political authority resonates with the specific social expectations tied to the authority role: Citizens may *expect* their political leaders to promote retaliation against a threatening enemy. If leaders do not respond accordingly, they risk losing approval by their followership (Hogg et al., 2012). However, vicarious retribution is not just expected from people in leadership positions. Rather, in-group members may perceive it as mandatory to retaliate on behalf of their fellow in-group members (e.g., when victims are not capable of defending themselves) and may perceive it as deviant or a sign of insufficient commitment to the group if one fails to meet these expectations (e.g., by refusing to execute or support vicarious retaliation; Shaw et al., 2017). Importantly, the degree to which people expect that an intergroup threat is responded to with vicarious retribution may be culturally shaped. More precisely, such a response may be perceived as more normatively appropriate (and thus expected) in some groups than in others. The extent to which (vicarious) retribution may be shaped by cultural norms is described in more detail in the next section.

## 2.4. CULTURAL ASPECTS

Retaliatory responses to norm violations can be more or less culturally prescribed. One cultural dimension that appears to be particularly relevant in that regard is "culture of honor" norms (Nisbett & Cohen, 1996). According to the anthropological literature, culture of honor norms have primarily developed in regions where (a) people were highly vulnerable to losing their entire wealth through theft and (b) the government was not adequately capable of preventing or prosecuting theft (Shackelford,

2015). One region where these conditions were present is the U.S. South. Historically, many people in this region worked as herdsman. Herding, compared to other forms of agriculture (e.g., farming), had a relatively high risk for theft. At the same time, the U.S. South was characterized by low population density, which made it difficult for authorities to prosecute crimes. This geographical structure might have sparked the emergence of an independent "system of order," in which people tried to deter norm violations such as theft by establishing a public image of being strong and "ready to retaliate," even against minor transgressions.

In a line of empirical research using the U.S. South as an exemplary culture of honor region, psychologists have demonstrated that men from these regions show stronger emotional, physiological, and behavioral responses to minor provocations (e.g., an insult) than men from northern regions (Cohen et al., 1996). Likewise, rates of homicide committed by White men are higher in the U.S. South compared to the North, but only for homicides resulting from brawls and not for felony-related homicides (e.g., those resulting from burglary; Nisbett & Cohen, 1996). Moving beyond the U.S. context, Kugler et al. (2013) have shown that compared to German participants, respondents from the United States and Canada—two "frontier societies"—were more lenient in their punishments of people who were reacting with extreme, often lethal, force in response to attacks on themselves, their neighbors, and their property, even when those attacks went far beyond the bounds of what the legal codes would allow.

How can this line of research inform punishment in international politics? In essence, these findings speak to the idea that retaliating in response to a norm violation can be culturally demanded or—viewed from the other angle—that *not* retaliating against transgressions might result in public perceptions as being weak and vulnerable. Thus, when conflict parties strongly endorse culture of honor norms, even small transgressions might escalate into severe, violent conflicts because both conflict parties are motivated to mutually demonstrate their strength and toughness. Applying this idea to conflicts in international politics, punishment might be particularly prevalent and harsh when honor is a central norm in at least one of the involved states. Moreover, drawing on the idea that cultures of honor emerged in regions with little capacity for governmental crime prosecution (Shackelford, 2015), we can expect that the conflict-escalating effects of honor norms might be particularly pronounced in contexts without capacity for official recourse to a superordinate authority (e.g., an intergovernmental organization such as the United Nations, which can apply sanctions to offending states).

## 2.5. RESTORATIVE JUSTICE

So far, we have discussed punitive responses that inflict damage or suffering on the offender. There are, however, alternative responses to injustice that may nonetheless fulfill similar justice goals. Key among these is the restorative justice paradigm, which arose in the criminal justice context to overcome limitations of traditional punitive approaches. Restorative justice theory and practices vary widely, but most commonly they invite the active participation of the offender, victim, and other affected parties in a process that aims to repair harm and restore the social relations broken by an offense. Parties collectively come to an understanding about what happened and what further action is required. The focus is on dialogue, healing, and consensus. Research consistently shows that victims view restorative justice practices as fairer and more satisfying than alternative procedures, and they report a reduced desire for revenge following these procedures (Latimer et al., 2005; Strang et al., 2013). But what makes this form of justice particularly compelling to victims?

People's motives for restorative justice are not entirely different from those for more retributive forms of justice, but the emphasis on the various goals differs. First, like more punitive responses, restorative justice can rebalance the harm done to victims. There is also some evidence that restorative justice offers a forum for communicating the offender's suffering, which gives some victims satisfaction (Batchelor, 2021). But rather than humiliating or degrading the offender, restorative justice is more often characterized as rebalancing harm through *constructive* actions that materially or symbolically repair the harm done to the victim, such as apology and restitution (Johnstone, 2011). The importance of avoiding the humiliation of the offender is key to the notion of "reintegrative shaming" (i.e., shaming the act, not the person; Braithwaite, 1989). Moreover, restorative justice can redress the power and agency lost by the victim as a result of the transgression through their active participation in the punishment process. Typically, victims have little say in formal punishment contexts such as the criminal justice system (Christie, 1977), and restorative practices provide victims—and any other affected parties, such as members of the community—with a voice in decision-making, which contributes to judgments of fairness (Beven et al., 2005; Tyler, 2006).

But the power of restorative justice is thought to lie primarily in its ability to achieve a renewed consensus about the shared values violated by the transgression (Wenzel et al., 2012; Wenzel & Thielmann, 2006). Gaining a shared understanding of what happened, whereby offenders endorse the validity of the violated values through remorse and apology, is central to restorative justice. In line with this, research has revealed that victims view restorative justice as a way to help the offender change (Doak & O'Mahony, 2006; Shapland et al., 2006), and in fact, an offender's stated intention to "do something" about their offending is seen as a form of reparation in itself (Shapland et al., 2008). And whereas for more punitive forms of justice, values are affirmed *against* the offender, in restorative justice they are affirmed through consensus *with* the offender (Wenzel et al., 2008). Thus, restorative justice, arguably more so than other forms of justice, ensures offenders truly "get the message" of moral condemnation.

In summary, restorative justice contains many of the same communicative elements of punishment explored in the previous sections of this chapter. The distinctive aspects of a restorative approach, however, are the underlying intention of constructive action (vs. deprivation or degradation) and the communal and consensual process through which consensus is achieved. This means that different forms of justice may be preferred under different circumstances. For example, empirical research suggests that people may opt for restorative over retributive forms of justice when the norm violation is less serious; but to achieve justice after more severe transgressions, people prefer both be deployed (Gromet & Darley, 2006).

Moreover, because restorative justice aims to validate values, it is likely to be more desirable and satisfying in contexts in which there is some existing shared framework that permits moral consensus to be achieved (Okimoto et al., 2009; Wenzel & Thielmann, 2006).

In the realm of international politics, restorative justice is perhaps most closely manifested in truth commissions and other forms of transitional justice that emphasize the rebuilding of social and political relationships (Amstutz, 2005). In this context, reparations may involve financial compensation to victims or reform of political institutions and practices. One example is the South African Truth and Reconciliation Commission, which framed itself as restorative as opposed to the more retributive Nuremberg trials (Allais, 2011). Although not without critics, such commissions have the potential to be a therapeutic tool to promote future peace and stability (Allan & Allan, 2000).

However, securing public support for restorative justice may be challenging on the world stage. Intergroup relations are normally characterized by differences between parties, rather than shared norms and values (which are necessary for restorative justice to be achieved). Nevertheless, even very different groups may have mutual values worth validating (e.g., basic human rights), and finding—and communicating—such common ground would be crucial in securing the legitimacy of restorative justice in these contexts. In addition, for restorative justice to make sense, there would need to be some motivation for coming to a shared moral understanding. Therefore, where people see little capacity or harbor little desire for a cooperative relationship going forward, they might seek more retributive forms of justice (Okimoto et al., 2010).

## 2.6. CONCLUSION

Our goal in this chapter was to introduce social psychological concepts, theories, and research findings that we believe are relevant to the topic of this book—punishment in international politics. Although social psychological theorizing has been largely focused on punishment episodes between individuals or groups, this literature may nonetheless be informative for a conceptual investigation of punishment between states, nations, or other social entities in international politics.

First, we differentiated between second-party (punisher = victim) and third-party punishment (punisher ≠ victim). This differentiation is relevant for our present purpose because in political conflicts, the punisher is rarely the immediate victim. Research on third-party punishment has shown that this type of punishment is most likely to occur when an out-group member transgresses against an in-group member (i.e., the intergroup bias in third-party punishment; see Yudkin et al., 2016) and when third-party punishers highly identify with their group (Lickel et al., 2006; Yzerbyt et al., 2003).

Next, we introduced the terms displaced, collective, and vicarious punishment. In all of these cases, a punitive reaction harms not (only) the transgressor but other individuals, who may be more or less affiliated with the original transgressor. Research shows that displaced and collective punishment are more likely to occur (and perceived as more justified) when the punishment target and the original transgressor are perceived as similar or belonging to the same social category (entitativity; Sjöström & Gollwitzer, 2015). Of course, such interchangeability or entitativity perceptions can also be construed post hoc by the punisher in order to justify a retaliatory response (scapegoating). The extent to which entitativity perceptions in real-world intergroup conflicts are causal predictors versus post hoc justifications for vicarious punishment is currently an open question. But whatever the causal role of perceived entitativity may be, it is clear that these perceptions play an important role also for punishment in politics. For instance, Americans' endorsement for punitive reactions in the aftermath of the 9/11 attacks were clearly exacerbated by the perception that "they" (i.e., Muslims) all deserve to be punished (Liberman & Skitka, 2019; Washburn & Skitka, 2015).

Entitativity is not an objective feature of groups; rather, it is socially construed. Thus, there are clearly contextual (and individual) circumstances under which entitativity construals (of a target group) are more versus less likely to occur. Specifically, it may be easier to view members of a distant, foreign state as highly entitative out-groups, relative to other intergroup contexts. Moreover, threats to one's nation (or ethnicity) carry strong symbolic value. This might make the desire for harsher and more displaced and/or collective punishment more common on the international stage than in other contexts. And as seen in the war on terror, such thinking may result in retributive acts on innocent targets, backed by the full destructive force of state punishment tools (e.g., military force).

Also in this chapter, we reviewed social psychological research on punishment goals and motives, and we particularly advocated the theoretical perspective that punishment (as most other post-transgression responses) aims at sending a message to the offender. In other words, punishment serves a communicative purpose. This notion has its roots in sociological and philosophical theories about the purposes of punishment (e.g., Duff, 2001; Feinberg, 1965). Although these theories are mainly concerned with punishment at the societal or institutional level, the idea that even interpersonal punishment serves a communicative purpose is in line with a number of empirical findings (e.g., Fischer et al., 2022; Funk et al., 2014; Gollwitzer et al., 2011; Sarin et al., 2021). These findings consistently show that punishment is particularly satisfying for the victim if there is reason to believe that offenders have learned their lesson (Funk et al., 2014). In intergroup conflicts, the communicative goal is not so much about effecting an intra-individual moral change in the offender but, rather, to send a signal of strength, power, and the ability to defend oneself ("Don't mess with us!"). Supporting this notion, research has shown that U.S. Americans' sense of justice achieved after the death of Osama bin Laden, the mastermind behind the 9/11 attacks, was most strongly predicted by the perception that his assassination has sent a message to other would-be terrorists not to mess with the United States (Gollwitzer et al., 2014). In addition, endorsing harsh punishment in intergroup conflicts not only sends a message on the intergroup level but also sends a signal of strength, power, and the existence of a "moral compass" to other people within one's group. In other words, political authorities can fortify their leadership position by demanding and executing harsh punishment against an out-group enemy.

In this context, we have touched upon the idea that the difficulty in enforcing sanctions against offending states, or to prosecute people through legitimate intergovernmental justice mechanisms (especially when a state protects its leaders), makes the desire for punishment on the international stage particularly difficult to fulfill. So what happens when the perpetrator cannot be easily brought to justice and the punitive urge is left unfulfilled? The feeling of injustice may be left simmering unresolved, inspiring displaced or vicarious punishment. For example, ironically, the mistreatment of Iraqi detainees in Abu Ghraib prison by U.S. forces during the invasion of Iraq (which was itself a form of vicarious punishment) became, in the words of a senior al Qaeda leader, the "greatest recruiting tool" for militant jihadist groups in the region (Johnson et al., 2016). Yet, it seems possible that such cycles of increasingly displaced punishment could have diminishing returns in terms of satisfaction. To the extent that the original offender does not understand they are the true target of the displaced punishment, punishment fails to achieve its communicative goal. This seems to create a capacity for escalating yet dissatisfying cycles of displaced and/or vicarious retribution.

A crucial difference between interpersonal punishment and international punishment episodes is that wrongdoing on the international political stage typically involves many perpetrators, not just one. But what does mass punishment look like? How does one do this using the apparatus of traditional (or even restorative) criminal justice? Bringing thousands of people to justice in a court is logistically impossible. Therefore, displacing the punishment to a few select perpetrators—those who are politically responsible—is typical (e.g., in many International Criminal Court trials). However, such displaced punishment may not be satisfying to some victims because they may perceive some offenders to have gotten away with their wrongdoings. To resolve the issue, people might be motivated to support a wider response that metes out punishment in broader brushstrokes across larger populations (e.g., war). Another difficult question related to this is the following: Who decides what form of justice is appropriate when there are multiple victims or when an entire nation views itself as a victim?

A citizenry may have discrepant views about whether they would seek retributive versus restorative justice or which message should be delivered to the perpetrator(s).

And, finally, what about long-standing ("intractable") conflicts in which it is no longer clear who the perpetrators and who the victims are? What happens when both parties are constantly trying to "send a message" to the other, and neither feels heard (because they both think they are the victim)? From a social psychological standpoint, intractable conflicts at the state level are particularly challenging because they are (a) often defined by impermeable group boundaries (i.e., nationality/ethnicity), which fuels hostility on both sides; and (b) often characterized by seemingly irreconcilable moral values, making restorative justice a potentially ineffective solution.

In this chapter, we also briefly discussed cultural aspects that have an impact on punishment goals, punitive attitudes, the likelihood of punitive responses (most notably, culture of honor norms in a society), and the concept of restorative justice, which aims at achieving the same goals as retributive punishment but with entirely different means. Restorative justice is about healing a relationship, and not merely about giving the victim a sense of justice achieved. It is about committing to procedural justice (i.e., by requiring an active participation of victims and transgressors in the process) rather than unilaterally imposed sentences by some authority. And, restorative justice is essentially about explicit communication between a victim and an offender rather than about implicit messages that may or may not be understood. Research has shown that restorative procedures outperform retributive sanctions regarding victims' degree of satisfaction and psychological closure after an offense, but a mutual willingness to heal and repair the relationship is also required. Assessing and securing this willingness are particularly difficult in intractable intergroup conflicts. Yet, difficult does not mean impossible: Restorative procedures on the international level (i.e., truth commissions and transitional justice) are essentially based on a shared hope that a conflict is resolvable. Without such hope, reconciliation is difficult to achieve.

# References

Aharoni, E., Simpson, D., Nahmias, E., & Gollwitzer, M. (2022). A painful message: Testing the effects of understanding and suffering on punishment judgments. *Zeitschrift für Psychologie, 230*(2), 138–151.

Allais, L. (2011). Restorative justice, retributive justice, and the South African Truth and Reconciliation Commission. *Philosophy & Public Affairs, 39*(4), 331–363.

Allan, A., & Allan, M. M. (2000). The South African Truth and Reconciliation Commission as a therapeutic tool. *Behavioral Sciences and the Law, 18*(4), 459–477.

Amstutz, M. R. (2005). *The healing of nations: The promise and limits of political forgiveness*. Rowman & Littlefield.

Bacon, F. (1985). *The essays*. Penguin. (Original work published 1601)

Batchelor, D. (2021). Talking punishment: How victim perceptions of punishment change when they communicate with offenders. *Punishment & Society, 25*(2), 519–536.

Bernhard, H., Fischbacher, U., & Fehr, E. (2006). Parochial altruism in humans. *Nature, 442*(7105), 912–915.

Beven, J. P., Hall, G., Froyland, I., Steels, B., & Goulding, D. (2005). Restoration or renovation? Evaluating restorative justice outcomes. *Psychiatry, Psychology and Law, 12*(1), 194–206.

Braithwaite, J. (1989). *Crime, shame and reintegration*. Cambridge University Press.

Bushman, B. J., Bonacci, A. M., Pedersen, W. C., Vasquez, E. A., & Miller, N. (2005). Chewing on it can chew you up: Effects of rumination on triggered displaced aggression. *Journal of Personality and Social Psychology, 88*(6), 969–983.

Campbell, D. T. (1958). Common fate, similarity, and other indices of the status of aggregates of persons as social entities. *Behavioral Sciences and the Law, 3*, 14–24.

Carlsmith, K. M., & Darley, J. M. (2008). Psychological aspects of retributive justice. *Advances in Experimental Social Psychology, 40*, 193–236.

Carlsmith, K. M., & Sood, A. M. (2009). The fine line between interrogation and retribution. *Journal of Experimental Social Psychology, 45*(1), 191–196.

Christie, N. (1977). Conflicts as property. *British Journal of Criminology, 17*(1), 1–15.

Cohen, D., Nisbett, R. E., Bowdle, B. F., & Schwarz, N. (1996). Insult, aggression, and the southern culture of honor: An "experimental ethnography." *Journal of Personality and Social Psychology, 70*(5), 945–960.

Cushman, F. A., Sarin, A., & Ho, M. (2022). Punishment as communication. In M. Vargas & J. Doris (Eds.), *The Oxford handbook of moral psychology* (pp. 197–209). Oxford University Press.

Darley, J. M., & Pittman, T. S. (2003). The psychology of compensatory and retributive justice. *Personality and Social Psychology Review, 7*(4), 324–336.

Denson, T. F., Lickel, B., Curtis, M., Stenstrom, D. M., & Ames, D. R. (2006). The roles of entitativity and essentiality in judgments of collective responsibility. *Group Processes & Intergroup Relations, 9*(1), 43–61.

Doak, J., & O'Mahony, D. (2006). The vengeful victim? Assessing the attitudes of victims participating in restorative youth conferencing. *International Review of Victimology, 13*(2), 157–177.

Duff, R. A. (2001). *Punishment, communication, and community.* Oxford University Press.

Ellsworth, P. C., & Ross, L. (1983). Public opinion and capital punishment: A close examination of the views of abolitionists and retentionists. *Crime & Delinquency, 29*(1), 116–169.

Fehr, E., & Fischbacher, U. (2004). Third-party punishment and social norms. *Evolution and Human Behavior, 25*(2), 63–87.

Feinberg, J. (1965). The expressive function of punishment. *The Monist, 49*(3), 397–423.

Fischer, M., Twardawski, M., Strelan, P., & Gollwitzer, M. (2022). Victims need more than power: Empowerment and moral change independently predict victims' satisfaction and willingness to reconcile. *Journal of Personality and Social Psychology, 123*(3), 518–536.

French, P. A. (2001). *The virtues of vengeance.* University Press of Kansas.

Funk, F., McGeer, V., & Gollwitzer, M. (2014). Get the message: Punishment is satisfying if the transgressor responds to its communicative intent. *Personality and Social Psychology Bulletin, 40*(8), 986–997.

Gaertner, L., Iuzzini, J., & O'Mara, E. M. (2008). When rejection by one fosters aggression against many: Multiple-victim aggression as a consequence of social rejection and perceived groupness. *Journal of Experimental Social Psychology, 44*(4), 958–970.

Gollwitzer, M. (2009). Justice and revenge. In M. E. Oswald, S. Bieneck, & J. Hupfeld-Heinemann (Eds.), *Social psychology of punishment of crime* (pp. 137–156). Wiley.

Gollwitzer, M., & Denzler, M. (2009). What makes revenge so sweet: Seeing the offender suffer or delivering a message? *Journal of Experimental Social Psychology, 45*(4), 840–844.

Gollwitzer, M., & Keller, L. (2010). What you did only matters if you are one of us: Offenders' group membership moderates the effect of criminal history on punishment severity. *Social Psychology of Political Polarization, 41*(1), 20–26.

Gollwitzer, M., Meder, M., & Schmitt, M. (2011). What gives victims satisfaction when they seek revenge? *European Journal of Social Psychology, 41*(3), 364–374.

Gollwitzer, M., & Sjöström, A. (2017). Revenge and retaliation: A social–functionalist approach. In B. Turner & G. Schlee (Eds.), *On retaliation* (pp. 29–46). Berghahn.

Gollwitzer, M., Skitka, L. J., Wisneski, D., Sjöström, A., Liberman, P., Nazir, S. J., & Bushman, B. J. (2014). Vicarious revenge and the death of Osama Bin Laden. *Personality and Social Psychology Bulletin, 40*(5), 604–616.

Gromet, D. M., & Darley, J. (2006). Restoration and retribution: How including retributive components affects the acceptability of restorative justice procedures. *Social Justice Research, 19,* 395–432.

Heider, F. (1958). *The psychology of interpersonal relations.* Wiley.

Hogg, M. A., van Knippenberg, D., & Rast, D. E. (2012). Intergroup leadership in organizations: Leading across group and organizational boundaries. *Academy of Management Review, 37*(2), 232–255.

Huddy, L., & Feldman, S. (2011). Americans respond politically to 9/11: Understanding the impact of the terrorist attacks and their aftermath. *American Psychologist, 66*(6), 455–467.

Johnson, D. A., Mora, A., & Schmidt, A. (2016). The strategic costs of torture: How "enhanced interrogation" hurt America. *Foreign Affairs, 95*(5), 121–132.

Johnstone, G. (2011). *Restorative justice: Ideas, values, debates* (2nd ed.). Routledge.

Kerr, N. L., Hymes, R., Anderson, A. B., & Weathers, J. (1995). Juror–defendant similarity and juror judgments. *Law & Human Behavior, 19*, 545–567.

Kugler, M. B., Funk, F., Braun, J., Gollwitzer, M., Kay, A. C., & Darley, J. M. (2013). Differences in punitiveness across three cultures: A test of American exceptionalism in justice attitudes. *Journal of Criminal Law and Criminology, 103*(4), 1071–1114.

Latimer, J., Dowden, C., & Muise, D. (2005). The effectiveness of restorative justice practices: A meta-analysis. *The Prison Journal, 85*(2), 127–144.

Leibbrandt, A., & López-Pérez, R. (2011). The dark side of altruistic third-party punishment. *Journal of Conflict Resolution, 55*(5), 761–784.

Liberman, P., & Skitka, L. (2019). Vicarious retribution in US public support for war against Iraq. *Security Studies, 28*(2), 189–215.

Lickel, B., Miller, N., Stenstrom, D. M., Denson, T. F., & Schmader, T. (2006). Vicarious retribution: The role of collective blame in intergroup aggression. *Personality and Social Psychology Review, 10*(4), 372–390.

Lickel, B., Schmader, T., & Hamilton, D. L. (2003). A case of collective responsibility: Who else was to blame for the Columbine High School shootings? *Personality and Social Psychology Bulletin, 29*(2), 194–204.

Lieberman, D., & Linke, L. (2007). The effect of social category on third party punishment. *Evolutionary Psychology, 5*(2), 289–305.

Lindén, M., Björklund, F., & Bäckström, M. (2016). What makes authoritarian and socially dominant people more positive to using torture in the war on terrorism? *Personality and Individual Differences, 91*, 98–101.

Luhtanen, R., & Crocker, J. (1992). A collective self-esteem scale: Self-evaluation of one's social identity. *Personality and Social Psychology Bulletin, 18*(3), 302–318.

Marcus-Newhall, A., Pedersen, W. C., Carlson, M., & Miller, N. (2000). Displaced aggression is alive and well: A meta-analytic review. *Journal of Personality and Social Psychology, 78*(4), 670–689.

Marques, J. M., Yzerbyt, V. Y., & Leyens, J.-P. (1988). The "black sheep effect": Extremity of judgments towards ingroup members as a function of group identification. *European Journal of Social Psychology, 18*(1), 1–16.

Miller, D. T. (2001). Disrespect and the experience of injustice. *Annual Review of Psychology, 52*, 527–553.

Morgan, G. S., Wisneski, D. C., & Skitka, L. J. (2011). The expulsion from Disneyland: The social psychological impact of 9/11. *American Psychologist, 66*(6), 447–454.

Newheiser, A.-K., Sawaoka, T., & Dovidio, J. F. (2012). Why do we punish groups? High entitativity promotes moral suspicion. *Journal of Experimental Social Psychology, 48*(4), 931–936.

Nisbett, R. E., & Cohen, D. (1996). *Culture of honor: The psychology of violence in the South*. Routledge.

Nozick, R. (1981). *Philosophical explanations*. Harvard University Press.

Okimoto, T. G., & Wenzel, M. (2009). Punishment as restoration of group and offender values following a transgression: Value consensus through symbolic labelling and offender reform. *European Journal of Social Psychology, 39*(3), 346–367.

Okimoto, T. G., Wenzel, M., & Feather, N. T. (2009). Beyond retribution: Conceptualizing restorative justice and exploring its determinants. *Social Justice Research*, 22(1), 156–180.

Okimoto, T. G., Wenzel, M., & Platow, M. J. (2010). Restorative justice: Seeking a shared identity in dynamic intragroup contexts. In E. A. Mannix, M. A. Neale, & E. Mullen (Eds.), *Fairness and groups* (Vol. 13, pp. 205–242). Emerald.

Pereira, A., Berent, J., Falomir-Pichastor, J. M., Staerklé, C., & Butera, F. (2015). Collective punishment depends on collective responsibility and political organization of the target group. *Journal of Experimental Social Psychology*, 56(1), 1–23.

Pfattheicher, S., Sassenrath, C., & Keller, J. (2019). Compassion magnifies third-party punishment. *Journal of Personality and Social Psychology*, 117(1), 124–141.

Rothschild, Z. K., Landau, M., Sullivan, D., & Keefer, L. A. (2012). A dual-motive model of scapegoating: Displacing blame to reduce guilt or increase control. *Journal of Personality and Social Psychology*, 102(6), 1148–1163.

Sarin, A., Ho, M. K., Martin, J. W., & Cushman, F. (2021). Punishment is organized around principles of communicative inference. *Cognition*, 208, Article 104544.

Shackelford, T. K. (2015). An evolutionary psychological perspective on cultures of honor. *Evolutionary Psychology*, 3(1), 381–391.

Shapland, J., Atkinson, A., Atkinson, H., Chapman, B., Colledge, E., Dignan, J., Howes, M., Johnstone, J., Robinson, G., & Sorsby, A. (2006). *Restorative justice in practice: The second report from the evaluation of three schemes*. University of Sheffield Centre for Criminological Research.

Shapland, J., Atkinson, A., Atkinson, H., Dignan, J., Edwards, L., Hibbert, J., & Sorsby, A. (2008). *Does restorative justice affect reconviction? The fourth report from the evaluation of three schemes*. UK Ministry of Justice.

Shaw, A., DeScioli, P., Barakzai, A., & Kurzban, R. (2017). Whoever is not with me is against me: The costs of neutrality among friends. *Journal of Experimental Social Psychology*, 7(1), 96–104.

Sjöström, A., & Gollwitzer, M. (2015). Displaced revenge: Can revenge taste "sweet" if it aims at a different target? *Journal of Experimental Social Psychology*, 56, 191–202.

Sjöström, A., Magraw-Mickelson, Z., & Gollwitzer, M. (2018). What makes displaced revenge taste sweet: Retributing displaced responsibility or sending a message to the original perpetrator? *European Journal of Social Psychology*, 48(4), 490–506.

Skitka, L. J., Bauman, C. W., Aramovich, N. P., & Morgan, G. S. (2006). Confrontational and preventative policy responses to terrorism: Anger wants a fight and fear wants "them" to go away. *Basic and Applied Social Psychology*, 28(4), 375–384.

Skitka, L. J., Saunders, B., Morgan, G. S., & Wisneski, D. (2009). Dark clouds and silver linings: Socio-psychological responses to September 11, 2001. In M. Morgan (Ed.), *The impact of 9-11 on politics and war: The day that changed everything?* (Vol. 3, pp. 63–80). Palgrave Macmillan.

Sommers, S. R., & Ellsworth, P. C. (2000). Race in the courtroom: Perceptions of guilt and dispositional attributions. *Personality and Social Psychology Bulletin*, 26, 1367–1379.

Stenstrom, D. M., Lickel, B., Denson, T. F., & Miller, N. (2008). The roles of ingroup identification and outgroup entitativity in intergroup retribution. *Personality and Social Psychology Bulletin, 34*, 1570–1582.

Stephen, J. F. (1985). *General view of the criminal law of England*. Rothman. (Original work published 1863)

Strang, H., Sherman, L. W., Mayo-Wilson, E., Woods, D., & Ariel, B. (2013). Restorative justice conferencing (RJC) using face-to-face meetings of offenders and victims: Effects on offender recidivism and victim satisfaction: A systematic review. *Campbell Systematic Reviews, 9*(1), 1–59.

Tajfel, H. (1981). *Human groups and social categories: Studies in social psychology*. Cambridge University Press.

Tajfel, H., & Turner, J. C. (1986). The social identity theory of intergroup behavior. In W. G. Austin & S. Worchel (Eds.), *Psychology of intergroup relations* (pp. 7–24). Nelson-Hall.

Taylor, T. S., & Hosch, H. M. (2004). An examination of jury verdicts for evidence of a similarity-leniency effect, an out-group punitiveness effect, or a black sheep effect. *Law & Human Behavior, 28*, 587–599.

Twardawski, M., Gollwitzer, M., Altenmüller, M. S., Kunze, A. E., & Wittekind, C. E. (2021). Imagery rescripting helps victims cope with experienced injustice. *Zeitschrift für Psychologie, 229*(3), 178–184.

Twardawski, M., Gollwitzer, M., Pohl, S., & Bosnjak, M. (2022). Editorial: What drives second- and third-party punishment? Conceptual replications of the "intuitive retributivism" hypothesis. *Zeitschrift für Psychologie, 230*(2), 77–83.

Tyler, T. R. (2006). Restorative justice and procedural justice: Dealing with rule breaking. *Journal of Social Issues, 62*(2), 307–326.

van Prooijen, J.-W. (2018). *The moral punishment instinct*. Oxford University Press.

van Prooijen, J.-W., & Lam, J. (2007). Retributive justice and social categorizations: The perceived fairness of punishment depends on intergroup status. *European Journal of Social Psychology, 37*(6), 1286–1297.

Vidmar, N. (2001). Retribution and revenge. In J. Sanders & V. L. Hamilton (Eds.), *Handbook of justice research in law* (pp. 31–63). Kluwer.

Vidmar, N., & Miller, D. T. (1980). Social psychological processes underlying attitudes toward legal punishment. *Law and Society Review, 14*(3), 565–602.

Walster, E., Walster, G. W., & Berscheid, E. (1978). *Equity: Theory and research*. Allyn & Bacon.

Washburn, A. N., & Skitka, L. J. (2015). Motivated and displaced revenge: Remembering 9/11 suppresses opposition to military intervention in Syria (for some). *Analyses of Social Issues and Public Policy, 15*(1), 89–104.

Wenzel, M., Okimoto, T. G., & Cameron, K. (2012). Do retributive and restorative justice processes address different symbolic concerns? *Critical Criminology, 20*(1), 25–44.

Wenzel, M., Okimoto, T. G., Feather, N. T., & Platow, M. J. (2008). Retributive and restorative justice. *Law and Human Behavior, 32*(5), 375–389.

Wenzel, M., & Thielmann, I. (2006). Why we punish in the name of justice: Just desert versus value restoration and the role of social identity. *Social Justice Research, 19*(4), 450–470.

Yudkin, D. A., Rothmund, T., Twardawski, M., Thalla, N., & Van Bavel, J. J. (2016). Reflexive intergroup bias in third-party punishment. *Journal of Experimental Psychology: General*, *145*(11), 1448–1459.

Yzerbyt, V., Dumont, M., Wigboldus, D., & Gordijn, E. (2003). I feel for us: The impact of categorization and identification on emotions and action tendencies. *British Journal of Social Psychology*, *42*(4), 533–549.

# 3

# The Fruits of Wrongdoing in International Law

## What Does (and Does Not) Happen When Laws Are Broken

STEPHEN C. NEFF

## 3.1. INTRODUCTION

It is widely agreed that when laws are violated, consequences should ensue. But what should these consequences be in the realm of international law? In national legal systems, there can be punitive action taken by governments and courts, on behalf of the community at large. It has even been contended that punitive action on behalf of society at large against wrongdoers is the very essence of orderly social life. "Government," the behavioral psychologist B. F. Skinner tersely pronounced, "is the use of the power to punish" (Skinner, 1953, p. 335).

In international law, however, things are more difficult. There is no global government or police system comparable to those in nation-states. It is even doubted whether there is any such thing as an international community in any meaningful sense of that term. There is, however, a system of laws, even if it is one that emerges from the bottom-up, from the states themselves, rather than being handed down from on high by a legislator. Our present concern is with what happens when those laws are violated—given the absence of central authority to inflict punishment. The short answer to that question is that a state which violates international law incurs a duty to make reparation for that violation to any injured party.

A deeper consideration of the subject, however, reveals that there are three possible classes of consequences that can befall a wrongdoing state—with punitive action in the proper sense being one of them. These three are identified here at the outset, along with several other important general points. The main discussion then comprises a broad exploration of how these consequences of legal violation have appeared and evolved through the history of international law. Illustrative examples are provided, with (of course) no pretense of comprehensiveness.

### 3.1.1. Three Classes of Consequences of Law Violations

The concept of punishment for legal violations can be viewed in either a broad or narrow sense. In its broadest sense, punishment might be thought of as any negative consequence that is visited upon an actor, by an outside authority (of some kind), as a response to some form of antisocial conduct on the actor's part. (The reference to an "outside authority" is necessary so as to exclude negative consequences that flow automatically or mechanically from the action itself, e.g., touching live electrical wires in violation of rules and being electrocuted.) Specifically, negative consequences of norm violations could usefully be broken down into three (more or less) distinct categories, of which only one can be regarded as punitive in a strict and proper sense.

The first category of consequences comprises a duty on the part of the wrongdoer to compensate any and all persons who suffered material injury from the wrongdoing. A second category of consequences arising from norm violations would focus not on "rescuing" the victims from material loss but, instead, on inducing the wrongdoer to behave in a more prosocial or law-abiding way in the future. This kind of reaction to norm violation is, by definition, future- rather than past-oriented. It could be labeled the rehabilitative approach; but it is suggested that "utilitarian" would be a better, and more general, tag. The purpose is to include in this category all kinds of measures that are taken for the purpose of achieving a stated goal. It immediately becomes apparent that measures which penalize the wrongdoer are justifiable to precisely the extent to which they contribute to the attainment of the goal—and not thereafter. It is easily seen that the utilitarian calculus differs in principle from the compensatory calculus.

Third and finally, there is the punitive response, properly speaking. Here, the essential focus is different yet: on the degree of moral turpitude of wrongdoer. "The punishment should fit the crime" (as even Gilbert and Sullivan recognized), in that the degree of unpleasantness inflicted onto the norm violator is commensurate to the degree of wickedness animating the act. This could be termed the retributive approach to norm violation. Here, the primary focus is on the injury done to the normative system of the society at large. It might be that material loss suffered by victims is slight or even nonexistent. (An automobile driver might drive in a highly reckless manner and chance not to hit anyone.) It may also be that the wrongdoer is genuinely remorseful over the act—but that there is still a feeling that they must nonetheless "pay their due" to society for their misconduct, if only to deter *other* persons from misbehaving in the future. This retributive response could therefore be said to be both backward- and forward-looking—backward-looking in that the moral guilt of the person at the time of the norm violation is regarded as the decisive factor in setting the punishment; but also forward-looking in the sense that a purpose of the punishment is to uphold the values of the society at large with a view to discouraging future misconduct by other persons.

In principle, this third class of consequences—the punitive one—is absent from the sphere of inter-state relations. In practice, however, as will be observed, there is some scope for punitive considerations to play a role, if only a modest one. Punitive elements can sometimes seep through cracks in the conceptual apparatus, so to speak. There have also been, as will also be seen, proposals to bring punishment of states directly and openly into international law, although these have not, as yet, actually borne fruit.

## 3.1.2. The Importance of Self-Help Remedies in International Law

When people think of law in a national context, images of police and courts spring readily to mind. Police and courts exist in the international sphere as well, but they are far less pervasive and powerful than their domestic counterparts. In particular, international courts have only a severely limited jurisdiction over states. They can only hear cases that states choose to bring before them. Not surprisingly, that leaves a very great deal of international activity outside the reach of judicial scrutiny. The result is that international law gives far greater scope for self-help remedies than do domestic legal systems. Much of international law enforcement is, accordingly, a do-it-yourself enterprise by purported victims of injustices of various sorts. Also unsurprisingly, this leaves a worrying degree of scope for abuses of various kinds.

This frightening scope for abuse of international law, fascinating though it is, is not the focus of this discussion. Our concern is with the normal consequences of violations of international law—and of the ways in which these can be classified as compensatory, utilitarian, or punitive. Courts can be expected to be relatively clear about this (as will be seen). Amid the welter of self-help measures mounted by various aggrieved states on their own initiatives, however, matters often become considerably less clear. The following section presents a brief—indeed very brief—exploration of that question as it has unfolded over the course of history since the European Middle Ages.

## 3.2. IN THE BEGINNING

In the European Middle Ages, the absence of international courts, and the extreme rarity of arbitration, meant that self-help remedies in cases of legal violation loomed very large indeed. These took three important forms: just wars; reprisals; and, more marginally, self-defense.

### 3.2.1. Medieval Just War

The classic just war, as inherited from doctrinal writings in the Middle Ages, was the quintessential illustration of self-help, by a victim of injustice against a wrongdoer (for a shorter account, see Neff, 2005; for a thorough treatment of medieval just-war doctrine, see Russell, 1975). It was, in principle at least, nonpunitive. This might seem odd, given that the force is directed against a legal wrongdoer—that is, against a party that is withholding the just party's legal entitlement. But it is not essential to the just-war scheme that the wrongful party be guilty of any kind of moral turpitude. The wrongful party might believe, sincerely and genuinely, that it is in the right and that the so-called entitlement being claimed is, in reality, not really owing. A ready analogy with litigation suggests itself. It clearly can occur that in a lawsuit—for example, a contest over title to property—both parties sincerely believe in the legal validity of their own respective stances. In the event, of course, one party will be held to be actually in the right, and the other in the wrong. The result of the contest is that the wrongful party yields up the disputed property to the rightful one. But the wrongful party cannot meaningfully be said, in the eyes of the law, to suffer punishment. The person simply relinquishes something that they lacked a legal right to hold. The wrongful party is merely being required to respect the legal rights of another person. But this is not punishment—any more than a shopper is being "punished" by not being allowed to shoplift.

A just war, then, was a resort to armed force to obtain a legal entitlement that was being withheld by another party. It was purely a matter of execution, because the legal entitlement must *already* be in existence prior to the taking of action. A just war was therefore backward-looking, in that it sought to rectify a past wrong. The wrong, of course, might be what lawyers call a continuing wrong, such as the taking of property coupled with a continued withholding of it from the rightful owner. Even though the unlawful withholding continues through time, it is nevertheless the case that the fundamental norm violation, the original taking, occurred in the past.

An important point to appreciate about medieval just-war doctrine is that it concerned a justification for resort to *offensive* force. It was therefore quite distinct from the concept of self-defense (discussed below). To be sure, just wars could be described as defensive in the loose sense that they are designed to enable victims of injustice to obtain redress against wrongdoers and to defend or vindicate the rule of law in general. The key point, however, is that just-war doctrine entitled the just party to take the initiative and to inaugurate the hostilities by striking the first blow. Here, too, the concept of just war as the execution of a legal right is helpful. Just as a police officer is entitled to take the initiative and hunt down a criminal, so is a just party entitled to pounce upon their foe at a moment of their own choosing.

### 3.2.2. Reprisals

Reprisal, to a layperson, immediately connotes vengeance: "an eye for an eye, a tooth for a tooth." This is not, however, the legal meaning of the term. The eye-for-an-eye policy has a different label: *retaliation*, meaning a mechanical infliction back upon a party of an act that an individual themself had earlier performed. In international law, the proper term is "retorsion."

Reprisal was something different. It was, in fact, basically the same thing, in spirit, as a just war—it is the obtaining of satisfaction legally owed, by means of self-help. It may be viewed as a nonmilitary form of just war. It differed from a just war in two notable respects: (a) Unlike a just war, it was carried out by nonviolent means and under judicial oversight; and (b) it was directed not against the actual wrongdoer but instead against a surrogate or stand-in for the wrongdoer, who was themself *not* guilty of any lawbreaking. This second feature, on its own, would ensure that reprisals do not qualify as punishment. Acts of reprisal, to be sure, might be *oppressive* acts causing hardship to the persons affected, but they cannot be said to be *punitive* acts. A brief explanation by way of a hypothetical illustration will make the point clear.

An archetypal reprisal case would involve a merchant who did business in a foreign country. In the process of this, the merchant was robbed or swindled by some private parties. The natural remedy would be for the victimized merchant to sue in the local courts for relief, in the form of a civil judgment against the wrongdoers. Suppose, however, that the local courts refused to entertain the action—perhaps because of an absence of jurisdiction over the matter or perhaps for less exalted reasons, such as anti-foreign prejudice or corruption. In either event, the key self-help requirement of necessity is now satisfied: an absence of any viable alternative remedy.

In cases of reprisal, the self-help remedy is somewhat roundabout. The merchant would return to his home country and apply to his own government for what was called (appropriately enough) a letter of reprisal. This letter of reprisal was, in effect, a license to the merchant to recover his losses by the (admittedly drastic) method of seizing property belonging to fellow nationals of the original wrongdoers. These unfortunate fellow nationals had to be located in the merchant's home country so that the action would be prosecuted entirely within the jurisdiction of the aggrieved merchant's home state. There was no pretense that these targets of the letter of reprisal were in any way personally involved in the original wrongful act. They simply happened to be in, as it were, the wrong place at the wrong time. Their ordinary right to safety and security was merely being subordinated to the higher priority goal of making the original victim whole. The reprisal taker would then, in effect, use the letter as a private search warrant, entering the premises of fellow nationals of the wrongdoers and seizing their property to reimburse him for his prior losses.

Some important protections were granted to the victims of this reprisal process. For one thing, in applying for the letter of reprisal, the injured merchant was expected to provide satisfactory evidence that the alleged wrongdoing really occurred and that redress had not been available in the foreign courts (i.e., that the prerequisite of necessity was duly satisfied). Moreover, the applicant had to quantify the loss. The letter of reprisal, if granted, would state that value. As a result, the aggregate value of the property seized could be no greater than that stated sum. To ensure that the reprisal taker did not overshoot, he was required, when taking property, to present it to the court for a valuation. When the total valuation of the property taken to the court matched the stated sum in the letter, the process stopped.

Here we have an example of a legal process that, in the purest manner, is compensatory rather than punitive in character. Seizures were permitted up to the precise value of the original loss, and no further. This feature was shared with just wars. But with reprisals, there was the additional consideration that the remedial acts were not directed against the actual wrongdoer but instead against surrogates or stand-ins.

One final point about reprisals remains to be made—that is, that the unfortunate victims of the reprisal action did not necessarily (at least in theory) bear the ultimate burden of compensating the merchant for his injury. They would be entitled to be indemnified for their losses by the actual wrongdoer in their home country. Consequently, at the end of the entire process, the effect would be that the original villain would (eventually) compensate his victim for the original unlawful act, albeit by a rather roundabout process.

### 3.2.3. Self-Defense

Self-defense is importantly different from both just wars and reprisals. For present purposes, a key point about it is that it is only somewhat tenuously or marginally concerned with norm violation. It is true that, in most cases, a self-defending state will be attempting to fend off an unlawful act of aggression. But any such unlawfulness does not figure in the actual definition of self-defense. Self-defense is instead regarded as an inherent right, arising out of the fundamental natural-law right to life. This means that self-defense is exercisable even when the attacker is not a law violator. An example is a just-war scenario. The just side would have the exclusive right to use force offensively (as noted above)—but the unjust side would, strictly speaking, retain its right to self-defense.

In addition, self-defense differs from the just war in that the self-defender's only legal entitlement is to fend off the attack—and nothing else. In a just war, the rightful party has the right to enforce, by armed force, their legal entitlement. For example, if his territory is being unlawfully occupied, he has the right forcibly to expel the wrongful occupant and thereby recover his rightful possession. A just war, in other words, is a means of bringing about a *change* in the status quo (provided, of course, that the just side is successful in its war). A self-defender, in contrast, is only entitled to restore the situation as it existed prior to the assault. The individual has no right to go beyond that and take anything from their assailant. Self-defense is therefore a much more conservative right, in the strict sense of that term. It is a restoration of the past situation, not the righting of a wrong. Self-defense action therefore cannot be considered as punitive—except in the extended and rather artificial sense that an aggressor may be said to suffer "punishment" if its wicked designs fail to bear fruit.

Self-defense is also importantly different from reprisals. For one thing, self-defense action, unlike reprisals, is taken against the actual person committing the wrong. There is no element of surrogacy. Also, self-defense action lacks any element of judicial oversight. It is therefore more purely of a self-help character.

One final feature of self-defense separates it sharply from just wars and reprisals—that is, that self-defense must occur as the attack occurs. It is designed for the beating back of an ongoing attack, rather than the rectification after the fact of a prior wrong (as is the case with both just wars and reprisals). Self-defense is accordingly quintessentially utilitarian in character, rather than compensatory or punitive. It is directed not toward compensation for a prior loss, or punishment of the attacker, but rather toward the attainment of a goal in the present or near future: the defeat of the attack.

### 3.2.4. The Early Modern Reformulation of Just-War Doctrine

It is a curious feature of medieval just-war doctrine, from our modern perspective, that it had strangely little concern with substantive legal justifications for war. Instead, its chief concern was with what we might think of as "side conditions" such as the requirements of necessity (meaning the absence of an alternative channel of redress) or the correct subjective frame of mind or motive. As to what the *actual* legal claim by the just party might be, medieval doctrine was largely silent. The effect was that any valid legal claim could suffice—provided, of course, that, in addition, all the side conditions were satisfied.

This gap was filled chiefly by the Dutch natural-law writer Hugo Grotius in his monumental treatise *On the Law of War and Peace* in 1625. Grotius' contribution was to shift the emphasis of just-war doctrine from the side conditions to the substantive legal claims. He identified three such substantive just causes for resorting to war (i.e., for taking the offensive) (Grotius, 1625/1925, pp. 171–172). First was to obtain what is legally owing—for example, compensation for an injury or territory wrongfully occupied. This was, in essence, the classic medieval just war—compensatory in nature. Second was what Grotius called defensive war. This did *not* mean self-defense. It meant pre-emptively attacking another party with a view to forestalling an impending attack by that party. (It does not count as self-defense because it does not concern resisting an *ongoing* attack but is instead preventive in nature.) This could be regarded as essentially utilitarian. Force is used for the attaining of a goal or, alternatively, as a kind of rehabilitative action, a forcible inducing of another party to refrain from committing a wrong. The key point is that this type of just war is future-oriented rather than past-oriented. The third type of just war was punishment for past, completed wrong. Here we see, for the first time, punishment accorded an explicit status in international law.

On the subject of punishment in general, Grotius (1625/1925, pp. 462–521) had a great deal to say. Two of his points, in particular, may be highlighted. One concerned cases of violations of natural law—that is, of rules that are applicable for the entire human race, as opposed to treaty rules or customary rules which arise out of voluntary arrangements between particular parties. For such violations, Grotius insisted that *any* member of the human community is entitled to impose a punishment onto the wrongdoer. It was not essential that the punishing party have sustained any kind of material damage from the misconduct (pp. 470–478). Punitive action was thereby seen as a vindication of the collective values of the society at large rather than as a mechanism for compensating victims. The other important point about punishment was the insistence by Grotius on proportionality. The punishment inflicted onto the wrongdoer should be proportionate to the wrong committed (p. 494).

## 3.3. THE 19TH CENTURY

In the 19th century, expounders of international law made a distinction between war properly speaking and what were commonly called "measures short of war." (On this topic, see generally Neff, 2005, pp. 215–249). War in the proper sense was held to be an essentially consensual affair, in the nature of a duel. It was an agreement on the part of the two states to settle some dispute between them by means of armed force. Viewing war in this way marked a very dramatic departure from the medieval and early modern views of the subject, chiefly in that the element of legal wrongdoing now played no definitional role in war. All that was needed was a dispute of some kind (any kind), coupled with the mutual decision on the contestants' part to settle the matter by force of arms. Instead of lawbreaking and law enforcement, war was now a contest of wills, a matter of challenge and response, an exercise of power rather than of right. The purpose of war in this modern sense was, therefore, not to uphold the rule of law (as in just-war doctrine) but, rather, to subject the opposing party to one's will. There is much to be said of this important change in the conception of the nature of war (Neff, 2005, pp. 167–214). For present purposes, only one point need be made: that war in this modern sense had nothing *definitionally* to do with punishment. Things stood very differently, however, regarding measures short of war. The principal forms that are considered here are armed reprisals.

### 3.3.1. Reprisals, 19th-Century Style

As in the pre-19th-century world, an essential prerequisite of a reprisal was some kind of prior unlawful conduct on the part of the target state. The 19th-century concept of armed reprisals was consequently the direct successor to the medieval just war. As such, it was a unilateral resort to offensive force by a party that had suffered some kind of prior legal wrong. At the same time, however, the practice of armed reprisals in the 19th century differed from its medieval predecessor in four notable ways. One is that reprisals, in the 19th-century usage, referred to acts against *states* rather than against private parties. A second important difference was that 19th-century reprisals frequently featured a recourse to military force rather than merely a taking of property from individuals. A third key difference was that the element of surrogacy was no longer present. Reprisal action was now directed against the very party that had committed the prior wrong and not against an innocent stand-in or substitute, as in the Middle Ages. Fourth, this new form of reprisal was not so scrupulously compensatory in nature as its medieval predecessor, with its clinical balancing of harm done and compensation obtained. Nineteenth-century reprisals were therefore a rather more rough and ready affair than their medieval ancestors. Given these differences, it is rather unfortunate that the term "reprisal" is applied to both of these phenomena.

An example of the resort to armed force for the extraction of a money indemnity occurred in the Don Pacifico incident of 1850, in which Britain took action against Greece. The home of a British national had been plundered by a Greek mob, for which Britain demanded indemnification from Greece. When this was not forthcoming, a fleet was dispatched to institute a blockade of Greek ports. This forced Greece to agree to arbitration (in which, interestingly, Britain was awarded a far smaller sum in damages than it had claimed—£150, as against an original claim of £21,295).

Forcible reprisals could take other forms than bombardments or blockades. Sometimes, they involved the occupation of a portion of a state's territory, as a not-so-subtle inducement to the state to rectify some past alleged wrong. An example occurred between Peru and Spain in 1862–1865.

It was sparked by the assaulting of some Spanish immigrants to Peru by Peruvian laborers. A demand for compensation by Spain was not met, so a Spanish force proceeded to seize the guano-producing Chincha Islands, owned by Peru, pending payment. Peru eventually agreed to pay 3 million pesos to Spain, and the islands were then duly returned to it. Similarly, in 1901, France occupied the Turkish island of Mytilene after Turkey showed itself to be excessively dilatory in satisfying French demands for redress over four earlier matters (Moncharville, 1902).

### 3.3.2. Reprisals as Punishment

As noted above, the "official" position in international law was that forcible reprisals could be employed (where no peaceful alternative was available) for compensatory or utilitarian ends but not for punitive ones. In actual state practice, however, these niceties were not always scrupulously observed. It is not difficult to find reprisals in state practice of the 19th century that do bear clear signs of being punitive in character. Perhaps the clearest example is the bombardment of Greytown, in Nicaragua, by U.S. naval forces in 1854. Anti-American sentiment was strong in that country as a result of pressure for permission to build a canal through the territory to link the Caribbean Sea and the Pacific Ocean. As the American minister attempted to restore calm, a bottle was thrown at him. He asked his government for a show of force against Nicaragua in response. This was provided in the form of a warship calling at Greytown, whose commander demanded an apology for the incident, in addition to an indemnity, from the Nicaraguan authorities. When these were not forthcoming, the commander unleashed a bombardment that effectively leveled the town.

Sometimes, punitive actions had long-term consequences. The most notable example was in Algiers, in the wake of the famous (or infamous) "fly whisk incident." This occurred in 1827 when the French consul in Algiers was meeting with the local ruler to discuss alleged misconduct by some French residents of Algiers. The discussion appears to have become rather heated, and in the course of it, the ruler struck the consul with a fly whisk. The consul indignantly withdrew to France, and the French government demanded an apology from the ruler of Algiers. When that was not forthcoming, France first mounted a naval blockade of Algiers and then proceeded, in 1830, to launch a full-scale invasion and takeover of the country. (French rule over Algeria lasted until 1962.)

## 3.4. BETWEEN THE WORLD WARS

Following the traumas of the Great War of 1914–1918, the range of possible reactions to violations of international law, identified above, remained in place—including, notably, the possibility of resort to armed reprisals. There were also, however, some innovations. The question of penalties for war-related acts was raised at the Paris Peace Conference of 1919 in several contexts. Following the conclusion of the Treaty of Versailles, two newly established institutions began to operate in this area. One was a permanently sitting World Court (or Permanent Court of International Justice, to give it its proper name). The other key institution was the League of Nations, which also had certain powers to take action against violators of law.

### 3.4.1. The Treaty of Versailles

The question of dealing with norm violations arose in several guises at the Paris Peace Conference and found its way into several provisions of the Treaty of Versailles.[1] In particular, there were three sanctions-related or punishment-related subjects that were dealt with. First was criminal penalties, in the true sense of that term, for persons who had committed violations of the laws of war during the recent conflict. These were to be

---

1. Treaty of Versailles, June 26, 1919. 225 C.T.S.188.

inflicted on individuals and not on states (as is still the position in international law).[2]

A second subject of interest was the treatment of ex-Kaiser William II. Here, the Treaty itself expressed that the victorious powers "publicly arraign William II . . . for a supreme offence against international morality and the sanctity of treaties." It envisaged that a "special tribunal" would be constituted to conduct the trial.[3] By "supreme offence against international morality and the sanctity of treaties" was meant Germany's violation of the neutrality of Belgium in 1914, of which Germany itself had been a guarantor. It should be appreciated that this envisaged trial was to be of William II personally, not of the state of Germany as such. In any event, the trial never took place because the Netherlands, to which the Kaiser had fled after his overthrow, declined to extradite him.

The third matter dealt with by the Treaty of Versailles was the legal responsibility of Germany as a state. Interestingly—and thoroughly in keeping with international legal doctrine—this matter was not covered in the section of the Treaty on "Penalties" (as the first two issues were). Instead, it was placed in a section appropriately labeled "Reparation." The key provision, for legal purposes, was Article 231, in which Germany expressly accepted its "responsibility . . . for causing all the loss and damage" suffered by the Allied and Associated states. This was the famous "War Guilt Clause"'—although a lawyer would quibble that it should more properly (if less snappily) be called the "Sole Responsibility Clause." It was admission on Germany's part not of criminal conduct but rather of civil liability—thereby triggering the automatic obligation to compensate injured parties for their losses. The task of quantifying the damage was entrusted to a separate commission. The dispiriting story of the German reparation payments has been extensively treated and need not be discussed here (see, e.g., Gomes, 2010; Trachtenberg, 1980).

---

2. Id., arts. 228–230.

3. Id., art. 227.

## 3.4.2. Judicial Action

Judicial action to deal with violations of international law was certainly not a novelty. Inter-state arbitration dates back as far as ancient Greece (see generally Ager, 1996). But arbitration had always been (and continues to be) a fitful affair, with panels formed for individual cases and then dissolved. What was new after the Great War was a permanently sitting court, which would build up a body of coherent case law over the passage of time—ideally meaning eternity. The World Court began sitting in 1922 in The Hague. It was the hope of idealists that this new institution would lead to progressively greater reduction in the importance of self-help measures in international law, in favor of objective adjudication by impartial judges on the basis of the rule of law. Unfortunately in the view of champions of the rule of law, the Court did not have compulsory jurisdiction over states. It was empowered to hear only cases that states brought before it. As a result, the Court played only a modest role—but still an important one—in the international affairs of the period.

In cases that were brought before it, however, the World Court was able to provide reparation—that is, to order restitution and to award money damages against countries. Punitive measures were not available to it. The first award of money damages by the Court was in 1923, in a case against Germany for refusing to allow a French ship with a munitions cargo to go through the Kiel Canal. The Court made an award against Germany of 140,750 French francs.[4] Information on the operation of the P.C.I.J. is readily available (see, e.g., Hudson, 1943), so further exploration of the subject is not called for in the present discussion.

## 3.4.3. Sanctions and the League of Nations

Another legacy of World War I was the League of Nations, which adopted, for the first time, a global program of collective security. It came with a

---

4. The S.S. Wimbledon, P.C.I.J., ser. A, no. 1 (1923).

sanctions provision attached. This was Articles 16 and 17 of the League Covenant, concerning states (whether League members or not) that resorted to war without first exhausting the various peaceful-settlement mechanisms outlined in the Covenant. In such an event, the wrongdoing state "shall ipso facto be deemed to have committed an act of war against all other Members of the League." These other member states then became obligated, immediately and automatically, to impose a range of economic and diplomatic measures against the offending member country—the severing of trade and financial relations, together with a ban on "all intercourse between their nationals and the nationals of the covenant-breaking State." In addition, the League Council was required to make recommendations regarding the deploying of armed force against the wrongdoer.

This provision was brought into play on one memorable occasion: in response to the invasion of Abyssinia by Italy in 1935 and 1936 (although it failed to prevent the conquest from succeeding).

For present purposes, Article 16 of the League Covenant is noteworthy because it is, at least arguably, an example of punishment for norm violation. This may be said because Article 16—unlike the guarantee provision of Article 10—is clearly oriented toward inflicting harm onto the wrongdoer, as well as toward rescuing the victim. Even the common label "economic sanctions" suggests punishment rather than rescue. There is, however, room for quibbling on this point because it could be credibly asserted that the underlying purpose of the sanctions was, in reality, to defeat the operation of the wrongdoing state and thereby to rescue the victim. Even accepting that assessment, it still remains fair to regard Article 16 as being, according to its terms, a punitive provision—and, as such, the first in multilateral treaty law.

## 3.5. SINCE 1945

The adoption of the United Nations (UN) Charter in 1945 introduced a new-modeled collective security system, along with an important new international norm: a general prohibition against the use of force in international affairs (with a notable exception for self-defense).[5] This prohibition is generally interpreted as barring the resort to forcible reprisals of the 19th-century sort. Regarding possible responses to violations of international law, a notable innovation was the provision for "enforcement action" by the UN or alternatively by coalitions of states under the general auspices of the UN. There was some hope, at the outset, that the UN might even evolve into a world government, with the Security Council wielding executive powers on a more or less continuous basis. If this were to happen, then reliance on self-help measures for enforcing international law would become obsolete. In appropriate cases, the Security Council could even take overtly punitive action against lawbreaking states, in the manner of police forces in national law.

For better or worse, these visions of world government have not (or not yet) come to pass. In reality, responses to violations of international law continue to be dealt with as in the past—meaning that the heavy reliance on self-help measures continues in force. One innovation, however, was the codification of the law in this area, by a subsidiary body of the UN General Assembly called the International Law Commission (composed of independent experts). The Commission produced, after many years of arduous effort, a codification of the law relating to state liability for wrongful conduct, including principles governing remedies, in the form of a set of Articles on State Responsibility in 2001.[6]

Within this established, and traditional, framework, however, there were a number of new developments that were not foreseen by the drafters of the UN Charter. One was the dangerous expansion of self-defense claims, which in some instances seemed so broad as, in effect, to resuscitate the supposedly deceased right to resort to armed reprisals. Another development, arising out of the new concern in international law for human rights, was the question of the lawfulness (or otherwise) of humanitarian

---

5. UN Charter, arts. 2(4), 51.

6. Int'l Law Commission, Report on Its 53d Session, UN Doc. A/56/10 (2001), at 43–59 (hereafter I.L.C., Articles on State Responsibility).

intervention in cases of serious human rights violation. There were also some voices in favor of the infusion of overtly criminal penalties, for the first time, into international law—either as punitive damage awards in judicial actions or as direct findings of criminal guilt of states. These developments are briefly surveyed.

### 3.5.1. Collective Security UN Style

After World War II, the League of Nations was replaced by the UN. Like its ill-starred predecessor, the UN has an important (or potentially important) collective security component, now operating under the guidance of the Security Council. The UN Charter explicitly empowers the Security Council to take "enforcement action" in the form of economic sanctions and even of the deployment of armed force. The Security Council is not, however, a law enforcement agency properly speaking. Its mission is not to enforce international law per se but, rather, to safeguard international peace and security generally.

To be sure, there is bound to be a large overlap between these two functions because threats to international peace could easily take the form of violations of the UN Charter's prohibition against the use of force. This point is illustrated by the two most notable instances in which the Security Council has authorized the deployment of armed force: the Korean War of 1950–1953 and the liberation of Kuwait from Iraqi occupation in 1990 and 1991. These were both in the nature of collective self-defense exercises, but at the same time they were responses to unlawful uses of force by North Korea and Iraq, respectively. The key point remains, however, that law enforcement is only, so to speak, a side effect of the Security Council's principal peacekeeping mission.

In the course of its peacekeeping mandate, the Security Council is certainly capable of making arrangements for the compensation of victims of legal wrongdoing. The case of Kuwait and Iraq is especially instructive. In addition to the physical expulsion of Iraqi forces from Kuwait's territory, provision was also made for monetary payments by Iraq, out of its oil revenues, for damages committed by it. A massive compensation program was devised and administered by a body called the UN Compensation Commission. Throughout the years, awards of more than $50 billion were approved by the Commission, for the benefit of approximately 1.5 million individual claimants. In addition, four countries (Kuwait plus Saudi Arabia, Jordan, and Iran) received awards.[7] These payments, however, were very carefully crafted so as to constitute indemnities for losses, as opposed to criminal-style fines for misconduct. They therefore cannot be regarded as punitive in character.

Most commonly, Security Council action, when it occurs, is primarily utilitarian in character. This is especially evident in cases in which the Council's goal has been to reduce suffering in armed conflicts—most typically by means of arms embargoes. During the Croatian and Bosnian civil strife of 1991–1995, an arms embargo was imposed against all parties to the conflicts.[8] Similarly, in the case of the Libyan civil war that began in 2011, an arms embargo was imposed.[9]

Some instances of Security Council action could even be said to be primarily punitive in character and only secondarily utilitarian. The best illustrations are the actions taken against Southern Rhodesia and South Africa in response to the racial policies of those countries. In 1966, the Security Council ordered UN member states to apply a broad range of economic measures against Southern Rhodesia.[10] In 1977, the Council ordered a mandatory arms embargo against South Africa.[11] Neither of these, however, was really a pure case of punishment. Regarding Southern Rhodesia, the sanctions certainly had a utilitarian, as well as a punitive, character. They were designed to bring about a change of government policy (or even a change of government). Similarly, in the South African

---

7. For full information on the operation of the UN Compensation Commission, see https://uncc.ch/home.

8. S. C. Res. 713, Sep. 25, 1991.

9. S. C. Res. 1970, Feb. 26, 2011.

10. S. C. Res. 232, Dec. 16, 1966.

11. S. C. Res. 418, Nov. 4, 1977.

case, there was, in addition to the punitive element, a utilitarian concern to blunt the country's power to do harm through the use of armed force.

### 3.5.2. The Sometimes Short Path from Self-Defense to Armed Reprisals

It was noted above that self-defense action is essentially nonpenal because it focuses entirely on the rescue of the person being attacked rather than on the moral turpitude of the attacker. Self-defense has been accepted as a lawful right of states since at least the Middle Ages, but only since 1945 has it come play an important part in international law. The reason is that self-defense is the sole permissible use of unilateral force to be explicitly recognized by the UN Charter.[12] As noted above, self-defense, at least in its purest form, is action taken in the very face of an ongoing armed attack, with a view to defeating the aggression and restoring the status quo.

There have been several instances in which action began as legitimate self-defense but then strayed beyond the limits allowed. In the Korean War, for example, the UN forces did not rest content with expelling the North Korean forces from South Korean territory. Instead, at the behest and under the leadership of the United States, the decision was made to carry the war into the North, with a view to unifying the peninsula under a single government. This ambition was, however, frustrated by the entry of Chinese forces (supposedly consisting solely of non-state-supported "volunteers"). Perhaps the most notorious case of enlargement of self-defense occurred in the Iran–Iraq conflict of 1980–1988. It began with an act of naked aggression by Iraq against Iran. Here too, the attack was repulsed. But Iran was not content with the status quo ante. It then counter-invaded Iraq, with an avowed goal of removing the government of Iraq from power.

There have even been occasions in which the presence of even an initial exercise of self-defense was doubtful. Perhaps the clearest example of

---

12. UN Charter, art. 51.

this was the American air attack on Libya in 1986. This was precipitated by a terrorist incident that occurred in a nightclub in West Berlin, in which a number of American nationals were killed. In response, the United States mounted an air attack on Libya, apparently with a view to killing the country's leader, Muammar Qaddafi. The action was justified as self-defense, although it clearly was not designed to prevent the terrorist bombing in Berlin from being carried to fruition. That attack was completed prior to the American air attack—which in any event was directed at a target very far from West Berlin. Notwithstanding the proffered American justification, it is difficult to see this incident in any other terms than as a punitive act.

### 3.5.3. Humanitarian Intervention

Perhaps the single most hotly contested topic in the whole of international law is the lawfulness, or otherwise, of humanitarian intervention—meaning the use of armed force, without UN Security Council authorization, to put a stop to serious violations of human rights. What is envisaged here is a kind of self-appointed rescue effort, in which a state takes it upon itself (perhaps in company with other like-minded states) to come to the rescue of some foreign population that is being oppressed by its own ruler. It is, in short, a self-help operation but one that is in the interest not of the acting state but, rather, of the population of some foreign country.

Fortunately, it is not necessary for present purposes to wade into the contentious debate over the lawfulness of such high-minded conduct (for a case against the lawfulness of humanitarian intervention, see Chesterman, 2002; for a case in favor, see Téson, 2005). It is only necessary to note that those who support the lawfulness of humanitarian intervention characterize it very explicitly in utilitarian rather than punitive terms. In this respect, it bears a distinct resemblance to self-defense, which (as noted above) is characterized legally as rescue rather than as punishment. Humanitarian intervention, of course, is not actually a form of self-defense because, by definition, it entails the rescue of persons outside the jurisdiction of the intervening state. But its advocates do view it as, in effect, an analogue of self-defense—and, as such, subject to the constraints of necessity and proportionality in essentially the same way as self-defense.

A clear case in which humanitarian intervention has been explicitly invoked occurred in 2018 when the United States and Britain mounted coordinated air strikes against Syria, in response to its use of chemical weapons in its civil war. As a legal justification of its action, the British government expressly invoked the right of humanitarian intervention. The operation was not described as punitive, however. The stated goal was "to alleviate overwhelming humanitarian suffering."[13]

As in the case of Security Council actions designed to alter the behavior of states, there is often little difficulty in espying at least a modest punitive component to humanitarian operations. The bombing campaign in Serbia in 1999, for example, can easily be given a double characterization—as designed both to punish the Serbian government for its repressive policies and to induce it to alter those policies. The same could be said of the Syrian attacks of 2018.

### 3.5.4. Modern-Day Reprisals (Countermeasures)

It has been observed that UN Charter's general prohibition against the use of force is generally understood to encompass armed reprisals. Nonforcible reprisal measures, however, continue to be permitted in international law—although under the new label of "countermeasures." There are restrictions on the resort to these measures, which substantially replicate the older law on reprisals as articulated in the Naulilaa case discussed above. Also carried over from the older law is the rejection—at least in principle—of any punitive character to countermeasures. Countermeasures can be

---

13. "Syria Action—UK Government Legal Position," Apr. 14, 2018, https://www.gov.uk/government/publications/syria-action-uk-government-legal-position/syria-action-uk-government-legal-position.

either utilitarian or compensatory, but not punitive. As the Commission stated in its official commentary on the State Responsibility Articles,

> Countermeasures may only be taken by an injured State in order to induce the responsible State to comply with its obligations..., namely, to cease the internationally wrongful conduct, if it is continuing, and to provide reparation to the injured State. Countermeasures are not intended as a form of punishment for wrongful conduct, but as an instrument for achieving compliance with the obligations [owed].[14]

This seems clear enough. Unfortunately, the matter becomes slightly less clear when the requirement of proportionality is considered. This is another feature that has been inherited directly from the law governing 19th-century reprisals. There has been debate as to the meaning of proportionality, between basically two schools of thought, which have been helpfully (if informally) labeled as the "equivalence" and the "cessation" positions (Etezazian, 2016, pp. 264–277). According to the equivalence view, proportionality means that the material injury inflicted by the countermeasures must be more or less equivalent, quantitatively, to the material injury caused by the original wrongful act. It need not be the same in *kind*, but it should be the same in *severity*. In that sense, it should be a tit-for-tat measure. According to the cessation view, in contrast, proportionality means that the injury done by the countermeasures is limited by the principle of necessity—that is, that as much injury may be inflicted onto the wrongdoing party as is necessary, under the circumstances, to induce that party to cease its wrongdoing and provide the required reparation. Any injury beyond that amount would be disallowed as mere gratuitous injury, which is clearly prohibited.

It may be noted that the equivalence viewpoint is backward-looking, in the sense that it looks to the prior injury to dictate the seriousness of the countermeasure allowed. This is in keeping with the idea of punishment,

---

14. Int'l Law Comm'n, Commentary on art. 49, in Report on Its 53d Session, UN Doc. A/56/10 (2001), at 130.

in which the severity of the sanction applied is governed, basically, by the severity of the wrongdoing that provoked it. To this extent, therefore, it may be said that the equivalence position implicitly embodies a retributive or punitive outlook. The cessation approach, in contrast, is clearly utilitarian. It is forward-looking, in the sense that the governing principle is to allow whatever injury is needed to bring about an appropriate change in the future conduct of the wrongdoing state.

Basically, the Articles on State Responsibility seek to strike a fine balance between the two positions—but it is fair to say that the greater support is given to the equivalence stance. Article 51, on proportionality, states, "Countermeasures must be commensurate with the injury suffered, taking into account the gravity of the internationally wrongful act and the rights in question [of the injured state]." This formulation basically adopts the equivalence position because countermeasures are to be "commensurate with the injury suffered." As a secondary matter, however, the injury can be adjusted upward or downward to take account of two other factors: the gravity of the original wrong and the value of the rights affected by that wrong. This appears to suggest that countermeasures do, in fact, have a somewhat punitive character, given that, as in the case of criminal punishments, there is a concern to match the response to the gravity of the offense.

It is not easy to reconcile Article 51 with the commentary on Article 49 quoted above, which appears to reject punitivity so decisively. Perhaps the best way to view the matter is to say that the material damage which can legally be inflicted by countermeasures is to be measured by the equivalence test (with appropriate adjustment)—but that, at the same time, the *purpose* of those countermeasures must be either compensatory or utilitarian (or both).

The conclusion may fairly be reached that, on this point, international law is in something of a muddle. The difficulty is mitigated, however, by the fact that, in reality, the conceptual crevice between the equivalence approach, on the one hand, and the compensatory and utilitarian strategies, on the other hand, is not so vast. Backward-looking measures that are "commensurate with the injury" are generally not really so different, in practice, from forward-looking measures that seek to induce a change of future conduct. Consequently, whether countermeasures are viewed as punitive or, alternatively, as utilitarian or compensatory will often lie only in the eye of the beholder.

### 3.5.5. Proposals for Punitive Damages Against States

If some uncertainties and ambiguities remain in the law of countermeasures, there are several areas of law that are decidedly more speculative in character. Two of these are briefly considered here: the possibility of punitive damages against states and the possibility of direct criminal responsibility of states. Consider first the subject of punitive damages. This expression is something of an oxymoron because the term "damages" refers to compensatory payments, which (as noted above) are, in principle, quite distinct from punitive action.[15] Punitive damages combine the two concepts. These are money payments imposed onto a state as a result of wrongdoing, which are explicitly above and beyond what is needed to rectify the injury done and to compensate the victim of the wrong. They are punitive in character in that (at least in principle) they reflect the moral turpitude of the wrongdoer rather than the material losses that arose from the wrong. They are appropriate in cases in which the compensatory payments are thought to be too light a "penalty" and that, consequently, some additional payment should be assessed.

Punitive damages are a feature of many domestic legal systems. But efforts to incorporate the concept into international law have met, so far, with minimal success.[16] "Compensation," cautioned the World Court in

---

15. See, to this effect, the Lusitania Cases Arbitration (*U.S.A. v. Germany*), 7 R.I.A.A. 32 (1923), at 39.

16. See, for example, the Manouba Arbitration (*France v. Italy*), 11 R.I.A.A. 463 (1913), at 475; and Arbitration on Acts Committed by Germany (*Portugal v. Germany*), 2 R.I.A.A. 1035 (1930), at 1076–77.

2018, "should not... have a punitive or exemplary character."[17] The Court reiterated the point in 2022, pronouncing it to be "well established in international law that reparation due to a State is compensatory in nature and should not have a punitive character."[18]

Even in the area in which punitive damages might be thought to be most appropriate—for violations of human rights law—no significant headway has been made. In a notable case in 1989, for example, the Inter-American Court of Human Rights was asked to impose punitive damages and declined to do so.[19] Similarly, the European Court of Human Rights has adopted a policy of not awarding punitive damages.[20] A very striking case in which punitive damages might have been justified was the case of the murder by poisoning of the Russian dissident Alexander Litvinenko in London in 2006. Credible evidence emerged that the perpetrators of the murder were in the employ of the Russian state. An action against Russia was brought in the European Court of Human Rights over the matter, in which Russia was found to be responsible for the death. Punitive damages against Russia were requested by the claimant but refused by the Court.[21]

Notwithstanding this firm and consistent rejection of punitive damages in international law up to the present time, it is not impossible that the future might be different. In the 2018 World Court case referred to above, one of the judges, Judge Bhandari, wrote in favor of allowing punitive damages in cases of serious damage to the natural environment.[22] It should also be noted that one country, the United States, has made provision for punitive damages against states in its domestic law. In 2008, the United States

---

17. Certain Activities in the Border Area (Compensation) (*Costa Rica v. Nicaragua*), 2018 I.C.J. Rep. 15, para. 31.

18. Armed Activities (Compensation) (*Congo v. Uganda*), Feb. 9, 2022, para. 102.

19. *Velásquez Rodríguez v. Honduras* (Reparations and Costs), July 29, 1989, American Convention on Human Rights, Ser. C, No. 7, para. 38; and 95 Int'l L. Rep. 315–16.

20. See, for example, *Greens v. the United Kingdom*, 53 E.H.R.R. 710 (2010), para. 97.

21. *Carter v. Russia* (21.9.21), 74 E.H.R.R. 354 (2021), para. 180.

22. Certain Activities in the Border Area (Compensation) (*Costa Rica v. Nicaragua*), 2018 I.C.J. Rep. 15, Op. of Judge Bhandari, at 96, paras. 16–21. I thank Professor James Harrison of the University of Edinburgh for drawing my attention to this opinion.

enacted legislation that makes punitive damages against states available to victims of state-sponsored terrorist acts.[23] One action brought against Sudan in 2014 resulted in a punitive damages award of approximately $4.3 billion.[24] It is not impossible that other countries might follow the United States' lead in allowing punitive damages against states, perhaps in areas other than terrorism (e.g., genocide or aggression). In that event, support could build for allowing them as a matter of customary international law (which is an outgrowth of state practice). But that will inevitably take some time, if it occurs at all.

## 3.6. CONCLUSION

We have observed that of the three classes of consequences of legal wrongdoing—the compensatory, the utilitarian, and the punitive—the punitive is very much the junior partner. It is not altogether absent from inter-state relations, but it has nowhere near the officially recognized respectability of the other two. It leads a somewhat shadowy existence, as befits a system of law that arises from below, out of the day-to-day practice of states, instead of being pronounced from above by crowned heads or parliaments or presidents. There scarcely be punishment without a punisher—that is, without a government—as B. F. Skinner candidly reminds us.

Such a conclusion might, however, be too glib. It should not be impossible for punishments to be collectively inflicted by the community at large on its own initiative. Collective actions such as shaming and shunning by community members as a whole can sometimes be devastatingly effective as punishments. Some religious groups, such as the Jehovah's Witnesses, the Amish, and the Hutterites, are known to use such methods

---

23. National Defense Authorization Act, 122 Stat. 3, §1083(a); 28 U.S. Code §1605A(c).

24. *Opati v. Republic of Sudan*, 60 F.Supp. 3d 68 (D.D.C., 2014), at 82. For later consideration of certain aspects of the case by the U.S. Supreme Court, see *Opati v. Republic of Sudan*, 140 S. Ct. 1601 (2020).

to great effect (Zippelius, 1986, pp. 159–166). But it is difficult to see collective tactics such as these working effectively in inter-state relations. It is not that spontaneous, community-wide sanctioning cannot work. The problem is more fundamental: the absence of a community in the first place. International society, as it is currently, is too fragmented and too egoistical to enable collective punishing to be feasible. That is not to say that this will always be so. It is not impossible that the states of the world may gradually gel into a true community united by a rich set of shared values and norms—in contrast to the present world in which states are bound by such fragile ties as treaty relations and customary practices in specific areas. At such a possible future time, there may be centralized institutions that can inflict punishments upon states in the name of the global community, as a day-to-day matter. Such a world, however, lies in the future (if at all) rather than in the present.

## References

Ager, S. L. (1996). *Interstate arbitrations in the Greek World, 337–90 B.C.* University of California Press.

Chesterman, S. (2002). *Just war or just peace? Humanitarian intervention and international law*. Oxford University Press.

Etezazian, S. (2016). The nature of the self-defence proportionality requirement. *Journal on the Use of Force and International Law*, 3(2), 260–289.

Gomes, L. (2010). *German reparations, 1919–32: A historical survey*. Palgrave Macmillan.

Grotius, H. (1925). *De Jure Belli Et Pacis* (F. W. Kelsey, Trans.). Clarendon. (Original work published 1625)

Hudson, M. O. (1943). *The Permanent Court of International Justice, 1920–1942*. Macmillan.

Moncharville, M. (1902). Le Conflit Franco–Turc De 1901. *Revue Générale de Droit International Public*, 9, 677–700.

Neff, S. C. (2005). *War and the law of nations: A general history*. Cambridge University Press.

Russell, F. H. (1975). *The just war in the Middle Ages*. Cambridge University Press.

Skinner, B. F. (1953). *Science and human behaviour*. Macmillan.

Téson, F. R. (2005). *Humanitarian intervention: An inquiry into law and morality* (3rd ed.). Transnational.

Trachtenberg, M. (1980). *Reparation in world politics: France and European economic diplomacy, 1916–1923*. Columbia University Press.

Zippelius, R. (1986). Exclusion and shunning as legal and social sanctions. *Ethology and Sociobiology*, 7(3–4), 159–166.

# 4

# Penal Logics in International Politics

*Nordic Foreign Policy on International Justice*

KJERSTI LOHNE

## 4.1. INTRODUCTION[1]

The sociology of punishment is the body of thought exploring the relations between punishment and society. It seeks to make sense of legal punishment as a social phenomenon, analyzing the role of punishment in social life. Although many consider Émile Durkheim as the grand old father of sociological approaches to punishment, the field has only come into form as an organized area of study in approximately the past two decades (Garland, 2018). According to Simon and Sparks (2013), it is not even a discipline but, rather, a *problématique*: a complex of questions addressed through different approaches. Although, as we shall see, such an open-ended approach to studies of punishment and society is useful, as a "complex of questions," the studies have been overwhelmingly dominated by the discipline of criminology, and with the journal *Punishment &*

---

1. This chapter is an output of the project "Promoting Justice in a Time of Friction: Scandinavian Penal Exports" (JustExports) funded by the Research Council of Norway.

Kjersti Lohne, *Penal Logics in International Politics* In: *Punishment in International Society*. Edited by: Wolfgang Wagner, Linet R. Durmuşoğlu, Barbora Holá, Ronald Kroeze, Jan-Willem van Prooijen, and Wouter Werner, Oxford University Press.
© Oxford University Press 2024. DOI: 10.1093/oso/9780197693483.003.0004

*Society* as its intellectual hub. There are certainly more advantages than drawbacks to this disciplinary predominance, but for our purposes, it also entails an epistemological chasm: The sociology of punishment is a body of thought deeply entrenched in the study of punishment and *national* society. As such, the sociological study of punishment in *international* society is largely unchartered territory (but see Franko, 2017; Lohne, 2019; Savelsberg, 2018).

This chapter offers an analysis of penal power when it is detached from its association with national justice and enters the realm of the international. The focus remains, however, on the *state's* penal power, its logics and rationalities when applying "penality"—the whole of the penal complex, its laws, discourses, norms, and practices (Garland, 2013)—as solutions to norm violations in international society. Specifically, the chapter contributes a comparative analysis of Nordic discourses driving penal power in two overlapping yet nonetheless distinct areas of transnational concern—namely the field of international criminal justice and the prosecution of foreign fighters. International criminal justice makes for an interesting case to study namely because it represents the primary example of punishment in international politics by constituting the international—rather than the nation-state—as the site of crime, justice, and community (McMillan, 2016). On the other hand, the issue of foreign fighters—especially in relation to the war in Syria—disrupts the national and international frame of justice and community alike, as it reveals the transnational and hybrid nature of contemporary forms of crime, punishment, and social order. It argues that whereas a humanitarian discourse drives the Nordic engagement in the larger field of international criminal justice, the discourse on foreign fighters is characterized by securitization (Buzan et al., 1998)—transforming the prosecution of international crimes into a matter of national security.[2] As such, the analysis raises interesting

---

2. The military defeat of the so-called Islamic State animated debates about what to do with the detained fighters in Syria, especially the approximately 800 European foreign fighters held in detention camps. Although many states remain less than enthusiastic to do so, many scholars argue that for moral and legal reasons, European states should repatriate foreign fighters and prosecute them in domestic courts. Because of the difficulties in gathering evidence for

questions about penal logics in international politics and about how penal power beyond the nation-state remains receptive to securitization despite political support for an international system of criminal justice.

Following this introduction, the chapter proceeds by outlining the analytical and methodological approach to connecting sociology of punishment with studies of the international. The third section delves into state discourses and logics of penality in foreign policy, focusing first on Norway's approach to international criminal justice and foreign fighters before turning to Sweden. The fourth section aims to situate the chapter's findings on penal logics beyond the national within a broader analytical framework, and it sketches out a preliminary research agenda for bridging sociology of punishment with international relations. As such, the chapter concludes by accentuating the need to "denationalize" the sociology of punishment by positing the study of punishment at the center of study of international society.

## 4.2. TOWARD A SOCIOLOGY OF PUNISHMENT FOR INTERNATIONAL POLITICS

Punishment in international politics is widely considered to refer to the field of international criminal justice, including war crimes trials and punishment of the so-called core international crimes: war crimes, crimes against humanity, genocide, and the crime of aggression. Alongside the institutionalization of international criminal justice through courts and tribunals, culminating in the establishment of the global and permanent International Criminal Court (ICC) in 1998, there has emerged an extensive literature and academic commentary on the field's development and practice (Christensen, 2015; Vasiliev, 2015), including on the justifications

prosecuting international crimes—war crimes, crimes against humanity, and genocide—in conflict, most prosecutions of foreign fighters today focus on charges related to membership in a terrorist organization, which has a much lower evidentiary threshold (Cuyckens & Paulussen, 2019).

and rationalities, consequences, and functions of punishment in international criminal justice (Drumbl, 2007; Hola et al., 2011; Stahn, 2020). Yet, in addition to the criminalization of core international crimes, there are a number of developments in need of more critical thinking regarding how questions of crime, punishment, and justice are becoming increasingly international.

For example, whereas the ICC promises global justice in case of "failed" national justice, there is simultaneously a less visibly and politically contested, global system of international organizations, nongovernmental organizations (NGOs), and donor and "rooster"-contributing nations offering bilateral or multilateral "penal aid" to other nation-states under the auspices and budgets of foreign affairs and humanitarian aid (Brisson-Boivin & O'Connor, 2013). At the regional level, there are internationalized courts (e.g., the African Court of Human and People's Rights) and transborder police and intelligence cooperation (Goldsmith & Sheptycki, 2007), but also the emergence of what we may consider as transnational penality: The European Union (EU), for example, has rapidly advanced into a politicolegal organ with its own distinctive court, law, regulations, prosecution office, and norms regulating policing and punishment within EU territory (Rafaraci & Belfiore, 2018). Along with global prohibition regimes (Nadelmann, 1990), transnational prison rental agreements (Pakes & Holt, 2017),[3] and international prisons,[4] these developments all suggest a conceptual and empirical disconnection between crime, punishment, and the nation-state. Indeed—and perhaps instead—they represent

---

3. The most recent example is Denmark's rent of 300 prison places in Kosovo, to where they will send their foreign criminals. See https://www.ft.com/content/42e396a5-82df-4e44-a883-18883 fb880c3.

4. After being brought before trial on universal jurisdiction charges in The Seychelles, Somali pirates are transferred to a prison in Somaliland that is funded by the United Nations (UN). https://www.unodc.org/unodc/en/press/releases/2011/March/unodc-open-somalilands-first-prison-in-50-years-to-further-tackle-piracy-scourge.html. Another example of an international prison is the international wing of Mpanga prison in Rwanda, which not only is funded by international donors but also exclusively hosts prisoners convicted by the Special Chambers of Sierra Leone.

emerging forms of transnational penal power, challenging us to examine contemporary penal governance through a much more complex lens.

As indicated above, there is empirical and theoretical work regarding some of these developments. However, a critical lack of overarching perspectives remains on how penal discourses, norms, and practices operate as expressions of power in international politics. At the same time, the sociology of punishment remains conspicuously absent from analytical engagement with how questions of criminal law and justice are becoming increasingly international (but see Aaronson & Shaffer, 2021; Franko, 2017; Lohne, 2019; Savelsberg, 2018). The lack of engagement with transnational penal power and punishment in international politics may be attributed to the sticky division of disciplinary labor between criminology and international relations in studying the national and international (Loader & Percy, 2012) and to the privileged role of the nation-state framework in the study of crime and punishment (Aas, 2012).

Paralleling the need for empirical engagement with contemporary, globalized forms of penal power is the need for a sociology of punishment that is global both in scale and in imagination—"disembedded" from the field's "methodological nationalism" (Aas, 2012; Beck, 2007). As concerns punishment in international politics, there are at least two features that disrupt the way punishment is conceptualized within national politics and the nation-state framework. First, there is no sovereign in international society. Yet in the sociology of punishment literature, it is not only more or less a truism that the power to punish rests with the state (Zedner, 2016) but also that—in the spirit of Max Weber—the nation-state itself is defined by its monopoly of violence. That punishment and penal power have expanded to the international not only upsets these epistemologies but also implies that punishment and penal power need to find justification and legitimacy in other functions and sources of authority than that of sovereign state power. Second, there is no public constituency of voters in international politics. This implies that penal mentalities, sensibilities, and discourses about crime, punishment, and justice must be mobilized by actors for other purposes than the pursuit of electoral votes and public accountability to one's constituency (Lohne, 2019). In lieu of the nation-state, questions need to be asked about what—and who—drives punishment and penal power at the international level.

For example, in international relations, there is a lack of attention to how penal power is deployed in foreign policy. Although there is a significant literature on international criminal justice (e.g., Kersten, 2016), sanctions of norm violations (e.g., Erickson, 2020), and the spread of punitive practices and solutions at the international level (e.g., Lang, 2009), there is a dearth of empirical knowledge and analytic scrutiny of penal power as part of the foreign policy toolbox. To begin to address this gap, this chapter analyzes expressions of penal values, discourses, and power in foreign policy and international aid, specifically those of Norway and Sweden. As we discuss later, the humanitarian character and "soft power" status of these two countries' foreign policies make them particularly apt for studying (penal) power in international politics in terms of norms and values, including the pursuits of justice and community (rather than studying power as mere expressions of anarchy and coercion in international society) (see Hoffmann, 2010). By analyzing Norway and Sweden's foreign policy positions on two aspects of punishment in international politics, namely international criminal justice and the prosecution of foreign fighters, the chapter argues that whereas a discourse on humanitarianism dominates their contribution to international criminal justice, the discourse on prosecution of foreign fighters is much more security-oriented.

The analysis is based on a close reading of Norway and Sweden's open-source government documents dealing with international criminal justice and foreign fighters, where particular attention has been given to government "speech acts," policies, legislation, and parliamentary debates. The author carried out a document search based on relevant key words in the two countries' online databases for government documents covering the years 2017–2021.[5] After the initial keyword search, relevance was identified manually by excluding repetitive boilerplate documents and

---

5. Keywords for Norway included "ICC," "internasjonal strafferett," "internasjonal straffedomstol," and "fremmedkriger." Keywords for Sweden included "ICC," "terroristresor," and "syrien + brott."

passing, insubstantial references to the ICC or foreign fighters. The data material subsequently analyzed includes 25 documents on Norway's position on international criminal justice, 19 documents on Norway's position on the prosecution of foreign fighters, 25 documents on Sweden's position on international criminal justice, and 9 documents on Sweden's position on the prosecution of foreign fighters. In addition, the data include a review of Norway and Sweden's statements at the ICC's annual Assembly of States Parties (ASP) meetings within the same period. The documents were analyzed with attention to discourse and "speech acts," focusing in particular on how assumptions and beliefs about punishment and penal power are communicated and the purposes of different types of language (Fairclough, 2013). As official policy documents, they relate to particular social, political, and historical contexts that were also considered when analyzing how these texts "do" foreign policy practice.

## 4.3. STATE DISCOURSES AND LOGICS OF PENALITY IN FOREIGN POLICY

### 4.3.1. Norway on International Criminal Justice and the Prosecution of Foreign Fighters

Norway has an extensive and long-standing foreign policy engagement with international criminal justice (Fife, 2000). It presents itself as a "staunch supporter" of the ICC and a "consistent partner" in the "fight against impunity."[6] Norway played an active role in the negotiation process of the Rome Statute of the International Criminal Court (Benedetti &

---

6. Norway Ministry of Foreign Affairs, 19th Session of the Assembly of States Parties to the Rome Statute of the International Criminal Court, The Hague, December 14–16, 2020, statement by Minister of foreign affairs, Ine Eriksen Søreide; Norway Ministry of Foreign Affairs, 18th Session of the Assembly of States Parties to the Rome Statute of the International Criminal Court, statement by Monica Furnes, Director, Ministry of Foreign Affairs; Norway Ministry of Foreign Affairs, 17th Session of the Assembly of States Parties to the Rome Statute of the International Criminal Court, statement by Monica Furnes, Director, Ministry of Foreign Affairs.

Washburn, 1999), and it has had a substantial diplomatic focus by, for example, engaging and leading several working group processes in the ICC's ASP. It has signed sentence transfer agreements with the ICC (and previous international criminal tribunals, such as the International Criminal Tribunal for the former Yugoslavia) and has implemented the Rome Statute in national law (Klamberg, 2023), ensuring that, according to the Ministry of Foreign Affairs (MFA), "Norwegian authorities can cooperate in full with the Court."[7]

The data further document Norway's driving logics behind its support for the ICC. As it makes clear in its priorities to the UN General Assembly,[8] Norway wants to support work for a world order based on international law and the UN Charter. As such, an "overarching" and "central" goal is to fight impunity and strengthen international criminal law through working for universal ratification of the ICC's Rome Statute and for a good working relationship between states and the Court. That Norway led the working group on legal amendments to the ICC's ASP must be seen to reflect this ambition.

As the Norwegian MFA makes clear in its annual budget, Norway views the ICC as "an important contribution to democratization, rule of law promotion and peace-building after armed conflict."[9] Although it views the "ICC [as] a fundamental part of the international peace and security architecture"[10] and "a fundamental part of rules-based international order that we have all benefited from,"[11] it also focuses on how "justice for

---

7. Prop. 1 S (2017–2018) - For budsjettåret 2018 under Utenriksdepartementet, Utgiftskapitler: 100–172 Inntektskapitler: 3100, 12.10.2017 Proposisjon Utenriksdepartementet. For a review of Norway's criminalization of international crimes—and the somewhat paradoxically scant case law—see Høgestøl (2020).

8. Norges prioriteringer til FNs 72. generalforsamling, 15.09.2017 Artikkel Utenriksdepartementet; Norges prioriteringer under FNs 73. generalforsamling, 11.09.2018 Artikkel Utenriksdepartementet.

9. Prop. 1 S (2017–2018) - For budsjettåret 2018 under Utenriksdepartementet, Utgiftskapitler: 100–172 Inntektskapitler: 3100, 12.10.2017 Proposisjon Utenriksdepartementet.

10. 17th Session of the Assembly of States Parties to the Rome Statute of the International Criminal Court, statement by Monica Furnes, Director, Ministry of Foreign Affairs.

11. 17th Session of the Assembly of States Parties to the Rome Statute of the International Criminal Court, statement by Monica Furnes, Director, Ministry of Foreign Affairs.

victims is increasingly being seen as a prerequisite for peace."[12] For these reasons, Norway is a substantial donor to the ICC's semi-independent Trust Fund for Victims. Indeed, most MFA statements to the ASP General Assembly meetings express financial support to the Fund, for instance, through statements such as "I am pleased to announce that Norway is ready to provide a voluntary contribution to the Trust Fund for Victims, earmarked for reparations to victims of the Al Mahdi case."[13] These earmarked contributions to restitution of cultural heritage are elsewhere presented as "contribution to the advance of rule of law principles."[14]

MFA statements to the ASP General Assembly meetings also emphasize the importance of "applying the full force of the law to address sexual and gender-based crimes and crimes against children"[15] and commend the Court's efforts to focus on these particular crimes.[16] In relation to the fight against impunity for sexual-based violence in conflict, Norway emphasizes its substantial financial contributions—for example, through the ICC's Victims Trust Fund. This focus on sexual and gender-based violence is also apparent in other areas of Norwegian foreign policy, such as through operational support in the form of police advisors and experts on the topic seconded to UN operations in Liberia and Haiti.[17]

However, in contrast to a discourse on the ICC characterized by humanitarian and liberal values of rule of law, democracy, and human rights—and on "justice for victims" and sexual and gender-based crimes

12. 17th Session of the Assembly of States Parties to the Rome Statute of the International Criminal Court, statement by Monica Furnes, Director, Ministry of Foreign Affairs.

13. 16th session (December 6–8, 2017) of the Assembly of States Parties to the Rome Statute of the International Criminal Court, Permanent Mission of Norway to the United Nations.

14. Prop. 1 S (2020–2021) - For budsjettåret 2021 under Utenriksdepartementet, Utgiftskapitler: 100–179 Inntektskapitler: 3100, 07.10.2020 Proposisjon Utenriksdepartementet.

15. 17th Session of the Assembly of States Parties to the Rome Statute of the International Criminal Court, statement by Monica Furnes, Director, Ministry of Foreign Affairs.

16. See also 16th session (December 6–8, 2017) of the Assembly of States Parties to the Rome Statute of the International Criminal Court, Permanent Mission of Norway to the United Nations.

17. Spørsmål og svar om kvinner, fred og sikkerhet, 15.11.2018 Artikkel Utenriksdepartementet.

and crimes against children—the discourse on foreign fighters in Syria is dominated by security concerns. As a white paper from the Norwegian MFA makes clear, "returned foreign fighters constitute a security risk."[18] As such, the reviewed documents focus heavily on the need to counter security threats through various means and especially international intelligence cooperation.

The identification of returned foreign fighters as security risks parallels the government's view that "prosecution of foreign fighters should generally be carried out where the crimes have been committed."[19] It stresses that Norwegian citizens who have committed crimes in Syria or Iraq must expect to be prosecuted there, and that Norway participates in international discussions regarding justice initiatives in the region and supports international mechanisms for the collection of evidence. Should foreign fighters nonetheless return to Norway, they will be prosecuted according to Norwegian penal law. According to the Norwegian MFA, Norwegian penal law provides a solid framework for prosecuting individuals who have supported ISIS or participated in crimes in Syria and Iraq.[20] Since 2016, Norway has incrementally criminalized the activities of foreign fighters, covering traveling and participation in foreign wars (on behalf of non-state parties) as well as participation in terror groups.[21]

To counter the risk of returned foreign fighters, the data highlight the need for increased international cooperation and to combine societal security and national preparedness against returned foreign fighters with the stabilization of foreign states. International cooperation must be strengthened at the Nordic, European, and UN levels, and the documents in various ways refer to Norway's role as a driving force for

---

18. Meld. St. 36 (2016–2017) - Veivalg i norsk utenriks- og sikkerhetspolitikk, 21.04.2017 Melding til Stortinget Utenriksdepartementet.

19. Prop. 1 S (2020–2021) - For budsjettåret 2021 under Utenriksdepartementet, Utgiftskapitler: 100–179 Inntektskapitler: 3100, 07.10.2020 Proposisjon Utenriksdepartementet.

20. Prop. 1 S (2020–2021) - For budsjettåret 2021 under Utenriksdepartementet, Utgiftskapitler: 100–179 Inntektskapitler: 3100, 07.10.2020 Proposisjon Utenriksdepartementet.

21. Høgestøl (2018); see also Chapter 18 of the Norwegian Penal Code.

such cooperation. For example, according to Norway, it has become one of the main actors working for a joint UN anti-terror strategy,[22] and in its current (2021–2022) seat at the UN Security Council, Norway heads the 1267 committee on sanctions for ISIS and al-Qaeda and is a member of the 1373 committee on counterterrorism.[23] Discursively, foreign fighters and the terror threat are discussed as part of both "global security threats" and transnational organized crime, invoking the need for both military and civil police cooperation and preparedness at local and global levels alike.[24] Although this justifies the need for strengthening international police and intelligence cooperation, and to implement stronger border police along Schengen's outer borders, it also justifies measures such as police capacity-building in foreign states. "As a contribution to the fight against impunity," Norway leads a French–Norwegian specialized police team in the UN operation Minusma in Mali.[25] In the words of the Norwegian MFA, "It is important for Norway to see development aid and security policy in connection with one another and to develop a coherent politics to meet these [global] security threats."[26] In other words, the "stabilization" of foreign states is particularly interesting because it links to wider debates—and "mission creeps"—between security and development.[27]

In summary, Norway views punishment of international crimes, including the prosecution of foreign fighters, through a variety of foreign policy discourses. Whereas the discourse on foreign fighters is more

22. Meld. St. 44 (2016–2017) - Noregs deltaking i den 71. ordinære generalforsamlinga i Dei sameinte nasjonane (FN), 21.06.2017 Melding til Stortinget Utenriksdepartementet.

23. Kontraterror, forebygging av voldelig ekstremisme, organisert kriminalitet, 29.11.2021 Artikkel Utenriksdepartementet.

24. For example, Regjeringens arbeidsprogram for samarbeidet med EU i 2017, 01.02.2017 Plan/strategi Utenriksdepartementet.

25. Kontraterror, forebygging av voldelig ekstremisme, organisert kriminalitet, 29.11.2021 Artikkel Utenriksdepartementet.

26. Prop. 1 S (2017–2018) - For budsjettåret 2018 under Utenriksdepartementet, Utgiftskapitler: 100–172 Inntektskapitler: 3100, 12.10.2017 Proposisjon Utenriksdepartementet.

27. See also Kontraterror, forebygging av voldelig ekstremisme, organisert kriminalitet, 29.11.2021 Artikkel Utenriksdepartementet: "Security and development must be seen in connection to one another."

explicit in its internal state security focus, Norway's foreign policy approach to international criminal justice is characterized by a humanitarian, victim-oriented discourse along with an overall emphasis on a rules-based international order.

### 4.3.2. Sweden on International Criminal Justice and the Prosecution of Foreign Fighters

International law is likewise core to Swedish foreign policy.[28] With increasing geopolitical friction and pushback against multilateralism and the liberal world order, Sweden considers it imperative to work for the protection of the rules-based international system as represented by the UN: "The rules-based system is essential for the safety of the world, but also for the safety of Sweden."[29] As such, Sweden is clear about the security motives that underlie its support for and work to strengthen international law and the liberal world order it depends on. Invoking the democratic peace theory, Sweden's foreign minister also professes that "democracies do not go to war with one another," that "there is a clear connection between international law and democracy," and that "to me, it is obvious that international law is a tool for democratic development."[30]

Sweden's statements at the ASP General Assembly meetings reiterate "its steadfast support"[31] for the ICC, how Sweden is a "strong proponent"

---

28. Tal vid UD:s Folkrättsdag Stockholm, 1 februari 2018. Det talade ordet gäller. 02 februari 2018 Tal från Utrikesdepartementet.

29. Tal vid UD:s Folkrättsdag Stockholm, 1 februari 2018. Det talade ordet gäller. 02 februari 2018 Tal från Utrikesdepartementet.

30. Tal av utrikesminister Margot Wallström vid UD:s folkrättsdag 2019, Stockholm den 5 april 2019 Det talade ordet gäller 08 april 2019 Tal från Utrikesdepartementet.

31. Government Offices of Sweden, statement by Her Excellency Ann Linde, Minister of Foreign Affairs, at the General Debate, 19th Session of the Assembly of States Parties to the Rome Statute, The Hague, December 6, 2021, Ministry of Foreign Affairs, Sweden; Government Offices of Sweden, statement by Her Excellency Ann Linde, Minister of Foreign Affairs, at the General Debate, 19th Session of the Assembly of States Parties to the Rome Statute, The Hague, December 14, 2020, Ministry of Foreign Affairs, Sweden.

of its important mandate, and that "impunity is unacceptable."³² These statements follow a similar form and structure as the statements made by Norway, which include thanks to and appreciation for the Court's officials, comments on the internal institutional processes going on at the Court, and concerns about current pushbacks and threats against the "rules-based order."³³ However, in comparison to Norway, Swedish statements are slightly longer and more explicit in their agenda. For example, Sweden repeatedly laments the absence of a Security Council referral of the situation in Syria to the ICC, and later also Myanmar.

The statements also maintain a strong gender perspective—for instance, through commenting on the representation of female staff at the Court and on the Court's work against sexual and gender-based crimes: "Rape, sexual slavery and other sexual and gender-based violence have been taken to new horrific levels. Unspeakable crimes continue to be committed in violent conflicts against women and girls, men and boys. They deserve justice."³⁴

Gender equality, translated in UN lingo to work on resolution 1325 on women, peace, and security, is core to Sweden's foreign policy, which, indeed, prides itself on representing a *feminist* foreign policy.³⁵ In addition to representation, participation, and strengthening references to resolution

---

32. Statement by Dr. Gustav Lind, Deputy Director-General, Head of the Department of International Law, Human Rights and Treaty Law, Ministry for Foreign Affairs, at the General Debate of the 16th Session of the Assembly of States Parties to the Rome Statute, New York, December 6, 2017.

33. For example, Statement by Ambassador Carl Magnus Nesser, Director-General for Legal Affairs, Ministry for Foreign Affairs, at the General Debate, 18th Session of the Assembly of States Parties to the Rome Statute, The Hague, December 2, 2019.

34. Statement by Dr. Gustav Lind, Deputy Director-General, Head of the Department of International Law, Human Rights and Treaty Law, Ministry for Foreign Affairs, at the General Debate of the 16th Session of the Assembly of States Parties to the Rome Statute, New York, December 6, 2017.

35. Tal vid UD:s Folkrättsdag Stockholm, 1 februari 2018. Det talade ordet gäller. 02 februari 2018 Tal från Utrikesdepartementet. See also Moss (2021). Sweden's 'feminist foreign policy' came to an abrupt end last year following the new rightwing government. See https://www.theguardian.com/world/2022/oct/18/swedish-government-scraps-countrys-pioneering-feminist-foreign-policy.

1325 in other UN resolutions and statements, the fight against impunity for sexual and gender-based violence is central to Sweden's work in this area. Sweden states,

> We must recognise that sexual and gender-based violence in conflict is a security challenge and a threat to development. Sexual violence in conflict is a tactic of war. It is a threat to security and durable peace that requires an operational security and justice response.[36]

Sweden's efforts in this area include, for example, the introduction of a separate listing criterion for this type of violence on the sanctions regime for the Central African Republic,[37] a call for the ICC prosecutor to give particular attention to sexual and gender-based violence,[38] and substantial financial contributions to the ICC's semi-independent Trust Fund for Victims.

Commenting on the importance of reparative justice for victims, all of the Swedish general statements at the ASP emphasize the country's financial contributions to the Victims Trust Fund, four of which add that Sweden is the Fund's largest donor, "with total contributions of approximately 3 million euros during the period 2019–2021."[39]

As mentioned previously, Sweden emphasizes accountability for crimes committed in Syria. In lieu of an ICC referral, Sweden repeatedly stresses the role that universal jurisdiction can play for prosecuting international crimes and that national courts can contribute to accountability alongside regional and international ones. There have been several war crimes

---

36. Tal vid UD:s Folkrättsdag Stockholm, 1 februari 2018. Det talade ordet gäller. 02 februari 2018 Tal från Utrikesdepartementet.

37. Tal vid UD:s Folkrättsdag Stockholm, 1 februari 2018. Det talade ordet gäller. 02 februari 2018 Tal från Utrikesdepartementet.

38. Sverige i FN:s säkerhetsråd - vecka 19 Veckan som gick i säkerhetsrådet: Syrien/kemvapen, Bosnien-Hercegovina, Sydsudan/UNMISS, 14 maj 2018 Artikel från Utrikesdepartementet.

39. Government Offices of Sweden, statement by Her Excellency Ann Linde, Minister of Foreign Affairs, at the General Debate, 19th Session of the Assembly of States Parties to the Rome Statute, The Hague, December 6, 2021, Ministry of Foreign Affairs, Sweden.

convictions in Sweden based on universal jurisdiction, including for crimes committed in Syria; Sweden was the first state to obtain convictions under universal jurisdiction.[40] Indeed, according to the Swedish foreign minister, "Swedish prosecutors have distinguished themselves internationally for a long time." As part of this, Sweden also emphasizes its financial support of the UN-created International, Impartial and Independent Mechanism, which has been set up to investigate and gather evidence for future prosecutions[41] that could also take place under universal jurisdiction.

It is also noteworthy that the data reveal how Sweden's regional strategy for the crisis in Syria aims to strengthen local resilience.[42] Swedish foreign policy is predominantly focused on its financial contributions to humanitarian aid in Syria—it claims to be one of the largest donors here too.[43] Moreover—and presumably as part of building local resilience—Sweden fronted an international initiative to establish an ad hoc tribunal to "prosecute people who fought for the terrorist group ISIS on the ground in Syria and Iraq."[44] However, the initiative received criticism from the international human rights community, which advised "against designing any accountability mechanism whose purpose is to deal only with crimes perpetrated by one faction in a conflict."[45] The initiative must also be seen

40. Tal vid UD:s Folkrättsdag Stockholm, 1 februari 2018. Det talade ordet gäller. 02 februari 2018 Tal från Utrikesdepartementet; Anförande av utrikesminister Ann Linde vid UD:s folkrättsdag 2021, Anförande av utrikesminister Ann Linde vid UD:s folkrättsdag 2021 i Stockholm den 1 oktober 2021. 01 oktober 2021 Tal från Ann Linde, Utrikesdepartementet.

41. Nytt svenskt stöd till mekanism för ansvarsutkrävande i Syrien, Regeringen har beslutat att bidra med 3,5 miljoner kronor till FN:s mekanism för allvarliga, 04 juli 2018, Artikel från Utrikesdepartementet.

42. Sveriges regionala strategi för Syrienkrisen ändras och förlängs till 2023, Idag beslutar regeringen att ändra och förlänga den regionala strategin för Syrienkrisen, för, 17 december 2020, Pressmeddelande från Utrikesdepartementet.

43. Sveriges regionala strategi för Syrienkrisen ändras och förlängs till 2023, Idag beslutar regeringen att ändra och förlänga den regionala strategin för Syrienkrisen, för, 17 december 2020, Pressmeddelande från Utrikesdepartementet.

44. https://www.government.se/press-releases/2019/06/sweden-to-host-expert-meeting-on-isis-tribunal.

45. https://www.justiceinitiative.org/newsroom/ngos-challenge-swedens-proposal-for-an-isis-only-war-crimes-tribunal.

in light of the fact that at the time, Sweden did not have sufficiently strong laws criminalizing participation in and travel to join terror organizations. However, recently, new legislation has been adopted and applied to prosecute Swedish foreign fighters (see Holm & Wistrand Johansson, 2022).

In summary, Sweden views punishment of international crimes as imperative and emphasizes the transnational character of international criminal justice where universal jurisdiction can play a part especially in situations in which neither the conflict-ridden state nor the ICC is able or willing to prosecute.[46] Syria is central—indeed, Sweden leverages conflicts on the international agenda. Although it emphasizes the importance of a rules-based order for security reasons, and the role of the ICC herein, Sweden's foreign policy on international criminal justice and foreign fighters is also heavily driven by humanitarian reasons. Victims are in focus—particularly women and children—and in official statements, Sweden stresses its generous financial contributions to world grievances more often than not. Regarding foreign fighters and Syria in particular, there appears to be much less securitization of the issue than is the case with Norway.

## 4.4. PENAL LOGICS BEYOND THE NATIONAL

This chapter is animated by the need to study punishment and penal power in international politics. As such, the data on which this analysis is based are limited, yet they nonetheless provide a useful point of departure for exploring hypotheses and further research. The overall aim of understanding better the logics and underlying arrangements of contemporary penal governance and the operations and structural foundations of transnational penality is not an intellectual exercise. Rather, such studies will begin to address a number of troubling blind

---

46. Gemensam debattartikel av 18 utrikesministrar om kampen för att de som begått brott i Syrien inte ska gå ostraffade, Publicerad 31 mars 2021., 31 mars 2021, Debattartikel från Ann Linde, Utrikesdepartementet.

spots in international relations and sociology of punishment alike. How does the study of punishment in international politics challenge epistemologies in sociology of punishment scholarship, which are only visible when punishment is dislodged from its national frame of justice? And how is transnational penality—the "global penal complex" of criminal laws, discourses, norms, and practices—constitutive of and by international politics?

There are, of course, several roads forward to bridge international relations and sociology of punishment—empirically and analytically, as well as methodologically and theoretically (Lohne, 2020b). For example, I have previously attempted to develop a sociology of punishment for international criminal justice through a study of human rights NGOs' role in mobilizing for global justice. Approaching transnational networks of NGOs advocating for the ICC as an ethnographic object, I explored how connections are made and how forces and imaginations of global criminal justice travel. In doing so, the analysis revealed how international criminal justice is situated in particular spaces, networks, and actors and how these structure the imaginations of justice circulating in the field. As a penal field driven by cosmopolitan sensibilities and justifications, I attempted there to describe, understand, and explicate what I called a *cosmopolitan penality* (Lohne, 2019). As such, a sociological approach to international criminal justice engages the study of society to make sense of international criminal justice but also, crucially, uses international criminal justice to understand society.

In contrast to a study of international criminal justice, the analysis offered in this chapter does not deal with penality when it is detached from the nation-state altogether. Rather, the focus has remained on the nation-state, yet when penal power is directed "outwards" toward a different set of constituencies than a domestic audience of state citizens. By studying penality as it shapes up and is shaped by foreign policy and international politics, penal power is directed toward either the citizens of foreign states or the international community of state and non-state actors. In other words, penality enters the realms of foreign and international—rather than domestic—politics.

This chapter has offered an analysis of penal discourses in Norwegian and Swedish foreign policy on two interlinked areas of concern—international criminal justice and the prosecution of foreign fighters. It found two dominant discourses, one invoking humanitarianism and the other security. Whereas Norwegian foreign policy documents conveyed humanitarian discourses on issues of international criminal justice and security discourses dominated "speech acts" dealing with the issue of foreign fighters, humanitarian and security discourses were more blended in Swedish foreign policy on international criminal justice and foreign fighters. A question must be asked about what can account for these two very different discourses driving penal power in Norwegian and Swedish foreign policy.

Humanitarianism is many things to many people, it is "one way to 'do good' or to improve aspects of the human condition by focusing on suffering and saving lives in times of crisis or emergency" (Ticktin, 2014, p. 274). Humanitarianism is also, however, a form of governance (Barnett, 2013), operating, as Fassin (2011) has argued, through a particular "humanitarian reason." This governmental logic has emerged at the crossroads of political necessity and contemporary ethical concern over a world charged with violence, suffering, and insecurities (see also Reid-Henry, 2014).

Building on this work, scholars in sociology of punishment have recently begun to advance the concept of "penal humanitarianism" as a particular form of governmental logic too. For example, Bosworth (2017) explains how humanitarian discourses in migration management facilitate the transfer of penal power beyond the territorial nation state, using the example of how the British government funds prison-building programs, prison training programs, resettlement assistance for deportees, and mandatory prisoner transfer agreements with Jamaica and Nigeria—under the aegis of humanitarian aid. In my work on international criminal justice, I expanded the empirical and analytic range of penal humanitarianism to demonstrate how penal power seems to be particularly driven by humanitarian reason when punishment is disembedded from the nation-state altogether (Lohne, 2020a). The moral imperative to "do something" about the suffering of distant others—and of global violence—is today channeled into a criminal justice frame, where ending impunity for human rights violations has become a mantra for the development and institutionalization of international criminal justice (see also Engle et al., 2016; Houge & Lohne, 2017). As also observed by others (Kendall & Nouwen, 2014), the representational centrality of the victim is central—constituting a form of "currency" for human rights NGOs and other actors operating in the moral economy of global criminal justice-making (Lohne, 2019). In short, I argued that penal power is particularly driven by humanitarian reason when punishment is disembedded from the nation-state altogether (Lohne, 2020a). A question can thus be asked if penal humanitarianism is complemented—or altogether replaced—with what we may call "penal securitization" as the (northern) nation-state becomes more entangled in international criminal justice through the issue of foreign fighters and their complicity in international crimes.

At the same time, a question must be asked whether penal humanitarianism is a particularly useful concept for understanding *Nordic* penal power beyond the nation-state too. Norway and Sweden's invocation of humanitarian discourses may reflect the genre and the field of international criminal justice as, essentially, a "peace project" (see Mégret, 2018). After all, as the documents make clear, both Norwegian and Swedish foreign policy view the fight against impunity for international crimes as linked to broader objectives of democratization, rule of law promotion, and peace-building rather than to objectives associated with penality, such as deterrence and/or retribution. However, it may also reflect an extension of the states' reputation as standing for a more humane approach to punishment and criminal justice relative to other established democracies (Cavadino & Dignan, 2006; Pratt & Eriksson, 2013), and which therefore aligns with their nation-state "identities" or "brands" (Browning, 2007). Combined with the fact that Norway and Sweden have both branded themselves as "humanitarian superpowers" through their foreign policy engagements across the fields of peace-building, human rights, sustainable development, and humanitarianism more broadly (de Bengy Puyvallée & Bjørkdahl, 2021), penal humanitarianism may provide a particularly good lens for understanding how penal power is put to work by Nordic foreign policy specifically (Lohne, 2023).

However, without delving into the ontology of the Nordics as "natural born friends of peace" (Leira, 2013), scholars have shown how Norway and Sweden assert moral authority as a way of status-seeking and strategic positioning in international politics (Wohlforth et al., 2018). In contrast to "big powers" such as China, Russia, and the United States, small and medium-size states are concerned with status as a differentiating feature in the international system, with status being maintained or increased by showing one's usefulness to dominant state powers and the hegemonic international order (De Carvalho & Lie, 2015). According to status theory, in the liberal international order, contributions to multilateral organizations, peace operations, state capacity-building, international development, etc. are viewed as an expression of being a "good" state, in the sense of doing (morally) good while behaving well vis-à-vis more powerful states in the international order (Lawler, 2013). Status-seeking through moral authority thus provides a theoretical lens for grasping why Norway and Sweden emphasize humanitarian discourses, donations, and other contributions to international criminal justice. Through penal humanitarianism, Norway and Sweden are able to leverage penal power onto their foreign policy objectives while reaffirming their brand as humanitarian superpowers and strategic positioning in the international order.

At the same time, the analysis revealed a continuous reference to, and support for, the liberal international order—a rules-based system considered, as stated above, as essential "to the safety of Sweden."[47] Indeed, the liberal world order has not only provided Norway and Sweden with prominent soft power status but also guaranteed their security. As this system comes under increasing threat, it is no wonder that security discourses remain prominent in Norway and Sweden's foreign policy. Thus, this duality of humanitarian and security discourses is not contradictory. Rather, national security interests have remained foundational for

---

47. Tal vid UD:s Folkrättsdag Stockholm, 1 februari 2018. Det talade ordet gäller. 02 februari 2018, Tal från Utrikesdepartementet.

Norway and Sweden's "staunch" and "steadfast" support of international criminal justice, albeit their engagements have stressed humanitarian reasons for doing so.

The duality of humanitarianism and security in Norwegian and Swedish state logics on punishment in international politics also, arguably, has its parallel in domestic criminal justice. The notion of "Nordic penal exceptionalism," the thesis positing that criminal justice systems in the region are both different from and better than the norm in other established democracies, has been criticized for obfuscating rather than shedding light on the complexities and the contradictions of Nordic criminal justice. For example, scholars such as Vanessa Barker have stressed the Nordics' "Janus-faced penal regime" (Barker, 2013), focusing on the "benevolent violence" of the welfare state and its regressive border control politics, including recent inventions of prison islands and immigrant prisons (Barker & Smith, 2021). Drawing on Bourdieu, Luis Wacquant's (2009a, 2009b) work on neoliberal penal regimes highlights the dual nature of the state's disciplinary logic. While the state's "feminine," "left hand" takes care of social welfare functions such as education, health, and housing, the "masculine," "right hand" deals with economic discipline, efficiency, and effectiveness (Levi, 2011). In other words, this duality between social welfare and economic order represents not so much separate entities but, rather, organic logics of the state. Similarly, we may wonder if humanitarian and security discourses play a similar dual function of penal state logics in international politics. If this is so, it remains to be seen which "hand" will play out in foreign policy discourses on international justice in the future and how that will reflect the strength—or weakness—of the liberal world order and its supporting, and dependent, Nordic states.

## 4.5. CONCLUSION

This chapter has begun an inquiry about the role of penal power in foreign policy. Through an analysis of Norway and Sweden's foreign policy discourse on international criminal justice and prosecutions of foreign fighters, it has uncovered the centrality of humanitarian and security discourses in facilitating criminal justice solutions to complex and globalized violence, injustice, and suffering. It further connected Norway and Sweden's contributions to penal humanitarianism as a form of status-seeking in international politics by asserting moral authority, and it suggested that security discourses are becoming more prevalent as the liberal international order is increasingly threatened. The attention to penal discourses, especially as a form of moral authority and status-seeking, begins to provide a fuller understanding of how penal power operates beyond the nation-state framework and enters the realms of international politics. By bridging the disciplines of criminology and international relations, the chapter has moreover attempted to "denationalize" the sociology of punishment by positioning the study of punishment at the center of study of international society.

The general insight from this empirical yet certainly limited enquiry can be found in its insistence on the importance of discourse for understanding the dynamics of penal power in international politics. In domestic politics, the penal field is a much more defined area of institutional practice, policy, and study—no doubt because of the prominent and institutionalized role of criminal justice and punishment in contemporary nation-state orders. In international politics, penality is a fragmented phenomenon, dispersed across different thematic areas such as intelligence cooperation, international justice, development aid, and human rights promotion. Understanding how penal power is put to work by and for these various international policies—and how, in turn, these policies not only justify but also reconfigure the meanings and functions of punishment in international politics—remains a quest for the sociology of punishment in international society. As discourses on crime and punishment seem to have become a much more prominent way of gauging morality in international politics in the past few decades, unpacking the work of penal discourses and identifying penal power in international politics becomes all the more important. Moreover, geopolitical frictions and changes to the international order shape international politics. Scholars of punishment and society may thus have much to learn about penal power by paying closer attention to the work it does in and for international order-making.

## References

Aaronson, E., & Shaffer, G. (2021). Defining crimes in a global age: Criminalization as a transnational legal process. *Law & Social Inquiry, 46*(2), 455–486.

Aas, K. F. (2012). "The earth is one but the world is not": Criminological theory and its geopolitical divisions. *Theoretical Criminology, 16*(1), 5–20.

Barker, V. (2013). Nordic exceptionalism revisited: Explaining the paradox of a Janus-faced penal regime. *Theoretical Criminology, 17*(1), 5–25.

Barker, V., & Smith, P. S. (2021). This is Denmark: Prison islands and the detention of immigrants. *British Journal of Criminology, 61*(6), 1540–1556.

Barnett, M. N. (2013). Humanitarian governance. *Annual Review of Political Science, 16*, 379–398.

Beck, U. (2007). The cosmopolitan condition: Why methodological nationalism fails. *Theory, Culture & Society, 24*(7–8), 286–290.

Benedetti, F., & Washburn, J. L. (1999). Drafting the International Criminal Court Treaty: Two years to Rome and an afterword on the Rome Diplomatic Conference. *Global Governance, 5*(1), 1–37.

Bosworth, M. (2017). Penal humanitarianism? Sovereign power in an era of mass migration. *New Criminal Law Review, 20*(1), 39–65.

Brisson-Boivin, K., & O'Connor, D. (2013). The rule of law, security-development and penal aid: The case of detention in Haiti. *Punishment & Society, 15*(5), 515–533.

Browning, C. S. (2007). Branding Nordicity: Models, identity and the decline of exceptionalism. *Cooperation and Conflict, 42*(1), 27–51.

Buzan, B., Wæver, O., & De Wilde, J. (1998). *Security: A new framework for analysis.* Rienner.

Cavadino, M., & Dignan, J. (2006). Penal policy and political economy. *Criminology and Criminal Justice, 6*(4), 435–456.

Christensen, M. J. (2015). From symbolic surge to closing courts: The transformation of international criminal justice and its professional practices. *International Journal of Law, Crime and Justice, 43*(4), 609–625.

Cuyckens, H., & Paulussen, C. (2019). The prosecution of foreign fighters in Western Europe: The difficult relationship between counter-terrorism and international humanitarian law. *Journal of Conflict and Security Law, 24*(3), 537–565.

de Bengy Puyvallée, A., & Bjørkdahl, K. (2021). Introduction: On the resilience of the Scandinavian humanitarian brand. In A. de Bengy Puyvallée & K. Bjørkdahl (Eds.), *Do-gooders at the end of aid: Scandinavian humanitarianism in the twenty-first century* (pp. 1–12). Cambridge University Press.

De Carvalho, B., & Lie, J. H. S. (2015). A great power performance: Norway, status and the policy of involvement. In B. De Carvalho & I. B. Neumann (Eds.), *Small states and status seeking: Norway's quest for international standing* (pp. 1–21). Routledge.

Drumbl, M. A. (2007). *Atrocity, punishment, and international law.* Cambridge University Press.

Engle, K., Miller, Z., & Davis, D. M. (2016). *Anti-impunity and the human rights agenda.* Cambridge University Press.

Erickson, J. L. (2020). Punishing the violators? Arms embargoes and economic sanctions as tools of norm enforcement. *Review of International Studies, 46*(1), 96–120.

Fairclough, N. (2013). Critical discourse analysis. In J. P. Gee & M. Handford (Eds.), *The Routledge handbook of discourse analysis* (pp. 9–20). Routledge.

Fassin, D. (2011). *Humanitarian reason: A moral history of the present.* University of California Press.

Fife, R. E. (2000). Elements of Nordic practice 1999: Norway and the International Criminal Tribunals 1994–2000. *Nordic Journal of International Law, 69,* 359–372.

Franko, K. (2017). Criminology, punishment, and the state in a globalized society. In A. Liebling, S. Maruna, & L. McAra (Eds.), *The Oxford handbook of criminology* (6th ed., pp. 353–371). Oxford University Press.

Garland, D. (2013). Penality and the penal state. *Criminology, 51*(3), 475–517.

Garland, D. (2018). Theoretical advances and problems in the sociology of punishment. *Punishment & Society, 20*(1), 8–33.

Goldsmith, A., & Sheptycki, J. (2007). *Crafting transnational policing: Police capacity-building and global policing reform.* Bloomsbury.

Hoffmann, M. J. (2010). Norms and social constructivism in international relations. In R. A. Denemark (Ed.), *Oxford research encyclopedia of international studies.* Oxford University Press.

Høgestøl, S. A. (2018). En Generell Kriminalisering Av Fremmedkrigere: Den Norske Modellen Og Påtaleskjønn I Straffeloven § 145. In A. Andersson, S. A. E. Høgestøl, & A. C. Lie (Eds.), *Fremmedkrigere.* Gyldendal Juridisk.

Høgestøl, S. A. E. (2020). A Norwegian perspective on the prosecution of international crimes. In L. Lundstedt (Ed.), *Investigation and prosecution in Scandinavia of international crimes* (pp. 407–434). Stockholm University Law Faculty.

Hola, B., Smeulers, A., & Bijleveld, C. (2011). International sentencing facts and figures: Sentencing practice at the ICTY and ICTR. *Journal of International Criminal Justice, 9*(2), 411–439.

Holm, F., & Wistrand Johansson, E. (2022). Hanteringen Av Svenska Is-Resenärer i Syrien Ur Folkrättsligt Perspektiv. *Svensk Juristtidning,* 2022(3), 250–277.

Houge, A. B., & Lohne, K. (2017). End impunity! Reducing conflict-related sexual violence to a problem of law. *Law & Society Review, 51*(4), 755–789.

Kendall, S., & Nouwen, S. (2014). Representational practices at the International Criminal Court: The gap between juridified and abstract victimhood. *Law and Contemporary Problems, 76*(3), 235–262.

Kersten, M. (2016). *Justice in conflict: The effects of the International Criminal Court's interventions on ending wars and building peace.* Oxford University Press.

Klamberg, M. (2023). Nordic perspectives on international criminal law and international humanitarian law. In M. J. Christensen, K. Lohne, & M. Hornqvist (Eds.), *Nordic criminal justice in a global context: Practices and promotion of exceptionalism* (pp. 59–76). Routledge.

Lang, A. F., Jr. (2009). *Punishment, justice and international relations: Ethics and order after the Cold War.* Routledge.

Lawler, P. (2013). The "good state" debate in international relations. *International Politics*, *50*(1), 18–37.

Leira, H. (2013). "Our entire people are natural born friends of peace": The Norwegian foreign policy of peace. *Swiss Political Science Review*, *19*(3), 338–356.

Levi, R. (2011). *Class and criminal justice in neoliberal times: Wacquant dissects the penal state*. SAGE.

Loader, I., & Percy, S. (2012). Bringing the "outside" in and the "inside" out: Crossing the criminology/IR divide. *Global Crime*, *13*(4), 213–218.

Lohne, K. (2019). *Advocates of humanity: Human rights NGOs in international criminal justice*. Oxford University Press.

Lohne, K. (2020a). Penal humanitarianism beyond the nation state: An analysis of international criminal justice. *Theoretical Criminology*, *24*(2), 145–162.

Lohne, K. (2020b). Towards a sociology of international criminal justice. In M. Bergsmo, M. Klamberg, K. Lohne, & C. Mahony (Eds.), *Power in international criminal justice: Towards a sociology of international justice* (pp. 47–78). TOAEP.

Lohne, K. (2023). Nordic penal humanitarianism: Status-building, brand-alignment, and penal power. In M. J. Christensen, K. Lohne, & M. Hornqvist (Eds.), *Nordic criminal justice in a global context: Practices and promotion of exceptionalism* (pp. 128–145). Routledge.

McMillan, N. (2016). Imagining the international: The constitution of the international as a site of crime, justice and community. *Social & Legal Studies*, *25*(2), 163–180.

Mégret, F. (2018). International criminal justice as a peace project. *European Journal of International Law*, *29*(3), 835–858.

Moss, S. M. (2021). Applying the brand or not? Challenges of Nordicity and gender equality in Scandinavian diplomacy. In E. Larsen, S. M. Moss, & I. Skjelsbæk (Eds.), *Gender equality and nation branding in the Nordic region* (pp. 62–73). Routledge.

Nadelmann, E. A. (1990). Global prohibition regimes: The evolution of norms in international society. *International Organisation*, *44*(4), 479–526.

Pakes, F., & Holt, K. (2017). The transnational prisoner: Exploring themes and trends involving a prison deal with the Netherlands and Norway. *British Journal of Criminology*, *57*(1), 79–93.

Pratt, J., & Eriksson, A. (2013). *Contrasts in punishment: An explanation of Anglophone excess and Nordic exceptionalism*. Routledge.

Rafaraci, T., & Belfiore, R. (2018). *EU criminal justice: Fundamental rights, transnational proceedings and the European Public Prosecutor's Office*. Springer.

Reid-Henry, S. M. (2014). Humanitarianism as liberal diagnostic: Humanitarian reason and the political rationalities of the liberal will-to-care. *Transactions of the Institute of British Geographers*, *39*(3), 418–431.

Savelsberg, J. J. (2018). Punitive turn and justice cascade: Mutual inspiration from *Punishment and Society* and human rights literatures. *Punishment & Society*, *20*(1), 73–91.

Simon, J., & Sparks, R. (2013). Punishment and society: The emergence of an academic field. In J. Simon & R. Sparks (Eds.), *The SAGE handbook of punishment and society* (pp. 1–20). SAGE.

Stahn, C. (2020). *Justice as message: Expressivist foundations of international criminal justice*. Oxford University Press.
Ticktin, M. (2014). Transnational humanitarianism. *Annual Review of Anthropology, 43*(1), 273–289.
Vasiliev, S. (2015). On trajectories and destinations of international criminal law scholarship. *Leiden Journal of International Law, 28*(4), 701–716.
Wacquant, L. (2009a). *Punishing the poor: The neoliberal government of social insecurity*. Duke University Press.
Wacquant, L. (2009b). *Prisons of poverty* (Vol. 23). University of Minnesota Press.
Wohlforth, W. C., De Carvalho, B., Leira, H., & Neumann, I. B. (2018). Moral authority and status in international relations: Good states and the social dimension of status seeking. *Review of International Studies, 44*(3), 526–546.
Zedner, L. (2016). Penal subversions: When is a punishment not punishment, who decides and on what grounds? *Theoretical Criminology, 20*(1), 3–20.

# 5
# Punishment Beyond Borders

*Attitudes Toward Punishment in Interpersonal and International Contexts*

LINET R. DURMUŞOĞLU, JAN-WILLEM VAN PROOIJEN, AND WOLFGANG WAGNER

Akin to domestic societies, the international system is imbued with norms, ranging from human rights to the acquisition of weapons and the use of force. Even if "almost all nations observe almost all principles of international law and almost all of their obligations almost all of the time" (Henkin, 1979, p. 47), norm violations occur frequently, which leads to the question of how the international community should respond. In this chapter, we contribute to the debate by examining the conditions under which citizens support the use of force in response to a violation of an international norm. We integrate the literatures in social psychology, international law, and political science to examine whether citizens' attitudes toward punishment of individual offenders generalize to the international level and whether the authorization of an independent third party, such as the United Nations (UN) Security Council, increases citizen support for punitive action.

There is a wealth of research on factors that predict people's punitiveness in interpersonal relations between a single transgressor and a victim in the context of a modern state (Carlsmith & Darley, 2008; van Prooijen, 2018). On the level of the international system, however, there is no equivalent to the sophisticated criminal law system and the sanctioning power of the state. Although international law gives the UN Security Council a monopoly to authorize the use of force (other than in cases of self-defense), it lacks coercive power of its own. Its leverage "resides almost entirely in the perceived legitimacy its decisions grant to forceful actions" (Voeten, 2005, p. 528; see also Hurd, 2008, p. 2). Similarly, international courts and tribunals have remained dependent on states' willingness to accept their jurisdiction and to support their proceedings, resulting in a highly selective practice of punishing individual international crimes.

Studies of American public opinion have found that retributiveness and revenge motives heightened support for the 1991 and 2003 wars against Iraq (Liberman, 2006; Liberman & Skitka, 2017), for a hypothetical invasion of Syria (Washburn & Skitka, 2015), and for the hypothetical use of nuclear weapons against Iran (Rathbun & Stein, 2020; Sagan & Valentino, 2017). Liberman (2006) found that supporters of the death penalty are also more hawkish with a view to international conflicts. Sagan and Valentino caution that "future research will be necessary to determine whether these findings hold only for Americans or whether they are generalizable to the citizens of other countries" (p. 75; see also Liberman, 2006, p. 714). On the level of state policies, Rachel Stein (2019) finds that "democracies with more vengeful citizens tend to behave more belligerently" (p. 166).

We further advance research into international punishment by examining whether the authorization of an independent third party, such as the UN Security Council, increases citizen support for punitive action. Previous research has shown that American citizens who value multilateral institutions and those who lack confidence in the President are more supportive of U.S. government use of force if there is a mandate by the UN Security Council (Grieco et al., 2011). Among European publics, the absence of a UN mandate depresses support for the use of force (Everts & Isernia, 2015, p. 213). Tago and Ikeda (2015) show that among Japanese citizens, even resolutions that obtained a majority but were nevertheless not adopted because of a veto from one of the permanent members increase support.

The sources of UN Security Council authority have been contested among scholars of international law and international relations. For scholars of international law, a mandate of the UN Security Council provides one of the few lawful exemptions on the general prohibition on the use of force. Its authority rests on the rejection of naked power and the invocation of an international community (Kennedy, 2006, p. 81). However, Voeten (2005) argues that citizens do not seek an independent judgment on the appropriateness of an intervention but, rather, "political reassurance about the consequences of proposed military adventures" (p. 528). Thompson (2006) argues that channeling coercive action through the UN "sends a signal of benign intentions to leaders of third-party states, thereby increasing the likelihood of international support" (p. 11). Chapman (2012) argues that UN Security Council approval serves "as a signal that a foreign policy proposal will not be exceedingly costly or overtly aggressive" (p. 7). In contrast, we argue that the punitive use of force with a UN Security Council mandate should be understood as a form of third-party punishment. We show that citizens generally prefer third-party over second-party punishment both within the context of the nation-state and internationally, even if the costliness and effects of the punishment are kept constant. As a consequence, military action with a Security Council mandate receives more support than unilateral military action. The study of international punishment has been hampered by the delegitimization of punitive practices in international law, which has led states to reframe punitive measures in nonpunitive terms (e.g., self-defense), especially when they include armed force (Wagner & Werner, 2018). To our knowledge, the studies we report on in this chapter constitute the first empirical comparison of punishment in interpersonal and international contexts to date. In this chapter, we investigate citizens' support for international punishment by comparing it with their support for punishment of individual offenders (i.e., interpersonal punishment). Notably, we propose that both forms of punishment are rooted in a similar desire to punish offenders, suggesting that support for interpersonal punishment and that for international punishment are positively correlated. Moreover, although in the context of interpersonal punishment, people accord more legitimacy to independent third parties than to directly involved second parties (Fehr & Fischbacher, 2004; Leventhal, 1980), we test whether, and to what extent, this generalizes to attitudes toward international punishment. Finally, we investigate to what extent attitudes toward interpersonal and international punishment are related with political ideology and confidence in punitive institutions.

## 5.1. INTERPERSONAL VERSUS INTERNATIONAL PUNISHMENT

There are various similarities and differences in people's support for interpersonal versus international punishment. One similarity is that at both levels of analysis, punishment is a motivated reaction to the violation of a community norm (Fehr & Fischbacher, 2004; Leventhal, 1980; van Prooijen, 2018). Whereas at the interpersonal level these community norms are defined by domestic societies, at the international level they are defined by the international community. Evolutionary biologists, social psychologists, behavioral economists, and sociologists have argued that punishment of transgressors in interpersonal settings is functional by stimulating cooperation (e.g., Balliet et al., 2011; Fehr & Fischbacher, 2004; Fehr & Gächter, 2000; Leventhal, 1980), restoring fairness (Fehr & Fischbacher, 2004; Johnson et al., 2009; Kahneman et al., 1986; Turillo et al., 2002), and affirming the normative order (Durkheim, 1982, 1984). Given that the desire to punish emerges as a reaction to a wide variety of transgressions (van Prooijen, 2018), it stands to reason that also international transgressions stimulate this punitivity. In other words, the killing of innocent civilians in a war outside a country's borders triggers the same punitive response in individuals as a murder within the borders of their country. Individuals' support for the punishment of individual transgressors is hence likely to be positively associated with their support for the punishment of offending nations.

We examine interpersonal and international punishment through the common distinction between second- and third-party punishment (Fehr & Fischbacher, 2004; Fehr & Gächter, 2000). Second-party punishment can be defined as the punishment of a transgressor by the victim of the transgression or a party close to the victim (e.g., revenge). Third-party punishment is the punishment of a transgressor by an independent and presumably objective third party, such as a judge. Most third-party punishment in modern societies has been delegated to institutions with the right and legal obligation to punish, and here we therefore specifically focus on institutionalized punishment as conceptualization of third-party punishment. Second- and third-party punishment takes place not only at the interpersonal level, however, but also at the international level (Wagner, 2014; Wagner & Werner, 2018). Here, second-party punishment takes the form of unilateral action by a retaliating state (e.g., by imposing economic sanctions or using military force), whereas third-party punishment refers to measures authorized by international courts or the UN Security Council.

For interpersonal punishment, people generally prefer third-party over second-party punishment due to concerns about fairness. One core precondition to enable fair punishment is the impartiality and objectivity of the "punisher" (see procedural justice theory; Leventhal, 1980; Thibaut & Walker, 1975)—that is, the absence of a personal stake in the outcome for the punisher (e.g., there should be no personal relationship with either the victim or the perpetrator) along with an objective, emotionally detached assessment of the evidence. Such impartiality and objectivity are absent in second-party punishment, as avengers are likely to be acting out of self-interest and motivated by moral emotions such as anger. Research indeed underscores the role of anger in retaliation (Ben-Shakhar et al., 2007; Bosman & Van Winden, 2002; Pillutla & Murnighan, 1996). An independent third party, in contrast, is more likely to be seen as impartial and objective, increasing their legitimacy as a punisher. This should especially be the case for punitive institutions, which have been accorded formal authority to enforce an established rule of law that reflects community norms and values.

But for international punishment, the distinction between second- and third-party punishment is arguably less straightforward. Here, we consider two important differences between interpersonal and international punishment, carried out by second versus third parties. The first difference concerns the perceived punitive authority of the victim. Whereas taking revenge on a perpetrator is often frowned upon at an individual level, at the international level the victim is a sovereign state in an anarchic international system with no monopoly of force above the level of the states. Notwithstanding the official prohibition of punitive use of force, the absence of an effective penal system above the state level may be seen as legitimizing self-help practices, akin to vigilantism or lynching in areas of weak statehood (Haas et al., 2014; Harnischfeger, 2003; Jackson et al., 2013; Nivette, 2016; Tankebe, 2009). This difference in punitive authority could mean that while citizens often oppose second-party punishment in an interpersonal context, they may often support it in an international context.

The second difference concerns the perceived comprehensiveness, legitimacy, and efficiency of the domestic versus international legal systems. It is plausible that the average citizen's understanding of the jurisprudence and procedures involved in domestic institutional punishment is higher than that of those involved in international institutional punishment, making it more difficult for them to establish the fairness of international punishment. Moreover, international institutions are more frequently seen as politicized, and their claim of impartiality is often contested. Actions by the UN Security Council can be blocked by any of the five permanent members whose veto power has been contested. In recent years, the International Criminal Court (ICC) has been accused of becoming a coercive tool to pursue political objectives (Tiemessen, 2016). In particular, the ICC has been criticized for a neocolonial policy of persecuting primarily African politicians while sparing Western states (Cole, 2013). As a consequence, several African countries announced plans to withdraw from the ICC, and Burundi became the first country to do so in 2017. In addition, international legal proceedings have proven to be exceptionally lengthy and expensive (Ford, 2014; Smeulers et al., 2013). Naturally, these issues could decrease public support for international third-party punishment, thereby leading to a lower difference in support between second- and third-party punishment in the international context compared to the interpersonal context.

The present research examined these possible similarities and differences between interpersonal and international punishment. We sought to assess (a) whether people's attitudes toward interpersonal punishment predict their attitudes toward international punishment; (b) relatedly, whether people's interpersonal and international punitive attitudes are similarly or differently related with intrapersonal characteristics relevant for punitiveness (i.e., political orientation and confidence in punitive institutions); and (c) whether second- or third-party punishment attracts higher support at both the interpersonal and international levels. To address these research questions, we conducted two studies[1] with online survey experiments. The first study included a sample of 618 participants from the United States, whereas the second study included a larger cross-national sample with 613 participants from the United States, 616 from the United Kingdom, and 627 from Germany. We chose these three countries because we want to have variation in domestic punitive practices. Such differences manifest themselves in different prison populations—that is, the share of citizens that a society imprisons as a consequence of their violation of community norms. The United States stands out for the highest prison population among liberal democracies, having 655 inmates per 100,000 citizens. In contrast, the figure is only 75 in Germany. The United Kingdom is in between the two, with 140 prisoners in England and Wales, 143 in Scotland, and 76 in Northern Ireland (Wamsley, 2018). The first study was a pilot study and had the objective to test the experimental manipulation and vignettes before expanding the number of participants in the second study. After evaluating the results and concluding that the experiment was successful, we then ran the second, larger study with a cross-national sample. In both studies, participants were presented with two vignettes (see

---

1. Detailed information on the design, analyses, and results of the studies can be found at https://osf.io/7rxke/?view_only=c745497fcb7c4c1c90d57ee1533af0c0.

Appendix 5.1 and the online materials), one describing an interpersonal conflict (i.e., between Person A and Person B) and one describing an international conflict (i.e., between State A and State B), and the subsequent punishment of the transgressor. The interpersonal scenario describes a car accident as a consequence of one individual's reckless driving, and the international scenario describes State B violating the rights of a minority population originating from State A. Furthermore, the punishment was carried out by either the victim (second party) or a third party. To exclude any confounding factors, such as differing severity of the punishment, consequences of the punishment were kept constant across the second- and third-party conditions in both scenarios (i.e., payment of 200 Euros in the interpersonal scenario, and bombardment of military infrastructure in the international scenario). Furthermore, the names of the actors were kept neutral (i.e., Person A, Person B; State A and State B). After reading the vignettes, participants rated their attitudes toward the punishment, including their support for the punishment and their perception of whether fairness had been restored. This design allowed us to differentiate between people's attitudes toward second- and third-party punishment at both the interpersonal and international levels of analysis.

In addition to attitudes toward the different types of punishment, we explored two intrapersonal factors that could influence individual judgments about second- and third-party punishment: political orientation and confidence in punitive institutions. Previous research in social psychology has shown that conservatives have a higher desire to punish than moderate or liberal individuals (Hofmann et al., 2018). This finding conforms with studies of public opinion on the use of force that have found Republicans to be more supportive about using military force and nuclear weapons in particular than Democrats (Gelpi et al., 2009, p. 84; Sagan & Valentino, 2017, p. 62). Possible explanations offered for this finding are that conservatism places a higher emphasis on personal agency and individual causality for crime. Because the conservative–liberal spectrum does not readily translate from the American to the European context, we tested whether the left–right political spectrum can explain differences in support for punishment. Similarly, confidence in the criminal justice system has been shown to affect attitudes toward punishment (e.g., Jackson et al., 2012; Tyler, 2006a, 2006b, 2011). Furthermore, trust in national courts correlates with trust in international courts (Voeten, 2013). Therefore, we tested whether confidence in the punitive institutions introduced in our vignettes predicted support for second- or third-party punishment.

## 5.2. RESULTS AND DISCUSSION

Five main findings follow from the two studies we conducted (see the online supplemental materials for detailed statistical results). First, we found that support for second-party punishment at the interpersonal level is a moderate to strong predictor of support for second-party punishment at the international level in all four samples. Thus, on average, citizens who endorse the use of force without a UN Security Council mandate are also more likely to support individual victims to take justice into their own hands domestically. The correlation between interpersonal third-party punishment and international third-party punishment was only significant in one of the two samples with U.S. citizens. Second, at both the interpersonal and international levels, institutional third-party punishment attracted higher support. Figure 5.1 visualizes the support for second- and third-party punishment in interpersonal and international contexts. It shows consistently higher levels of support for punishment that is mandated by a court (interpersonal context) or the UN Security Council (international context). Figure 5.2 shows a very similar picture with regard to the restoration of fairness. Respondents in all four studies found that punishment that is mandated by a court (interpersonal context) or the UN Security Council (international context) performs better in restoring fairness.

This resonates with the finding by Grieco and colleagues (2011), who attributed the UN Security Council's authority to being "a second opinion from a trusted outsider" (p. 564). We contribute to this line of reasoning by noting that citizens value the Security Council not only as an additional source of information but also as a third party whose punitive authority

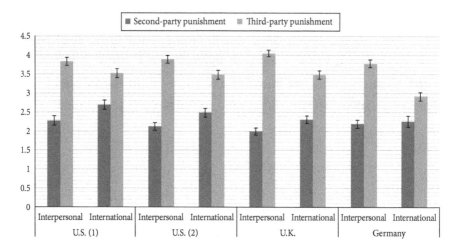

**Figure 5.1** Mean support ratings for second- and third-party punishment at the interpersonal and international level of analysis with confidence intervals.

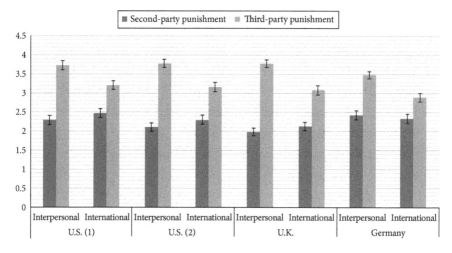

**Figure 5.2** Mean fairness restoration ratings for second- and third-party punishment at the interpersonal and international level of analysis with confidence intervals.

exceeds that of any second party because it is not a party to the conflict itself and thus is impartial.

Third, the effects of type of punishment (second vs. third party) on support for punishment and fairness ratings were stronger in the interpersonal than international contexts in all samples. This is also visualized in

Figures 5.1 and 5.2, in which larger difference between second- and third-party punishment appear on the interpersonal level. The contrast between the sophisticated criminal law system and the sanctioning power of the state, on the one hand, and the absence of any coercive power of the UN, on the other hand, thus impacts on the degree to which citizens disapprove of second-party punishment and prefer an impartial third party to punish norm violations instead. As theories of international relations emphasize, international politics takes place in an anarchic self-help system, and our results show that this notion resonates in citizens' higher rates of acceptance of second-party punishment among states compared to interpersonal relations.

Fourth, confidence in punitive institutions (i.e., the national criminal justice system and the UN Security Council) positively predicted support for third-party punishment at the respective level the institutions operate at in all four samples. Moreover, in the British and German samples, confidence in punitive institutions negatively predicted support for second-party punishment. In other words, even though the UN does not have any coercive power, confidence in its monopoly to authorize the use of force makes states' self-help strategies less acceptable.

Last, results from our first study revealed no differences in affective responses (i.e., anger and disgust) to the perpetrator across conditions (see online supplementary materials), excluding the possibility of "affective confounding" (i.e., differences in anger and disgust toward the perpetrator depending on the type of punishment).

Our studies make several novel theoretical contributions to the literature on international punishment and on the use of force in international relations. As a first contribution, the current findings support the notion that people's punitivity transcends contexts. Particularly support for second-party punishment between individuals appears to be closely associated with support for second-party punishment between states. Due to mixed findings, it remains unclear whether people also have a general tendency to support third-party punishment regardless of its context. As a second contribution, results revealed that, consistent with procedural justice theory (Leventhal, 1980; Thibaut & Walker, 1975), across contexts people strongly prefer punitive decisions to be made by an objective third party as opposed to a vindictive second party. Yet, this distinction appears to be more pronounced at the domestic level (i.e., when evaluating interpersonal disputes) than at the international level (i.e., when evaluating a dispute between two states). There are at least two possible (and not mutually exclusive) explanations for this. One explanation is that people have less confidence in international compared to domestic punitive institutions, decreasing their support for international third-party punishment. The lack of coercive powers of the UN, which contrasts starkly with the monopoly of force of the states in our studies, contributes to the lower level of confidence regarding the UN. Furthermore, the five UN Security Council permanent members' veto power and the resulting selectivity in responding to violations of international norms possibly lead to a lower level of confidence in this institution as an actor in third-party punishment. Another explanation is that people consider second-party punishment a more viable alternative at the international than at the interpersonal level, in light of a higher perceived authority of the "victim state" and the absence of a supranational monopoly of power. Given that the present studies had functionally different offenses at the interpersonal and international levels, it is impossible to assess these explanations with the current data. Future studies could be designed to more directly examine these issues.

As a third contribution, our findings show that confidence in punitive institutions plays an important role in determining a person's support for second- and third-party punishment independent of the context. Although this is an exploratory finding, confidence in punitive institutions and institutional punishment suggests that confidence in institutions may be an important factor in citizens' support for third-party punishment across settings. This finding is in accordance with the literature on compliance and cooperation with the criminal justice system (Jackson et al., 2012; Tyler, 2006a, 2006b, 2011). Moreover, it has important implications for policymakers, legal professionals, and law enforcement agencies because it stresses the importance of the public image of punitive institutions.

Our findings were inconclusive regarding the effect of political orientation on attitudes toward punishment. In Study 1, right-wing political orientation positively predicted agreement with second-party punishment (i.e., revenge). In Study 2, however, we could only replicate this finding in the German sample. In the American sample, right-wing political orientation positively predicted support for revenge only in the interpersonal context, whereas for the British sample, there was only a significant effect in the international context. Still, where there was an effect of political orientation, it was in the predicted direction. There may be moderators of these effects and differences in sample characteristics that we did not consider. The exact relationship between political orientation and support for different types of punishment at the domestic and international levels remains to be clarified by future research.

The current studies provide a better understanding of attitudes toward punitive measures administered by states and international institutions. Furthermore, both studies had high power to detect even small effect sizes, and our second study was pre-registered and included cross-national samples. Although the three samples in Study 2 are culturally proximate (i.e., Western and individualistic), they still display substantial variation in domestic punitivity. All of this suggests that the findings observed here are robust and likely to replicate in follow-up studies.

Even so, we cannot determine with certainty how well they generalize across other countries and offenses. Future research may replicate these findings with a broader range of offenses among nationally representative samples and also include countries with more radical differences in punitive practices. These could be countries in which, for instance, vigilantism is more widespread, or countries that were subjected to international punitive measures by the UN Security Council or international courts in recent years. A second and related limitation of our studies concerns the use of vignettes. Although the use of vignettes allowed us to isolate the effect of the type of punishment and the level of analysis while keeping the characteristics and consequences of the transgressions constant, this approach is not representative for most real-world settings. The information participants would come across in media reports is likely to include more details about the context of the transgression. Moreover, the identical outcomes of second versus third party would be unlikely to occur, while outcome differences are relevant for punitive judgments (see the literature on distributive justice; e.g., Deutsch, 1985).

Future studies could also investigate to what extent country characteristics, such as international standing and power position, form of government and political system, cultural proximity, and perceived group cohesion of the actors, could be influential for attitudes toward punishment in international contexts. In line with this, previous research has confirmed the relevance of a target state's political system (Falomir-Pichastor et al., 2007, 2012; Pereira et al., 2015) and group entitativity (Pereira & van Prooijen, 2018) or the support for collective punishment and international military interventions. Another possible next step in research on international punishment could focus on the underlying motives for punitive preferences—specifically whether impartiality and legitimacy indeed are important reasons to prefer third-party over second-party punishment, and particularly how these considerations play out at the international level of analysis.

## 5.3. CONCLUSION

The context of norm violations and punishment differs substantially between the level of domestic societies and the international level. Exceptions in weak or failed states notwithstanding, domestic societies typically have a sophisticated criminal law system that is backed by the sanctioning power of the state. In contrast, second-party punishment remains a common practice in international politics, as the UN and the international courts and tribunals remain highly dependent on the cooperation of the member states to sanction the violation of international norms. The prospect of overcoming second-party punishment between states depends, among other things, on public support.

In two high-powered experimental studies, we have examined citizens' responses to second- and third-party punishment in international and interpersonal relations and find both similarities and differences between these levels of analysis. Citizens' support for international punishment corresponds closely to their support for punishment of individual offenders. At both levels of analysis, they consider the delegation of punishment to a third party more legitimate than second-party punishment. Even so, the difference in support between second- and third-party punishment is more pronounced at the domestic level than at the international level. We conclude that although people's punitivity has a range of similar implications both interpersonally and internationally, punishment between states also adds a layer of complexity that makes it unique from punishment of individual offenders. In general, however, the strengthening of third-party punishment in international politics can count on a supportive public.

## ACKNOWLEDGMENT

We are grateful to the VU Association for its generous support of our research for this chapter.

## APPENDIX 5.1 VIGNETTES IN SURVEY EXPERIMENT

### INTRODUCTION

Following, you will be presented with a fictional scenario of a conflict between two [individuals/states]. Please take your time and read this scenario carefully. After you have finished reading the scenario, continue to the next page. There, you will be asked a few questions in connection with what you have read. There are no right or wrong answers to these questions—we are solely interested in your honest opinion.

## INTERPERSONAL LEVEL

**Second-party punishment condition.** Person A and Person B are driving on the highway. Because of Person B's reckless tailgating, they almost get into an accident, only prevented by an evasion manoeuvre. This leads both cars to drift off the road. While the cars are not damaged, Person B's reckless and illegal behaviour causes substantial distress for Person A. Person A is so enraged that he decides to take matters into his own hands and, instead of calling the police, punish Person B for the shock he experienced. He forcefully grabs the wallet of Person B and takes out 200 Euros as compensation for personal suffering.

**Third-party punishment condition.** Person A and Person B are driving on the highway. Because of Person B's reckless tailgating, they almost get into an accident, only prevented by an evasion manoeuvre. This leads both cars to drift off the road. While the cars are not damaged, Person B's reckless and illegal behaviour causes substantial distress for Person A. Person A is so enraged that he decides to call the police and the case is brought to court. The judge decides over Person B's punishment for the shock he caused, and Person B pays 200 Euros as compensation for Person A's personal suffering.

**Comprehension checks.** "Does the victim call the police?" ("*Yes*" or "*No*") and "Who punishes the perpetrator?" ("*A judge*" or "*The victim*").

## INTERNATIONAL LEVEL

**Second-party punishment condition.** During a peaceful protest, the police force of State B uses excessive force against a minority originally coming from State A. This use of excessive force leads to countless individuals dying and others ending up heavily injured. After these events have unfolded, State A, which closely followed what happened, decides to punish State B for the injustice they have committed. Instead of consulting the United Nations Security Council (as prescribed by international law), State A independently bombs State B's military infrastructure.

**Third-party punishment condition.** During a peaceful protest, the police force of State B uses excessive force against a minority originally coming from State A. This use of excessive force leads to countless individuals dying and others ending up heavily injured. After these events have unfolded, State A, which closely followed what happened, decides to refer this situation to the United Nations Security Council. To punish State B for the injustice they have committed, the United Nations Security Council passes a resolution leading to the bombardment of State B's military infrastructure.

**Comprehension checks.** "Did the victim state consult the United Nations Security Council about the perpetrator state's behaviour?" ("*Yes*" or "*No*") and "Who punished the perpetrator state?" ("*The United Nations Security Council*" or "*The victim state*").

## References

Balliet, D., Mulder, L. B., & Van Lange, P. A. M. (2011). Reward, punishment, and cooperation: A meta-analysis. *Psychological Bulletin*, 137(4), 594–615.

Ben-Shakhar, G., Bornstein, G., Hopfensitz, A., & Van Winden, F. (2007). Reciprocity and emotions in bargaining using physiological and self-report measures. *Journal of Economic Psychology*, 28(3), 314–323.

Bosman, R., & Van Winden, F. (2002). Emotional hazard in a power-to-take experiment. *The Economic Journal*, 112(476), 147–169.

Carlsmith, K. M., & Darley, J. M. (2008). Psychological aspects of retributive justice. *Advances in Experimental Social Psychology*, 40, 193–236.

Chapman, T. L. (2012). *Securing approval: Domestic politics and multilateral authorization for war*. University of Chicago Press.

Cole, R. J. (2013). Africa's relationship with the International Criminal Court: More political than legal. *Melbourne Journal of International Law*, 14(2), 670–698.

Deutsch, M. (1985). *Distributive justice: A social-psychological perspective*. Yale University Press.

Durkheim, É. (1982). *The rules of the sociological method*. Free Press.

Durkheim, É. (1984). *The division of labour in society*. Palgrave Macmillan.

Everts, P., & Isernia, P. (2015). *Public opinion, Transatlantic relations and the use of force*. Palgrave Macmillan.

Falomir-Pichastor, J. M., Pereira, A., Staerklé, C., & Butera, F. (2012). Do all lives have the same value? Support for international military interventions as a function of political system and public opinion of target states. *Group Processes & Intergroup Relations*, 15(3), 347–362.

Falomir-Pichastor, J. M., Staerklé, C., Depuiset, M.-A., & Butera, F. (2007). Perceived legitimacy of collective punishment as a function of democratic versus non-democratic group structure. *Group Processes & Intergroup Relations*, 10(4), 565–579.

Fehr, E., & Fischbacher, U. (2004). Third-party punishment and social norms. *Evolution and Human Behavior*, 25(2), 63–87.

Fehr, E., & Gächter, S. (2000). Cooperation and punishment in public goods experiments. *American Economic Review*, 90(4), 980–994.

Ford, S. K. (2014). Complexity and efficiency at international criminal courts. *Emory International Law Review*, 29, 1.

Gelpi, C., Feaver, P. D., & Reifler, J. (2009). *Paying the human costs of war: American public opinion and casualties in military conflicts*. Princeton University Press.

Grieco, J. M., Gelpi, C., Reifler, J., & Feaver, P. D. (2011). Let's get a second opinion: International institutions and American public support for war. *International Studies Quarterly*, 55(2), 563–583.

Haas, N. E., de Keijser, J. W., & Bruinsma, G. J. N. (2014). Public support for vigilantism, confidence in police and police responsiveness. *Policing and Society*, 24(2), 224–241.

Harnischfeger, J. (2003). The Bakassi Boys: Fighting crime in Nigeria. *Journal of Modern African Studies*, 41(1), 23–49.

Henkin, L. (1979). *How nations behave: Law and foreign policy* (2nd ed.). Columbia University Press.

Hofmann, W., Brandt, M. J., Wisneski, D. C., Rockenbach, B., & Skitka, L. J. (2018). Moral punishment in everyday life. *Personality and Social Psychology Bulletin*, 44(12), 1697–1711.

Hurd, I. (2008). *After anarchy: Legitimacy and power in the United Nations Security Council*. Princeton University Press.

Jackson, J., Bradford, B., Hough, M., Myhill, A., Quinton, P., & Tyler, T. R. (2012). Why do people comply with the law? Legitimacy and the influence of legal institutions. *British Journal of Criminology*, 52(6), 1051–1071.

Jackson, J., Huq, A. Z., Bradford, B., & Tyler, T. R. (2013). Monopolizing force? Police legitimacy and public attitudes toward the acceptability of violence. *Psychology, Public Policy, and Law*, 19(4), 479–497.

Johnson, T., Dawes, C. T., Fowler, J. H., McElreath, R., & Smirnov, O. (2009). The role of egalitarian motives in altruistic punishment. *Economics Letters*, 102(3), 192–194.

Kahneman, D., Knetsch, J. L., & Thaler, R. H. (1986). Fairness and the assumptions of economics. *Journal of Business*, 59(4), S285–S300.

Kennedy, D. (2006). *Of war and law*. Princeton University Press.

Leventhal, G. S. (1980). What should be done with equity theory? In K. J. Gergen, M. S. Greenberg, & R. H. Willis (Eds.), *Social exchange* (pp. 27–55). Springer.

Liberman, P. (2006). An eye for an eye: Public support for war against evildoers. *International Organization*, 60(3), 687–722.

Liberman, P., & Skitka, L. J. (2017). Revenge in US public support for war against Iraq. *Public Opinion Quarterly*, 81(3), 636–660.

Nivette, A. E. (2016). Institutional ineffectiveness, illegitimacy, and public support for vigilantism in Latin America. *Criminology*, 54(1), 142–175.

Pereira, A., Berent, J., Falomir-Pichastor, J. M., Staerklé, C., & Butera, F. (2015). Collective punishment depends on collective responsibility and political organization of the target group. *Journal of Experimental Social Psychology*, 56(1), 1–23.

Pereira, A., & van Prooijen, J.-W. (2018). Why we sometimes punish the innocent: The role of group entitativity in collective punishment. *PLoS One, 13*(5), e0196852.

Pillutla, M. M., & Murnighan, J. K. (1996). Unfairness, anger, and spite: Emotional rejections of ultimatum offers. *Organizational Behavior and Human Decision Processes, 68*(3), 208–224.

Rathbun, B. C., & Stein, R. (2020). Greater goods: Morality and attitudes toward the use of nuclear weapons. *Journal of Conflict Resolution, 64*(5), 787–816.

Sagan, S. D., & Valentino, B. A. (2017). Revisiting Hiroshima in Iran: What Americans really think about using nuclear weapons and killing noncombatants. *International Security, 42*(1), 41–79.

Smeulers, A., Hola, B., & Van Den Berg, T. (2013). Sixty-five years of international criminal justice: The facts and figures. *International Criminal Law Review, 13*(1), 7–41.

Stein, R. M. (2019). *Vengeful citizens, violent states*. Cambridge University Press.

Tago, A., & Ikeda, M. (2015). An "A" for effort: Experimental evidence on UN Security Council engagement and support for US military action in Japan. *British Journal of Political Science, 45*(2), 391–410.

Tankebe, J. (2009). Self-help, policing, and procedural justice: Ghanaian vigilantism and the rule of law. *Law & Society Review, 43*(2), 245–270.

Thibaut, J. W., & Walker, L. (1975). *Procedural justice: A psychological analysis*. Erlbaum.

Thompson, A. (2006). Coercion through IOs: The Security Council and the logic of information transmission. *International Organization, 60*(1), 1–34.

Tiemessen, A. (2016). The International Criminal Court and the lawfare of judicial intervention. *International Relations, 30*(4), 409–431.

Turillo, C. J., Folger, R., Lavelle, J. J., Umphress, E. E., & Gee, J. O. (2002). Is virtue its own reward? Self-sacrificial decisions for the sake of fairness. *Organizational Behavior and Human Decision Processes, 89*(1), 839–865.

Tyler, T. R. (2006a). Psychological perspectives on legitimacy and legitimation. *Annual Review of Psychology, 57*, 375–400.

Tyler, T. R. (2006b). *Why people obey the law*. Princeton University Press.

Tyler, T. R. (2011). Trust and legitimacy: Policing in the USA and Europe. *European Journal of Criminology, 8*(4), 254–266.

van Prooijen, J.-W. (2018). *The moral punishment instinct*. Oxford University Press.

Voeten, E. (2005). The political origins of the UN Security Council's ability to legitimize the use of force. *International Organization, 59*(3), 527–557.

Voeten, E. (2013). Public opinion and the legitimacy of international courts. *Theoretical Inquiries in Law, 14*(2), 411–436.

Wagner, W. (2014). Rehabilitation or exclusion? A criminological perspective on policies towards "rogue states." In W. Wagner, W. G. Werner, & M. Onderco (Eds.), *Deviance in international relations* (pp. 152–170). Springer.

Wagner, W., & Werner, W. (2018). War and punitivity under anarchy. *European Journal of International Security, 3*(3), 310–325.

Wamsley, R. (2018). *World prison population list* (12th ed.). Institute for Crime & Justice Policy Research.

Washburn, A. N., & Skitka, L. J. (2015). Motivated and displaced revenge: Remembering 9/11 suppresses opposition to military intervention in Syria (for some). *Analyses of Social Issues and Public Policy, 15*(1), 89–104.

# 6

# Why Sanctioning?

## The Rise and Purpose of Sanctions in International Politics

MICHAL ONDERCO

## 6.1. INTRODUCTION

It has become a truism to state that sanctions are becoming increasingly the policy instrument of choice. According to a review by Felbermayr et al. (2020), the number of sanction regimes increased from less than 20 in 1950 to well over 400 in the 2010s. At the time of this writing, the European Union (EU) has no fewer than 45 different sanctions regimes in place. Sanctions are, however, applied by a wide variety of actors—by states (as bilateral or unilateral sanctions), regional institutions (e.g., the EU), or international institutions (e.g., the United Nations).

Despite their growing popularity, a question remains as to why sanctions are so popular. "[The] reliance on economic sanctions would be natural if they were especially effective at getting other countries to do what Washington wants, but they're not," wrote Daniel Drezner (2021, p. 142) in a *Foreign Affairs* article reviewing the U.S. sanctioning practice. The mainstream international relations scholarship on sanctions overwhelmingly concludes that if the success of sanctions is measured

Michal Onderco, *Why Sanctioning?* In: *Punishment in International Society*. Edited by: Wolfgang Wagner, Linet R. Durmuşoğlu, Barbora Holá, Ronald Kroeze, Jan-Willem van Prooijen, and Wouter Werner, Oxford University Press.
© Oxford University Press 2024. DOI: 10.1093/oso/9780197693483.003.0006

by the change of the behavior by sanctions' target, the sanctions do not work (Bapat & Kwon, 2015; Brooks, 2002; Drezner, 1999, 2003; Pape, 1998; Peksen, 2019; Portela, 2012; van Bergeijk, 1994). If we view sanctions as a strategic exchange between the sanctions' sender and their target, then the target is most of the time unlikely to comply. Existing scholarship gives some caveats on when sanctions may work—for example, Drezner (1999) argues that they work if the target expects long-term economic exchange with the sender. However, the instances of sanctions' success are few, and they are often debated (Klotz, 1999). The targets of sanctions often develop special relationships—or elaborate schemes—to avoid and compensate for sanctions (Early, 2015). Sanctions also often contribute to suffering of the population in the target country (Early & Peksen, 2022). The political science scholarship on sanctions demonstrates a clear problem-solving focus and an interest in the consequences of sanctions.

But if sanctions "do not work," why are they increasingly popular? Drezner's (2021) answer in the above-cited *Foreign Affairs* piece—that sanctions are popular because America is in a military decline—cannot really explain their growing popularity worldwide. This is the question that this chapter seeks to answer. It seeks to answer this question with the help of the broader interdisciplinary scholarship on punishment, with the goal of connecting the political science insights on sanctions with broader scholarship of sanctions. Already in the late 1980s, Kim Nossal (1989) argued that sanctions are a form of international punishment. With sanctions often being imposed on countries that are described in the language of deviance and exclusion (Geldenhuys, 2004; Litwak, 2000; Smetana, 2020; Wagner & Onderco, 2014; Wunderlich, 2020), sanctions are explicitly and implicitly being linked to punishment. Examining the interdisciplinary scholarship on punishment along with the political science work on sanctions may hence link the two fields.

In doing so, the practice of sanctioning countries reflects three contributions of the punitive lens on international politics, as described in Chapter 1 of this volume: It shows which norms are at the core of international order (and deserve to be protected by the punitive responses), it demonstrates structures of power and authority (and the right to sanctions), and it shows where the potential for cooperation is in international politics.

This chapter discusses the purpose of sanctioning. It sets the political science scholarship on sanctioning within the broader interdisciplinary work on punishment, and it links the two with the most recent trends in the practice of international sanctions.

The remainder of the chapter continues as follows: Section 6.2 introduces the political science scholarship on sanctions and the purpose of sanctions. Section 6.3 examines the more recent shift toward targeting and individualization of sanctions, and how this implementation is actually not as targeted as desired. Section 6.4 concludes the chapter by discussing the growing contestation of sanctions, both domestically and internationally.

## 6.2. THINKING ABOUT SANCTIONS LIKE A POLITICAL SCIENTIST

As mentioned in the introduction, the most traditional and basic way to think about whether sanctions "work" is to focus on whether they produce the desired change in the target's behavior (Hufbauer et al., 2007; Pape, 1997). However, political scientists studying sanctions often consider three ways in which sanctions can "work":

- Sanctions can *coerce*. This is what most scholars mean when they think about the effect of sanctions. Sanctions can coerce the target to change the policy due to the pressure (Giumelli, 2013a; Sjoberg, 2006). Even the skeptics of sanctions, such as (Pape, 1997), for example agree that the sanctions imposed by the United States and Canada on South Korea in 1975 were successful in persuading the country to cancel plans to purchase a nuclear fuel reprocessing plant from France (see also Hufbauer et al., 2007). As mentioned in the introduction, however, the political science scholarship is skeptical of this argument by now.

- Sanctions can *constrain*. The target might not decide to abandon the sanctioned policy, but executing that policy might become increasingly more complicated and costly, and the progress toward that policy might become slower and more complicated (Giumelli, 2013a; Sjoberg, 2006). For instance, Moret et al. (2016) argue that the sanctions which the EU adopted against Russia in 2014 forced Russia to change its military strategy.
- Sanctions can *signal*. They can be used by the sender to indicate that a particular type of behavior is viewed as particularly reprehensible. As a signaling device, sanctions indicate commitment to and highlight the importance of a particular international norm (Giumelli, 2011, 2013a). Laura Sjoberg (2006) argues that sanctions help the socialization of states. For instance, the work of Nicholas Miller (2014) demonstrated that although the U.S. sanctions against the proliferators of weapons of mass destruction did not stop these countries from developing the weapons, the sanctions dissuaded other countries from pursuing such programs.

Naturally, these explanations are not mutually exclusive. Scholars, at times, see multiple reasons for imposing sanctions. Moret et al. (2016), in their work regarding whether imposition of sanctions changed the behavior of Russia, explicitly present multiple outcomes that one can expect from sanctions on Russia imposed by the United States and the EU—from withdrawal from Crimea to deterring other actions—and assess the likelihood of any of them occurring. By recognizing multiple reasons for sanctioning, often possibly complimentary, the views of political scientists fit well in the existing social science scholarship, which acknowledges that there is no such thing as a single or unitary theory of punishment—there is no single reason why societies throughout the world punish wrongdoers (Duff, 2003; Garland, 2001). In the remainder of this section, I unpack the three fundamental ways in which sanctions can function and link them to the existing political science scholarship and also interdisciplinary scholarship in social sciences.

## 6.2.1. Sanctions as a Coercive Device

Thinking about sanctions as a coercive device is at the very root of considering sanctions' "effectiveness." This logic underlies the interest in whether sanctions deliver the desired behavioral change.

Perhaps the oldest expression of the belief that sanctions can coerce states to change their behavior comes from the argument made by U.S. President Woodrow Wilson in 1919. Wilson (1919), juxtaposing sanctions vis-à-vis war, argued that

> a nation that is boycotted is a nation that is in sight of surrender. Apply this economic, peaceful, silent, deadly remedy and there will be no need for force. It is a terrible remedy. It does not cost a life outside the nation boycotted but it brings a pressure upon the nation which, in my judgment, no modern nation could resist. (p. 23)

During this period of time, sanctions became seen as a part of the New World Order, where war (as a means of enforcement in the Old World Order) was replaced by economic warfare, which was also used for means such as debt enforcement (Hathaway & Shapiro, 2017). As Nicholas Mulder (2019) notes, however, the increased use of sanctions also meant that the border between wartime and peacetime became more blurred, and the scope of what was permissive in peacetime became widely expanded. Mulder (2022) argues that inflicting pain on norm-breakers was the point of sanctions and that civilians often were purposely made to suffer.

Based on this logic of sanctions as a coercive device, generations of scholars have devoted energy to correlating the costs of sanctions, in one way or another, with their chance of success (Drury, 1998; Hufbauer et al., 1997, 2007; Morgan et al., 2009, 2014), focusing on issues such as institutional features like regime type (McGillivray & Stam, 2004) or a nation's trade structure (Baldwin, 1985; Drezner, 1999, 2003; Hirschman, 1945/1980; van Bergeijk, 1994). In more recent years, this research has focused on the effectiveness of EU sanctions and the correlates and determinants thereof (Giumelli, 2011, 2013a, 2013b; Portela, 2012, 2014, 2015a, 2015b).

Scholars have also measured and calculated the costs of sanctions for individual countries (Giumelli, 2017) and, at a lower level, firms (Onderco & van der Veer, 2021).

Although I address this point in more detail later in the chapter, the discussion about the costs of sanctions touches upon viewing sanctions as a coercive as well as a constraining device. The goal of sanctions can be simultaneously to coerce governments into changing policy by inflicting high personal costs and to constrain state capacity. For example, a country might be under different sanctions regimes, including personal sanctions against its leaders (e.g., visa bans or asset freezes), and under sanctions that are aimed to constrain the country's ability to engage in particular activities (e.g., export bans or embargoes). However, the original idea of constraining a country's resources through sanctions led to the rise of comprehensive sanctions regimes that aimed to coerce the sanctioned country by inflicting increasingly severe economic pain (Weiss, 1999). This idea was most clearly articulated in the case of Iraq in the 1990s when UN sanctions imposed on Saddam Hussein led to the death of approximately half a million Iraqis (Alnasrawi, 2001).

There are four main reasons why using sanctions as a coercive device might not lead to the desired outcomes. First, in line with the understanding of international politics based on rational choice theories, one could argue that expecting sanctions to affect the target's behavior is not reasonable—if the target was concerned about the impact, they would not even engage in a sanctionable behavior. Instead, the target engages in a sanctionable action *despite* the sanctions because the benefits from the behavior outweigh the costs of sanctions (Rowe, 2010). Second, the goal of sanctions is often left unarticulated or poorly articulated. What kind of behavior is expected from the target in order to remove the sanctions is often left unspecified. Imagine Russia deciding now (this chapter was written in July 2022) to comply with the EU's demands so that sanctions would be withdrawn. What would that mean? Stopping fighting? Withdrawing from Ukraine? Withdrawing from Crimea? Compensating Ukraine for all damage? All of the above? The goals are fairly unclear. Third, not all desired end goals are created equal. It might be easier to release some political prisoners than to give up an important part of the national technological research program, especially one that is a source of national pride or seen as indispensable for national security (or both, such as a nuclear weapons program). Fourth, the sanctions may backfire and lead to the "rally around the flag" effect. In other words, sanctions might inflict real pain, but rather than fuel a backlash against the leader, the population in the target state blames the sanctioner and/or rallies around the regime (Alexseev & Hale, 2019; Grossman et al., 2018).

Thinking about sanctions as a coercive device finds its parallel in the broader thinking of punishment as a coercive device in social sciences. The idea of punishment as a coercive device is at the core of the rehabilitative theories of punishment. These theories assume that punishment makes the wrongdoer a better person, and the wrongdoer will not repeat any more offenses (Hampton, 1984; Morris, 1981). Similarly, applying sanctions as a coercive device assumes that, somehow, the sanction target will cease its offending activities and will seek a way to resolve the issue. The idea of coercion is linked to the idea that although sanctions and punishment communicate censure (more on this aspect below; see also Becker, 1963; Duff, 2003), signaling the moral aspects is not enough. This is why humans require what Von Hirsch (1993) calls "prudential supplement," in addition to the communication of the moral. Psychologists also recognize the educative and rehabilitative functions of punishments (van Prooijen, 2018). Mild punishments provide a way to enforce rules when raising small children. Punishment must be moderate in order to be effective, however.

## 6.2.2. Sanctions as a Constraining Device

In addition to coercion, sanctions can also serve as a constraining device, with the goal to constrain actors' ability to exercise certain actions—for example, prevent governments from being a threat to their own population or to neighboring countries.

The early scholarship on sanctions was rather skeptical about the ability of sanctions to function as a constraining device. Scholars often viewed sanctions as easy to bypass, through sanctions busting, and hence unable to constrain actors (Crawford & Klotz, 1999; Early, 2015; Galtung, 1967). Even in cases in which sanctions were effective, they often led to more undesirable outcomes, such as increased participation of criminal elements in the economy (Andreas, 2005).

Constraining sanctions can take multiple forms. The most common way to use sanctions as a constraining device is to employ tools such as embargoes and export sanctions, which are meant to prevent export of particular goods to particular actors (Martin, 1992, 1994). As is often the case, the situation is not always clear-cut: For example, sanctions can be used as a constraining and coercive device, especially if they are imposed by a (quasi)monopolist supplier (see, e.g., Gheorghe [2019] regarding the monopolist structure of the nuclear market). Such constraints may be official (e.g., UN weapons embargoes) or unofficial (e.g., placing Huawei on the U.S. Commerce Department Entity List in 2019, effectively banning the sale of U.S.-designed semiconductor chips to the Chinese telecom company). However, as Giumelli (2011, 2013b) argues, coercive sanctions with conditions that are not likely or possible to be met can also be used as constraining devices. For example, when the EU freezes assets of third-country dignitaries which thus requires them to effectively either relinquish power or even go to jail, the effect of sanctions is not to coerce the target but, rather, to constrain their ability to act. This is the point of such sanctions—restricting actors' ability to exercise certain actions.

Using punishment to constrain the wrongdoer is in line with the long-standing view in criminology and psychology that incapacitation is a way to protect society. Incapacitation is in practical thinking associated with prisons (van Prooijen, 2018). Putting wrongdoers in prison incapacitates those who wish to do ill to others, with a goal to decrease crime.

Incapacitation is associated with a decrease in crime. Quite logically, once individuals are locked up, they cannot commit crimes (Levitt, 2004). However, this practice leads to pathological outcomes, such as overcrowded prisons in the United States. Another difficulty with using punishment as a constraining device is that long prison sentences may result in repeat offending, although the research has not yet produced conclusive results (Berger & Scheidegger, 2021). Existing criminological research is also on the fence regarding whether the length of incarceration leads to a stronger deterrent effect (Meade et al., 2012; Roach & Schanzenbach, 2016).

### 6.2.3. Sanctions as a Signaling Device

The third explanation of the purpose offered by sanctions concerns the signaling value of sanctions. In the positive retributionist narrative, "we *should* punish the guilty, because they deserve it" (Duff, 2003, p. 340). However, once applied, sanctions signal to others (beyond the sanctioner-target dyad) that the sanctioner cares about the norm and rule. Such behavior can then deter future wrongdoing by others because it sets clear boundaries. Just as signaling is very important for deterrence in general, it is also important with regard to sanctions (Fearon, 1994, 1997).

The work of Nicholas Miller, cited above, may serve as a good illustration. Miller argues that the sanctions against proliferators of weapons of mass destruction (WMD) are successful because they deter other countries from pursuing WMD. Hence, even if sanctions do not stop one particular WMD program, they may prevent others from being started or advancing (Miller, 2014, 2018). Moret et al. (2016) provide another illustration. In their work on the effect of EU and U.S. sanctions on Russia, they argued that although these sanctions did not persuade Russia to withdraw from Crimea, they may have persuaded Russia from occupying an even bigger chunk of Ukraine back in 2014.

If we think about states as a community, then such sanctions might fulfill a very important social function. In line with the constructivist theorizing in international relations, sanctions might be seen as a way to enforce certain norms in the international community (Homolar, 2011; Wagner et al., 2014). Sanctioning wrongdoers casts them aside, isolates them, and then punishes them for their behavior. Viewing sanctions in this manner dates back to the 1980s (Nossal, 1989), but it has been more recently revived in work on "rogue states" as well as on stigmatization in international politics (Adler-Nissen, 2014; Koschut, 2018; Smetana, 2020; Zarakol, 2014). In Chapter 8 in this volume, Hellquist advances a similar argument. She argues that sanctions alter the "normal" interaction between the sender and the target. Through the alteration of this normalcy, the sender's ability to impose sanctions also signals the normative authority in the international system.

By casting states as "rogue," the international community (and particularly its leading members) can adopt different tools of isolation to signal norm-breaking and communicate opprobrium associated with such actions (Wagner, 2014). Yet, this process is not automatic, and the likelihood of opprobrium being applied to states depends on how deeply a particular norm is embedded within the international community (Merlingen et al., 2001). In this view, the norm-breakers receive punishment not only because their action is reprehensible but also because public sanction sends a signal to the broad community that a particular action is unacceptable and that the underlying norms that were violated are important to the community as such (Geldenhuys, 2004).

In examining the application of sanctions in the setting of the European Monetary Union, scholars have recently problematized which actors become sanctioned and why. These scholars engaged with the following key question: Who is the audience to whom the European Commission, as the sanctioner, sends the signals—the norm-breaking countries (those not complying with the Growth and Stability Pact criteria) or the norm-complying countries? The tentative answer offered by these scholars is that the same countries can be both the target and the audience simultaneously (van der Veer, 2020; van der Veer & Haverland, 2018). Because this scholarship is thus far only tangentially connected to other political science work on sanctions, one may only hope that future work will develop a deeper connection to the broader political science scholarship on sanctions.

Another area in which an important signaling function of sanctions can be seen is regional sanctions, which have recently been used by a number of regional organizations. Regional organizations in Africa, for example, have repeatedly used sanctions to enforce pro-democracy norms in the region (Charron & Portela, 2015; Hellquist, 2014). Grauvogel et al. (2017) argue that even a threat of sanctions can stimulate anti-regime protests in Africa.

Viewing sanctions as a signaling device is in line with the sociological literature on punishment as a means to enforce norms, the key idea behind the interactionist perspective on deviance in sociology (Durkheim, 1973). The interactionist school argues that deviance must be constructed and enforced for it to be effective (Becker, 1963). Because such a process is socially constructed, it is also naturally time- and space-dependent since it reflects norms that are time- and space-dependent (Ben-Yehuda, 1990). Such a process then also leads to adaptation and learning, as individuals learn where the boundaries of norm-breaking are. Existing criminological research argues that one of the purposes of punishment is to communicate censure, which also means that it communicates which acts may lead to censure (Duff, 2003). By punishing individual wrongdoers, society signals that certain values are important and that certain actions (and actors) deserve punishment (van Prooijen, 2018).

Yet, as psychologists note, relying on the deterrent effect of punishment is problematic. Most crime is committed by actors who do not premeditate (plan) their actions, and perpetrators often have limited capacity for rational thinking (van Prooijen, 2018). One could argue that because states wield complex bureaucracies, they should be necessarily more rational in their decision-making and hence the deterrent effect of punishment should be higher. However, there is sufficient evidence that states do not always act completely rationally, and hence we should also be skeptical about the degree to which the deterrent effect of sanctions influences states.

## 6.3. SHIFT TOWARD TARGETED SANCTIONS

One of the most important trends in the sanctions practice in the post-Cold War period has been the shift toward more tailored sanctions, also known as targeted or smart sanctions (Drezner, 2011). The main spur for this shift has been the harsh sanctions regime that targeted Iraq after the First Gulf War. The comprehensive sanctions, imposed by the United Nations, led to suffering of the Iraqi civilian population while not changing the calculus of the Iraqi regime (Weiss, 1999). One of the major difficulties for sanctioning (punishing) in international politics is to impact those who decide on policy, not the general public. The targeted logic should lead to punishing selected individuals and companies while not affecting the population at large.[1]

This shift represents individualization of punishment, moving away from the collective punishment of comprehensive sanctions. The narrative of the "collective punishment" of the population by comprehensive sanctions led to the change in sanctioning practice in the first place. However, this change would not have been possible if the international system did not shift its attention to the individual as a relevant subject of international politics. If we think about international politics as a game among states, collective punishment does not really matter. However, once we start considering individuals as relevant referent objects, and once their suffering becomes a salient point, then collective punishment becomes problematic. The argument that the individual has become relevant for international policy has been made in relation to humanitarian intervention (Wheeler, 2000), but it can be generalized more broadly in the liberal tradition of international relations (Moravcsik, 1997).

The emergence of targeted sanctions, in this way, should somehow signify individualization of the punishment. This should, in theory, lead to

---

1. At the time of this writing (July 2022), a major sanctions debate in Europe is about targeting Russia with sanctions. The targeted nature of the sanctions, however, seems not to play a major role; indeed, there are some who express hope to inflict as much punishment as possible on Russia as a whole, in the hope that this would somehow lead to a surge of domestic opposition against the Russian leadership. These preferences might have to do with the especially egregious way Russia broke the international norms or with the support that Russians have shown for President Putin over time and after the start of the war. This is in line with the view among some scholars of punishment who argue that collective punishment becomes an acceptable way to punish democratic countries in which citizens have a larger role in determining who their leaders are. See Tännsjö (2007).

a more morally appropriate way of punishing wrongdoers. Currently, the targeted sanctions take the form of asset freezes of particular individuals and companies, travel bans, or export bans for particular items (often dual-use or military goods).

In abstract, this practice fits the idea of using sanctions as a constraining or coercive device. The use of sanctions to restrict individuals' access to their assets, or to restrict companies from trading, is in theory meant to either coerce them to stop norm-breaking or restrict their ability to do so. However, even then, it is difficult to avoid the strong punitive undercurrent, which comes with the selection of particular targets for censure and opprobrium.

The use of targeted sanctions also leads to another, more conceptual problem. The purpose of sanctions is punish the norm-breaker (coerce, constrain, or censure them). However, individualization of punishment in international politics leads to the use of domestic administrative tools (and domestic legal systems) to settle international conflicts, which challenges the traditional understanding of sovereignty (and sovereign equality). At the most superficial level, the individualization of sanctions leads to conflicts between states over the abuse of the domestic bureaucratic apparatus and also over the abuse of markets to enforce national interests (Farrell & Newman, 2019). Stated bluntly, if the sender restricts the assets of the target who happens to be a dignitary in another country for actions conducted by the dignitary in the target's country, such action violates the nominal sovereign equality of states. Of course, for political scientists, the fact that states have little respect for each other's sovereignty is not particularly shocking or new (Krasner, 1999). But once one censures and sanctions a head of state, it is difficult to pretend that one is targeting only an individual person. International legal scholars have for a long time highlighted that pursuing heads of states, for example, is normatively not very different from punishing states as such (Werner, 2014). Sanctions then become a tool in the domestic political struggle, and so the sender's action becomes embroiled in the domestic political conflict. Again, this is something that legal scholars long ago recognized happens in the field of international criminal justice—once investigation involves active politicians, the international tribunal itself becomes an actor in domestic political contest (Nouwen & Werner, 2010). Examining the current case of Belarus confirms that such a dynamic tends to happen also in situations in which only political leaders are targeted by "smart sanctions," but the imposition of such sanctions becomes a salient issue in the domestic political discussion.

There is also another, more palpable, consequence. Even if we overlook the conceptual issues, imposing sanctions on individual actors may lead to a spillover effect that will affect society more broadly. Consider targeting the Iranian Revolutionary Corps Guards (IRCG). The IRCG is deeply embedded in the Iranian economy, controlling major portions of it (Forozan & Shahi, 2017; Wehrey et al., 2009). Even if perfectly designed surgical sanctions were meant to cut the IRCG off from international finance (and in the subsequent paragraph, I argue that most of the sanctions are not that targeted), the spillover effect would affect the Iranian economy more broadly. Therefore, considering targeted sanctions as somehow a cleaner option means that one is avoiding the messy reality on the ground in many countries.

However, the major problem with the implementation of targeted sanctions is that although the idea might appear neat in theory, in practice, sanctions often end up being less than perfectly tailored. This is often the case because states "outsource" the enforcement of sanctions to private actors but threaten them with high costs (fines) in case of imperfect implementation. States outsource the sanctions enforcement because implementation of targeted sanctions requires a deep level of knowledge about clients and their activities, which private actors—such as banks, insurance companies, or shippers—have more readily available compared to governments. However, the threat of steep fines leads such actors to overcompliance, especially in situations in which governments provide detailed oversight and control.[2] In such situations, the targeted sanctions

---

2. There are, in fact, significant differences in the degree to which sanctions are being enforced, even within a relatively normatively uniform region such as the EU. This is one of the reasons why the EU supported emergence of an EU-wide sanctions enforcement agency. See Fleming and Bounds (2022).

might appear to be more similar to the comprehensive sanctions in practice (Giumelli, 2018; Giumelli & Onderco, 2021). This practical outcome of targeted sanctions highlights the community aspect of sanctioning in general.

## 6.4. GROWING CONTESTATION

To conclude, we examine the growing contestation of sanctions in the real world. If we take the idea of sanctions as having a signaling purpose, then we must understand that the community decides what is acceptable and what is not, and how and when the rules should be enforced. Sanctions contestation can reveal deeper contestation of core international norms but also a clash of potential penal philosophies.

Sanctions can be contested domestically as well as by other international actors. The imposition of sanctions is becoming increasingly contested by the domestic public. The growing contestation of foreign policy domestically is not a particularly novel phenomenon (Börzel & Zürn, 2021). Citizens may reject sanctions because they may have different views about the appropriateness of punishment (Onderco, 2017), and firms may contest them because they view them as impacting their bottom line (Onderco & van der Veer, 2021). At the regional level, regional organizations might adopt sanctions because they wish to highlight different norms or to explicitly challenge global sanctioners. In that way, they might signal either particular regional norms or contestation of the global ones.

However, at a more fundamental level, contestation of sanctioning raises in practice questions about appropriateness and wider sharing of norms. Whereas in the domestic society the costs of incarceration or norm enforcement more generally rarely are included in the discussion about punishment, such costs are very prominent in discussions concerning punishing international wrongdoing. Such variation highlights that although domestic punitive attitudes might influence how individuals think about foreign policy (Liberman, 2007; Wagner & Onderco, 2014), there might also be important limits to such thinking.

The contestation by other states links to the broader contestation of international norms, a field that has attracted much scholarly attention in recent years (Deitelhoff & Zimmermann, 2018; Smetana & Ondrco, 2018; Wiener, 2014). Such contestation by other countries can take different forms: They can contest the application of the norms, their legitimacy, or their relative weight vis-à-vis other norms (for more on this typology, see Smetana & Ondrco, 2018). As states contest the meaning of norms, they also contest whether the sanction should be imposed—if there is no wrong, there should also be no sanction. By contesting the norm's applicability, the audience contests the link between the specific meaning of the norm and the action. This leads to sharpening of the meaning of both the norm and its boundaries. By contesting the norm's justification, the validity and legitimacy of the norm (and the social order to which it is connected) are being contested. And if the norm is subject to hierarchical contestation, the audience re-enacts the positions of individual norms vis-à-vis one another. All three forms of contestation of norms—and of sanctioning—have an effect on the international normative order.

The growing contestation of the applicability of international norms (and appropriateness of sanctioning) reflects the growing contestation of some domestic sanctioning practices. Just as racial and class-based prejudices are becoming increasingly highlighted and contested domestically, they are similarly becoming contested internationally. As Martha Finnemore (2005) states,

> An argument that says, "I won't play by the rules" is a political loser. It is much more palatable and effective politically to fight rules with rules and argue, "I am playing by the rules; they just aren't your rules, and your rules are wrong." (p. 197)

Such debates, naturally, open discussions about the origins of the rules and also the fairness of such rules (Anghie, 2007). Here, too, the domestic and international contestations of sanctions might find fruitful cross-fertilization in the future.

One area in which political scientists have yet to catch up with the broader scholarship on punishment is the serious engagement with alternative logics of justice. In Chapter 8 in this volume, Hellquist makes some initial steps in this direction by arguing that because sanctions are inherently relational, different approaches to sanctions underlie different punitive logics. Gollwitzer et al. (see Chapter 2 in this volume) highlight and outline different ideas of justice. As Hellquist argues, one of the reasons why African Union sanctions are very short, as opposed to the EU's rather lengthy sanctions, is that the African Union follows a different logic—that of restorative justice. Of course, the logic of restorative justice is not immediately available for the United States and Iran. However, further research on the different ideas of justice, and their link to the existing (or alternative) sanctioning practices, offers a fruitful path for the future of the academic study of sanctions.

Based on the discussion in this chapter, it can be seen that international punishment is not entirely different from punishment in domestic societies. Some of the basic logics of punishment as well as purposes of punishment apply in the international system. However, numerous contextual factors make the comparison imperfect. As argued above, individualization of sanctions is very imperfect because of the way in which the international system is built and how it functions. Similarly, targeting of sanctions to individuals is difficult in a world in which the referent object is still a group—the state. At the same time, these differences should not hinder future interdisciplinary research on international sanctioning, which would leverage insights from other scientific fields.

## REFERENCES

Adler-Nissen, R. (2014). Stigma management in international relations: Transgressive identities, norms and order in international society. *International Organisation, 68*(1), 143–176.

Alexseev, M. A., & Hale, H. E. (2019). Crimea come what may: Do economic sanctions backfire politically? *Journal of Peace Research, 57*(2), 344–359.

Alnasrawi, A. (2001). Iraq: Economic sanctions and consequences, 1990–2000. *Third World Quarterly, 22*(2), 205–218.

Andreas, P. (2005). Criminalizing consequences of sanctions: Embargo busting and its legacy. *International Studies Quarterly, 49*(2), 335–360.

Anghie, A. (2007). *Imperialism, sovereignty, and the making of international law* (Cambridge Studies in International and Comparative Law). Cambridge University Press.

Baldwin, D. A. (1985). *Economic statecraft*. Princeton University Press.

Bapat, N. A., & Kwon, B. R. (2015). When are sanctions effective? A bargaining and enforcement framework. *International Organization, 69*(1), 131–162.

Becker, H. S. (1963). *Outsiders: Studies in the sociology of deviance*. Free Press.

Ben-Yehuda, N. (1990). *The politics and morality of deviance: Moral panics, drug abuse, deviant science, and reversed stigmatization*. State University of New York Press.

Berger, E., & Scheidegger, K. S. (2021, May). *Sentence length and recidivism: A review of the research*. Criminal Justice Legal Foundation. https://www.cjlf.org/publications/papers/SentenceRecidivism.pdf

Börzel, T. A., & Zürn, M. (2021). Contestations of the liberal international order: From liberal multilateralism to postnational liberalism. *International Organization, 75*(2), 282–305.

Brooks, R. A. (2002). Sanctions and regime type: What works, and when? *Security Studies, 11*(4), 1–50.

Charron, A., & Portela, C. (2015). The UN, regional sanctions and Africa. *International Affairs, 91*(6), 1369–1385.

Crawford, N. C., & Klotz, A. (1999). How sanctions work: A framework for analysis. In N. C. Crawford & A. Klotz (Eds.), *How sanctions work: Lessons from South Africa* (pp. 25–42). Palgrave Macmillan.

Deitelhoff, N., & Zimmermann, L. (2018). Things we lost in the fire: How different types of contestation affect the robustness of international norms. *International Studies Review, 22*(1), 51–76.

Drezner, D. W. (1999). *The sanctions paradox: Economic statecraft and international relations*. Cambridge University Press.

Drezner, D. W. (2003). The hidden hand of economic coercion. *International Organization, 57*(3), 643–659.

Drezner, D. W. (2011). Sanctions sometimes smart: Targeted sanctions in theory and practice. *International Studies Review, 13*(1), 96–108.

Drezner, D. W. (2021). The United States of sanctions. *Foreign Affairs, 100*(5), 142–154.

Drury, A. C. (1998). Revisiting economic sanctions reconsidered. *Journal of Peace Research, 35*(4), 497–509.

Duff, R. A. (2003). Punishment. In H. LaFollette (Ed.), *The Oxford handbook of practical ethics* (pp. 331–357). Oxford University Press.

Durkheim, E. (1973). Two laws of penal evolution. *Economy and Society, 2*(3), 285–308.

Early, B. R. (2015). *Busted sanctions: Explaining why economic sanctions fail*. Stanford University Press.

Early, B. R., & Peksen, D. (2022). Does misery love company? Analyzing the global suffering inflicted by US economic sanctions. *Global Studies Quarterly, 2*(2), ksac013.

Farrell, H., & Newman, A. L. (2019). Weaponized interdependence: How global economic networks shape state coercion. *International Security, 44*(1), 42–79.

Fearon, J. D. (1994). Signaling versus the balance of power and interests: An empirical test of a crisis bargaining model. *Journal of Conflict Resolution, 38*(2), 236–269.

Fearon, J. D. (1997). Signaling foreign policy interests. *Journal of Conflict Resolution, 41*(1), 68–90.

Felbermayr, G., Kirilakha, A., Syropoulos, C., Yalcin, E., & Yotov, Y. V. (2020). The Global Sanctions Data Base. *European Economic Review, 129*, article 103561.

Finnemore, M. (2005). Fights about rules: The role of efficacy and power in changing multilateralism. *Review of International Studies, 31*(Suppl. S1), 187–206.

Fleming, S., & Bounds, A. (2022, July 5). Brussels pushes for tougher sanctions enforcement via EU-wide body. Financial Times.

Forozan, H., & Shahi, A. (2017). The military and the state in Iran: The economic rise of the Revolutionary Guards. *The Middle East Journal, 71*(1), 67–86.

Galtung, J. (1967). On the effects of international economic sanctions, with examples from the case of Rhodesia. *World Politics, 19*(3), 378–416.

Garland, D. (2001). *The culture of control: Crime and social order in contemporary society*. Clarendon.

Geldenhuys, D. (2004). *Deviant conduct in world politics*. Palgrave Macmillan.

Gheorghe, E. (2019). Proliferation and the logic of the nuclear market. *International Security, 43*(4), 88–127.

Giumelli, F. (2011). *Coercing, constraining and signalling: Explaining UN and EU sanctions after the Cold War*. ECPR Press.

Giumelli, F. (2013a). How EU sanctions work: A new narrative (Chaillot Papers No. 129). EU Institute for Security Studies. https://www.iss.europa.eu/sites/default/files/EUISSFiles/Chaillot_129.pdf

Giumelli, F. (2013b). *The success of sanctions: Lessons learned from the EU experience*. Ashgate.

Giumelli, F. (2017). The redistributive impact of restrictive measures on EU members: Winners and losers from imposing sanctions on Russia. *Journal of Common Market Studies, 55*(5), 1062–1080.

Giumelli, F. (2018). The role of for-profit actors in implementing targeted sanctions: The case of the European Union. In O. Bures & H. Carrapico (Eds.), *Security privatization: How non-security-related private businesses shape security governance* (pp. 123–141). Springer.

Giumelli, F., & Onderco, M. (2021). States, firms, and security: How private actors implement sanctions, lessons learned from the Netherlands. *European Journal of International Security, 6*(2), 190–209.

Grauvogel, J., Licht, A. A., & von Soest, C. (2017). Sanctions and signals: How international sanction threats trigger domestic protest in targeted regimes. *International Studies Quarterly, 61*(1), 86–97.

Grossman, G., Manekin, D., & Margalit, Y. (2018). How sanctions affect public opinion in target countries: Experimental evidence from Israel. *Comparative Political Studies, 51*(14), 1823–1857.

Hampton, J. (1984). The moral education theory of punishment. *Philosophy & Public Affairs, 13*(3), 208–238.

Hathaway, O. A., & Shapiro, S. J. (2017). *The internationalists: How a radical plan to outlaw war remade the world*. Simon & Schuster.

Hellquist, E. (2014). *Regional organizations and sanctions against members: Explaining the different trajectories of the African Union, the League of Arab States, and the Association of Southeast Asian Nations* (KFG Working Paper Series, No. 59). https://ideas.repec.org/p/erp/kfgxxx/p0059.html

Hirschman, A. O. (1980). *National power and the structure of foreign trade*. University of California Press. (Original work published 1945)

Homolar, A. (2011). Rebels without a conscience: The evolution of the rogue states narrative in US security policy. *European Journal of International Relations, 17*(4), 705–727.

Hufbauer, G. C., Elliott, K. A., Cyrus, T., & Winston, E. (1997). US economic sanctions: Their impact on trade, jobs, and wages (Working paper). Peterson Institute for International Economics.

Hufbauer, G. C., Schott, J. J., & Elliott, K. A. (2007). *Economic sanctions reconsidered* (3rd ed.). Peterson Institute for International Economics.

Klotz, A. (1999). Making sanctions work: Comparative lessons. In N. Crawford & A. Klotz (Eds.), *How sanctions work: Lessons from South Africa* (pp. 264–282). Macmillan.

Koschut, S. (2018). Naming, shaming and reintegration: Beyond stigmatization in international politics [Paper presentation]. The 58th ECPR General Conference, Hamburg, Germany.

Krasner, S. D. (1999). *Sovereignty: Organized hypocrisy*. Princeton University Press.

Levitt, S. D. (2004). Understanding why crime fell in the 1990s: Four factors that explain the decline and six that do not. *Journal of Economic Perspectives, 18*(1), 163–190.

Liberman, P. (2007). Punitiveness and U.S. elite support for the 1991 Persian Gulf War. *Journal of Conflict Resolution, 51*(1), 3–32.

Litwak, R. (2000). *Rogue states and U.S. foreign policy: Containment after the Cold War*. Woodrow Wilson Center Press.

Martin, L. L. (1992). Interests, power, and multilateralism. *International Organization, 46*(4), 765–792.

Martin, L. L. (1994). *Coercive cooperation: Explaining multilateral economic sanctions*. Princeton University Press.

McGillivray, F., & Stam, A. C. (2004). Political institutions, coercive diplomacy, and the duration of economic sanctions. *Journal of Conflict Resolution, 48*(2), 154–172.

Meade, B., Steiner, B., Makarios, M., & Travis, L. (2012). Estimating a dose–response relationship between time served in prison and recidivism. *Journal of Research in Crime and Delinquency, 50*(4), 525–550.

Merlingen, M., Mudde, C., & Sedelmeier, U. (2001). The right and the righteous? European norms, domestic politics and the sanctions against Austria. *Journal of Common Market Studies, 39*(1), 59–77.

Miller, N. L. (2014). The secret success of nonproliferation sanctions. *International Organization, 68*(4), 913–944.

Miller, N. L. (2018). *Stopping the bomb: The sources and effectiveness of US nonproliferation policy*. Cornell University Press.

Moravcsik, A. (1997). Taking preferences seriously: A liberal theory of international politics. *International Organization, 51*(4), 513–553.

Moret, E., Biersteker, T., Giumelli, F., Portela, C., Veber, M., Bastiat-Jarosz, D., & Bobocea, C. (2016, October 12). *The new deterrent: International sanctions against Russia over the Ukraine crisis.* http://repository.graduateinstitute.ch/record/294704/files/The%20New%20Deterrent%20International%20Sanctions%20Against%20Russia%20Over%20the%20Ukraine%20Crisis%20-%20Impacts,%20Costs%20and%20Further%20Action.pdf

Morgan, T. C., Bapat, N., & Kobayashi, Y. (2014). Threat and imposition of economic sanctions 1945–2005: Updating the ties dataset. *Conflict Management and Peace Science, 31*(5), 541–558.

Morgan, T. C., Bapat, N., & Krustev, V. (2009). The threat and imposition of economic sanctions, 1971–2000. *Conflict Management and Peace Science, 26*(1), 92–110.

Morris, H. (1981). A paternalistic theory of punishment. *American Philosophical Quarterly, 18*(4), 263–271.

Mulder, N. (2019). The rise and fall of Euro-American inter-state war. *Humanity, 10*(1), 133–153.

Mulder, N. (2022). *The economic weapon: The rise of sanctions as a tool of modern war.* Yale University Press.

Nossal, K. R. (1989). International sanctions as international punishment. *International Organization, 43*(2), 301–322.

Nouwen, S. M. H., & Werner, W. G. (2010). Doing justice to the political: The International Criminal Court in Uganda and Sudan. *European Journal of International Law, 21*(4), 941–965.

Onderco, M. (2017). Public support for coercive diplomacy: Exploring public opinion data from ten European countries. *European Journal of Political Research, 56*(2), 401–418.

Onderco, M., & van der Veer, R. A. (2021). No more gouda in Moscow? Distributive effects of sanctions imposition. *Journal of Common Market Studies, 59*(6), 1345–1363.

Pape, R. A. (1997). Why economic sanctions do not work. *International Security, 22*(2), 90–136.

Pape, R. A. (1998). Why economic sanctions still do not work. *International Security, 23*(1), 66–77.

Peksen, D. (2019). When do imposed economic sanctions work? A critical review of the sanctions effectiveness literature. *Defence and Peace Economics, 30*(6), 635–647.

Portela, C. (2012). *European Union sanctions and foreign policy: When and why do they work?* Routledge.

Portela, C. (2014, March 11). The EU's use of 'targeted' sanctions: Evaluating effectiveness [Working document]. Centre for European Policy Studies. http://www.ceps.eu/system/files/WD391%20Portela%20EU%20Targeted%20Sanctions.pdf

Portela, C. (2015a). How the EU learned to love sanctions. In M. Leonard (Ed.), *Connectivity wars: The geo-economic battlegrounds of the future* (pp. 36–42). European Council on Foreign Relations.

Portela, C. (2015b). Member states resistance to EU foreign policy sanctions. *European Foreign Affairs Review, 20*(2/1), 39–61.

Roach, M. A., & Schanzenbach, M. M. (2016). *The effect of prison sentence length on recidivism: Evidence from random judicial assignment* (Northwestern Law & Econ Research Paper No. 16-08). SSRN. https://papers.ssrn.com/sol3/papers.cfm?abstract_id=2701549

Rowe, D. M. (2010). Economic sanctions and international security. In R. A. Danemark (Ed.), *The international studies encyclopedia*. Blackwell. https://www.oxfordreference.com/display/10.1093/acref/9780191842665.001.0001/acref-9780191842665-e-0070

Sjoberg, L. (2006). *Gender, justice, and the wars in Iraq: A feminist reformulation of just war theory*. Lexington Books.

Smetana, M. (2020). *Nuclear deviance: Stigma politics and the rules of the nonproliferation game*. Palgrave Macmillan.

Smetana, M., & Onderco, M. (2018). Bringing the outsiders in: An interactionist perspective on deviance and normative change in international politics. *Cambridge Review of International Affairs, 31*(6), 516–536.

Tännsjö, T. (2007). The myth of innocence: On collective responsibility and collective punishment. *Philosophical Papers, 36*(2), 295–314.

van Bergeijk, P. A. G. (1994). *Economic diplomacy, trade, and commercial policy: Positive and negative sanctions in a new world order*. Elgar.

van der Veer, R. A. (2020). Audience heterogeneity, costly signaling, and threat prioritization: Bureaucratic reputation-building in the EU. *Journal of Public Administration Research and Theory, 31*(1), 21–37.

van der Veer, R. A., & Haverland, M. (2018). Bread and butter or bread and circuses? Politicisation and the European Commission in the European Semester. *European Union Politics, 19*(3), 524–545.

van Prooijen, J.-W. (2018). *The moral punishment instinct*. Oxford University Press.

Von Hirsch, A. (1993). *Censure and sanctions*. Clarendon.

Wagner, W. (2014). Rehabilitation or exclusion? A criminological perspective on policies towards "rogue states." In W. Wagner, W. G. Werner, & M. Onderco (Eds.), *Deviance in international relations* (pp. 152–170). Springer.

Wagner, W., & Onderco, M. (2014). Accommodation or confrontation? Explaining differences in policies towards Iran. *International Studies Quarterly, 58*(4), 717–728.

Wagner, W., Werner, W., & Onderco, M. (2014). Rogues, pariahs, outlaws: Theorizing deviance in international relations. In W. Wagner, W. G. Werner, & M. Onderco (Eds.), *Deviance in international relations* (pp. 1–14). Springer.

Wehrey, F., Green, J. D., Nichiporuk, B., Nader, A., Hansell, L., Nafisi, R., & Bohandy, S. R. (2009). *The rise of the Pasdaran: Assessing the domestic roles of Iran's Islamic Revolutionary Guards Corps*. RAND Corporation.

Weiss, T. G. (1999). Sanctions as a foreign policy tool: Weighing humanitarian impulses. *Journal of Peace Research, 36*(5), 499–509.

Werner, W. G. (2014). International law, renegade regimes, and the criminalization of enmity. In W. Wagner, W. Werner, & M. Onderco (Eds.), *Deviance in international relations: "Rogue states" and international security* (pp. 193–213). Palgrave Macmillan.

Wheeler, N. J. (2000). *Saving strangers. Humanitarian intervention in international society*. Oxford University Press.

Wiener, A. (2014). *A theory of contestation* (Springer Briefs in Political Science). Springer

Wilson, W. (1919). *Addresses delivered by President Wilson on his western tour, September 4 to September 25, 1919, on the League of Nations, Treaty of Peace with Germany, industrial conditions, high cost of living, race riots, etc.* (66th Congress, 1 Session, Document No. 120). Government Printing Office.

Wunderlich, C. (2020). *Rogue states as norm entrepreneurs: Black sheep or sheep in wolves' clothing?* Springer.

Zarakol, A. (2014). What made the modern world hang together: Socialisation or stigmatisation? *International Theory*, 6(2), 311–332.

# 7

# Supporting the Punishment of Atrocity Crimes

## *A Broad Coalition Among a Narrow Elite*

MIKKEL JARLE CHRISTENSEN

## 7.1. INTRODUCTION

The study of punishment has been an object of sociological inquiry beginning with Durkheim (1893). Since Durkheim, a multitude of sociological studies have focused on crime and punishment. These studies have deepened our understanding of how crimes are affected by and affect society (Foucault, 1975; Garland, 1993), including how the power of the state to define crime and punishment (Garland, 2013) often has considerable effects that are not distributed evenly across society and its different social, economic, racial, and gendered groups. Whereas social science was originally focused on crime and punishment inside of the state, more recent scholarship has turned its attention to the forms of punishment that play out at a more global level. As the post-Cold War era saw considerable expansion of international law and courts (Alter, 2014) that included new international criminal tribunals (Cryer et al., 2019), a new scholarship has emerged around the study of international crime and punishment (Bantekas & Mylonaki, 2014; Drumbl, 2003; Hagan, 2003; Lohne,

Mikkel Jarle Christensen, *Supporting the Punishment of Atrocity Crimes* In: *Punishment in International Society*. Edited by: Wolfgang Wagner, Linet R. Durmuşoğlu, Barbora Holá, Ronald Kroeze, Jan-Willem van Prooijen, and Wouter Werner, Oxford University Press. © Oxford University Press 2024. DOI: 10.1093/oso/9780197693483.003.0007

2018; Parmentier, 2011; Roberts & McMillan, 2003; Rothe & Friedrichs, 2006; Smeulers & Haveman, 2008). Conceptualizing and analyzing this new form of criminal justice that was to different degrees unmoored from the state (Christensen & Levi, 2017), this literature took the emergence of a "cosmopolitan penality" as its object (Lohne, 2019). This chapter shows how this particular form of cosmopolitan penality is rooted sociologically in a globalized group of elite agents that is dominated by agents from the Global North, most of whom are men. As such, the chapter demonstrates how a particular version of punishment in international law and politics is driven by a relatively narrow elite of stakeholders, among which there is broad agreement that the internationalized punishment of specific crimes structured around international criminal courts and specific criminal law technologies is an important social good.

Previous scholarship has studied how such forms of globalized penality were driven by the emergence of new networks, organizations, and institutions that invested in international prosecution, adjudication, and, ultimately, punishment. Outside of the international criminal courts that were created to adjudicate criminal responsibility for core international crimes (war crimes, crimes against humanity, genocide, and the crime of aggression), a range of stakeholders, including civil society organizations working in human rights, turned their attention to supporting punitive criminal justice ideas and practices (Engle, 2014; Haddad, 2018; Lohne, 2019). Investing symbolically and materially in international criminal justice, professionals employed in human rights nongovernmental organizations (NGOs), typically headquartered in the Global North, became an important fixture in this social space, commenting on and supporting agents working directly for or in the international criminal courts (Batesmith, 2021; Hagan & Levi, 2004; Hagan et al., 2006). In addition, academics invested in international criminal justice (Christensen, 2016), with some of them being directly involved in the creation of new institutions and organizations in this social space. Such groups supplemented the agents working with international crimes and their punishment in both national and international jurisdictions. Collectively, these agents populate what has been referred to by some scholars as the field of international criminal justice (Christensen, 2015b; Dixon & Tenove, 2013; Hagan & Levi, 2005), a metaphor that also guides the analysis of this chapter. The social groups active in this field compete to define, among other things, what punishment in the global realm should look like. Whereas the punitive character of international criminal law coexists with other ideals and goals—for instance, those related to providing reparations to victims of international crimes (Christoph, 2012; Dixon, 2016; Sperfeldt, 2017, 2022)—the focus on prosecuting perpetrators for the sake of victims has become the rallying call of this field. The focus of this chapter is on the different social groups involved in the contest to define and develop punitive sanctions in the field of international criminal justice. Specifically, the chapter analyzes the core forms of expertise that specific social groups invest in punishment outside of the state. Whereas many of these investments target the creation of criminal law cases and the development of international criminal justice, they aim to affect also international politics in particular by trying to end impunity or more precisely working and advocating to ensure that political stakeholders, no matter their position, be prosecuted and, if found guilty, punished for their involvement in atrocity crimes. As such, these investments and the expertise on which they build form the sociological foundation of battles to define international criminal justice and its forms of punishment, something often done in the name of wider, societal interests. Making reference to and ostensibly working to promote and secure such interests, elites investing expertise in international criminal justice often represent, or perceive themselves to represent, specific groups, goals, and values.

The remainder of the chapter is divided into three sections. Section 7.2 discusses previous literature and how it relates to the perspective of this chapter. This section also introduces the concepts and methods used in the chapter. Section 7.3 analyses the elites engaged in the fight to define the legal machineries in and around the international criminal courts that help produce a form of global punishment that was designed to, at least potentially, disregard political power. Legitimating also their investments as representing particular interests, such as the interests of victims or the values of international society, the elites active in defining international criminal justice bring specific patterns of capital into the field. The differences between elites active in this field, their investments, and the stakes they (claim to) represent are indicative of the wider stakes of international criminal justice prosecution, adjudication, and, ultimately, punishment. Section 7.4 summarizes the findings of the chapter and points toward its potential significance for further studies of elites in the space of international punishment as well as the claims of representation that they build their positions on. Most significantly, this section shows how the elite of international punishment active in the field of international criminal justice is dominated by Global North agents that build their investments on particular forms of professional expertise. This means that visions of punishment in this field are dominated by specific perspectives developed as part of career paths in the Global North, its universities, legal institutions, and NGOs. Although embedded in a narrow elite, the support of international punishment of atrocity crimes is spread out across this elite; in fact, it has broad support to the point of being almost matter of fact.

## 7.2. STUDYING AGENTS SUPPORTING INTERNATIONAL PUNISHMENT

Crime and punishment continue to capture both the scholarly and popular imagination. The prevalent position of crime and punishment in societal imaginaries is underscored, among others, by French sociologist Luc Boltanski, who highlights the emergence of the crime mystery as a central characteristic of the modern imaginary (Boltanski, 2012). As part of this project, Boltanski also emphasized how the crime mystery shares with sociology the presupposition of a need to look for underlying structures and patterns to explain the state of the world (Boltanski, 2009). In the international realm, crime and punishment have also been the objects of scholarly attention. In a global setting in which no single state holds the legitimate monopoly to use physical force (Weber, 2007, pp. 77–78), scholarly thinking about internationalized punishment has both built on classic scholarship and produced new concepts. Generally, two different broad approaches to global punishment as tied to international criminal justice can be identified. The first literature generally takes an institutional and functionalist approach to legal processes and to the theoretical and jurisprudential underpinnings of international criminal punishment. This scholarship has also contributed important critical perspectives. The second approach is focused less on the institutions and functions of international criminal justice and instead takes a critical perspective on the agents active in and around such processes. Consequently, this scholarship often zooms in on the professionals and forms of power involved in creating and implementing punishment beyond the state.

The first strand of literature, arguably the most dominant and influential also outside of scholarship (e.g., in policy and public debates), focuses on the legal structures of international criminal punishment and its theoretical and jurisprudential underpinnings. In this broad category, most legal scholarship builds on specific assumptions about the relation between functions and effects (often conceptualized as retributive, deterrent, and expressive). Such assumptions are arguably shared by practitioners in and around the international criminal courts as well as by other stakeholders of this field, including at the political level. Whereas some scholars have built or provided support for retributive theories (Fichtelberg, 2005; Haque, 2005), others have questioned the potential practical implications of international criminal justice (Greenawalt, 2013). In addition, some scholars have argued that the inherent selectivity of prosecutions targeting international crimes makes claims of the retributive effects of international criminal law difficult to maintain (Drumbl, 2003, p. 270), selectivity being of continued importance in understanding how international criminal courts work (van Sliedregt, 2021). As part of a wider debate about the functions and effects of international punishment, in particular the deterrent effects of international criminal justice have been the topic of frequent debates (Dancy, 2018; Dietrich, 2014; Holtermann, 2010, 2021; Jo & Simmons, 2016; Mennecke, 2007) that still reverberate and were the object of a symposium in the *Journal of International Criminal Justice* (Dothan et al., 2021). As demonstrated by the special issue, there is still significant scholarly disagreement as to whether or not the International Criminal Court (ICC; and similar institutions) can be claimed to deter atrocity crimes (Dothan, 2021; Hodgson, 2020; Mégret, 2020; Whiting, 2021). Perhaps as a reaction to the lack of consensus about retributive and deterrent effects, a range of scholars have focused on the expressive functions of the international criminal courts that dole out punishment (Bringedal Houge, 2019; DeGuzman, 2012; Fisher, 2020; Luban, 2013; Sander, 2019a, 2019b; Sloane, 2017; Stahn, 2020). Others have studied expressive functions and effects outside of the international criminal courts (Palmer, 2020), including in responses to their practices (Clarke, 2019). These studies have contributed important findings on the functions and potential effects of international criminal justice and its mission to enforce punishment of atrocity crimes. However, they have often focused less on the agents and elites that work with this form of justice and whose power relations and choices have significant effects on its impact.

The second stream of literature is less directly concerned with the functions and potential effects of international punishment and instead takes a more agentic perspective studying the professionals that drive legal processes and those that are the subjects of international criminal justice. Such scholarship has, for instance, focused on how victims participate in legal proceedings before the international criminal courts (Beets, 2005; Hobbs, 2014; Moffett, 2015; Pena & Carayon, 2013; Sperfeldt, 2013; Wheeler, 2016). As such, this scholarship also touches on reparations to victims as well as on broader reparative dimensions of international criminal justice (Christoph, 2012; Combs, 2007; Dixon, 2016; Nickson, 2016; Popovski, 2000; Travis, 2015). Other scholarship, often linked to wider criminological perspectives (Holá et al., 2011; Smeulers et al., 2013, 2015), have focused on the perpetrators of international crimes and how international criminal justice deals with and punishes them (Holá & Van Wijk, 2014; Smeulers et al., 2019; van Wijk & Holá, 2017). In addition to scholarship on perpetrators and victims, sociological research (Christensen, 2015a) has focused on the elites and professionals active in the field of international criminal justice, both in the international criminal courts and in other types of organizations that work with atrocity crimes in different ways, such as NGOs, think tanks, and law firms. With regard to the professionals in the courts, research has highlighted the importance of elite agents who make decisions in these institutions (Batesmith, 2021; Christensen, 2019; Hagan & Levi, 2004; Hagan et al., 2006; Levi et al., 2016; Powderly, 2020) as well as those active around them—for instance, in some of the NGOs that have gained an important position in international criminal justice (Burgis-Kasthala, 2019; Cakmak, 2006; Christensen, 2021; Durham, 2012; Engle, 2014; Glasius, 2006; Haddad, 2018; Koleva & Vigh, 2021; Lohne, 2019; Sperfeldt, 2013). A smaller number of studies have focused on the role of academics in this field, at times relying on Schachter's old (and, from a sociological perspective, not very apt) concept of an "invisible college" (Schachter, 1977) of "international criminal lawyers" (Kreß, 2014). Other studies focused on academics have shown how the international criminal courts rely on scholarship in their legal decision-making (Manley, 2016; Stappert, 2018) or have studied the different types of scholars active in international criminal justice (Burgis-Kasthala, 2016; Christensen, 2016). Collectively, this research has investigated the elites and professionals active in the daily workings of international criminal justice. These agents often collaborate to build legal cases of atrocity crimes, for instance, as agents in the international criminal courts rely on evidence collected by others or build on academic arguments to support specific legal arguments. These patterns of cooperation also imply that these agents are not always in agreement with regard to how international criminal justice should unfold in practice, on which norms it should build, or how it should develop over time.

This chapter contributes a critical sociological study of the elite agents active in pushing for or against international criminal justice punishment. Building on an original multiple correspondence analysis (MCA; Le Roux, 2010), the analysis zooms in on the expertise of different social groups active in and around international criminal justice, its institutions and main sites of organized labor. Simply stated, the MCA measures differences between elite agents active in the field of international criminal justice. For instance, one variable measures whether or not agents hold a master's degree from a top university (folded into the variable edu_eliteuni). The top university variable here means an institution ranked in the top 10 in the world across three different university ranking systems. If one agent held such a degree and another did not, they would be placed at opposite ends of a spectrum. Whereas the constructed variables were often more complex than a simple binary (e.g., the edu_eliteuni shows how many degrees from elite institutions agents hold), the distribution of capital depicted in the map follows the logic of placing agents who differ in terms of their capital in different locations. In other words, distance between different forms of capital means that they are not statistically associated with each other. The variables were built to best be able to measure the differences in expertise embodied in elites in the field of international criminal justice, which can be used to study what forms of capital they are able to invest toward specific goals—most important in the present context the goal of punishing perpetrators for atrocity crimes. Specifically, the analysis focuses on the embodied expertise of elite social groups engaged in this field and how this expertise may affect elites' position-taking on punishment beyond the state. In other words, the analysis focuses on how particular accumulations of capital might format perceptions about what such punishment should look like. The idea is to study the forms of expertise that are active in battles to define what international punishment looks like, patterns of expertise that are mobilized also in representation of specific interests in global society—for instance, those of victims of atrocity crimes.

The conceptual point of departure for the chapter is inspired by the sociology of Pierre Bourdieu. Following his thinking, the embodied expertise of elite agents is conceptualized as capital (Bourdieu & Wacquant, 1992). Identifying central forms of capital—economic, social, and cultural—Bourdieu also highlighted how specific combinations of embodied expertise had distinct value in specific fields of practice—for instance, in the French fields of law (Bourdieu, 1986), academia (Bourdieu, 1984), and the state field of power (Bourdieu, 1989). Defined as a social space characterized by the objective relations between its different positions, the concept of a field has also been used to study international criminal justice, as mentioned above (Batesmith, 2021; Christensen, 2015b; Dezalay, 2017;

Dixon & Tenove, 2013; Hagan & Levi, 2005), but these studies typically relied on more qualitative methods. Using MCA, a quantitative method, allows the chapter to tease out the forms of capital invested in the field of international criminal justice by diverse elite social groups and to build ideas about how this can affect how and what different groups think about the punishment of international crimes and what values it represents. In this context, it is important to note that in both national and international social spaces, forms of capital can be of particular field-specific value in the sense that they are related to embodied expertise accumulated in this field that is not directly transferable to other social spaces, at least not without considerable depreciation (Christensen, 2015b, 2021).

To study the objective relations between different forms of capital that characterize connections and differences between elites in international criminal justice, an MCA was developed on the basis of sampling of specific agents active in this field. Four broad sampling techniques were used. The first sampling collected profiles of individuals highly ranked in the international criminal courts (judges, prosecutors, and defense counsel appearing in court). The second sampling collected profiles of agents working (or who had worked) in large international NGOs (where they worked with international criminal justice, for instance, having spoken at important diplomatic meetings or side events). The third sampled from agents in attendance at the negotiations of the Rome Statute. And, finally, the fourth sampled from academics who published on international criminal justice either in field-specific journals or in more general international law journals. Sampling began in 2019 and used data available in the public realm, often through online curriculum vitae, from 2018. The final MCA includes data on 365 elite agents (264 men and 101 women). Most of the agents were from the Global North, with 40% from Europe and 25% from North America. For the individuals who were included in the final sample, career biographies were built in a standardized way. Upon completion of the biographies, the capital of the sampled agents was coded. We coded across variables that measured, for instance, whether agents had obtained master's degrees and where they had spent their careers (international/national judiciaries, political appointments, and NGOs).

We built in intercoder reliability tests to ensure uniform and consistent coding. The resulting MCA is organized around 20 active variables with a total of 72 modalities. The variables cut across the three core forms of capital originally identified by Bourdieu: economic, cultural, and social. In addition, measures for symbolic/network capital were included: one for participation in the negotiation of the Rome Statute and one for mentions in large, international media outlets. As with the variable on attainment of master's degrees in elite universities, all agents were scored across all of these variables. Importantly, however, the form of capital that has the most variables in the current analysis, that of social capital, is also characterized by having a secondary form of field-specific capital. Variables that measure this form include being employed in the international criminal courts or serving as defense counsel before them, the former type of expertise seemingly different to transfer to other fields of practice (Christensen, 2018, 2020a). On the basis of quantification of capital produced by the MCA (Lebaron, 2009), a visualization of the field of international criminal justice focused on its elites.

Three dimensions format distinctions between the accumulated capital of different elites in the field of international criminal justice. Simply stated, these three dimensions account for the difference between different elite groups in this social space. In this chapter, we focus on the axis that accounts for most variation between accumulated capital in the field. This axis accounts for 45% of the total adjusted inertia in this field and is visualized across the horizontal plane in Figure 7.1. Across this axis, agents on the left of the field have mainly academic/research capital, whereas those on the right have their main expertise from legal practice and from working in legal institutions. This highlights the structuring effect of a distinction between practical expertise from working with (international) criminal law and punishment, on the one hand, and academic expertise accumulated through systematizing and commenting on such practices, on the other hand, which has previously been highlighted in scholarship (Christensen, 2020c). Variance along the horizontal axis of Figure 7.1 was created by isolating the modalities that contribute to the variance.

Supporting the Punishment of Atrocity Crimes

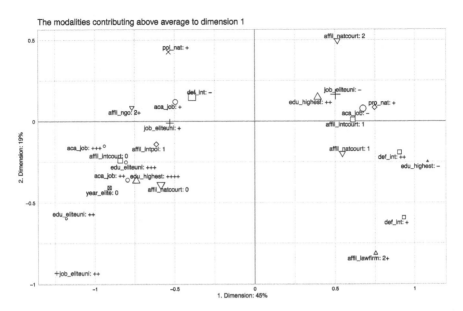

**Figure 7.1** The modalities contributing above average to Dimension 1.

In Figure 7.1, across the variables, a "+" refers to the accumulation of specific forms of capital, whereas a "–" refers to the lack of accumulation. Multiple "+"s refer to agents having accumulated more capital of this type. "affil_" variables refer to the number of times agents have been affiliated with specific institutions: "natpol" refers to national political positions; "intpol" to international politics; and "intcourt" and "natcourt" to domestic or international courts, respectively. "lawfirm" refers to affiliations with law firms. "aca_job" refers to employment in universities. "edu_ " variables refer to the education of agents: "edu_highest" refers to the number of degrees agents have obtained from universities; "eliteuni" refers to the top 10 universities across three different global rankings. "def_int" refers to agents who have defended cases before international criminal national courts, and "pro_nat" refers to agents who have prosecuted cases in national jurisdictions. The different symbols, such as the triangles, refer to the specific types of variables and aim to make the map easier to decipher.

On the right side of Figure 7.1, elite agents have mainly accumulated capital from working in the engine rooms of law: as practitioners of criminal and international criminal justice at either the national or the international level. On the left side, and in contrast, elites have mainly built expertise from academia or, to a lesser extent, from working in the civil society sector, often in NGOs. In other words, the sociological distance between agents who build their elite status on practical capital and those who build it on analyzing and commenting on international criminal justice formats the contest to define international criminal justice as a form of globalized punishment aimed at perpetrators of atrocity crimes. The groups active in international criminal justice each invest different forms of expertise into the stakes of this field that help structure this contest to define prosecution, adjudication, and punishment. The next section outlines the forms of capital invested in punishment for atrocities across the different elites.

## 7.3. CAPITAL INVESTMENTS IN INTERNATIONAL CRIMINAL PUNISHMENT

As embodied expertise, capital can be invested in different social spaces, including in the field of international criminal justice. Such investments shape how different elites engage with atrocity crime punishment and what positions they take on its direction. This is also, to a certain extent, related to the interests they represent, building their symbolic position, for instance, on being the representatives of victims of atrocity crimes as is the case for NGOs.

In Figure 7.1, the right side of the horizontal axis is dominated by agents with practical (international) criminal law capital. Many of these agents have worked with criminal law in a domestic setting, mostly in the Global North, often before moving into more international adjudication. This dynamic also highlights how these elites have often invested considerable parts of their careers in criminal justice at both the national level and the international level. As shown in Figure 7.1, practical capital was built into careers that led to being prosecutors and defense counsel at the international criminal courts. Although the capital of elites who are included in these groups is also differentiated, for instance, through career affiliations with law firms, their expertise was generally tied to working with criminal law. In general, the expertise of elites at different sides of the courtroom—prosecutors and defense attorneys—was often similar. However, prosecutors were more specialized in criminal law, whereas agents working as defense counsel typically had more diverse legal expertise related, for instance, to human rights or immigration law, a combination of different forms of legal capital they were often able to reproduce in this role because it allowed them to diversify their portfolio by mixing, for instance, cases before the international criminal courts and those before other courts, be they international, regional, or national. In contrast, elites in prosecution often had a narrower profile, having often specialized in criminal law, although they frequently worked with different forms of crime, typically organized crime or other forms of transborder criminality, such as terrorism. In addition, they were more likely to have worked in the public court system.

The capital accumulated by these elites reflects a wider structure of criminal justice systems in which prosecution and defense represent the different parties to a conflict. This structure divides agents who prosecute atrocity crimes on behalf of the state—or in the case of international criminal justice, the groups of states that founded and funded its institutions—and agents who represent the accused of such crimes. Most debates on the role of defense attorneys and prosecutors have focused on matters related to the equality of arms of these groups (Fedorova, 2012; Negri, 2005)—debates that are in some cases also driven by these very groups and, to a certain extent, mirror the battle between them inside the courtroom. Whereas this distinction is formally fundamental, often overlooked is how the representation of the parties of criminal cases at the international level is supported by different accumulations of expertise, even if discreet. The slight variations in the capital of prosecutors and defense attorneys mean, for instance, that the former has extensive expertise often built around criminal law specifically, whereas the latter has a broader legal experience that includes working with human rights. Although this difference is subtle and these groups are generally similar in their expertise, the distinction between them might affect their perspectives on international punishment as well as the knowledge and resources they are able to invest in winning their cases. For instance, although not directly visible from the data, prosecutors are likely to be focused on retributive justice, whereas defense might argue for more restorative perspectives. From their position in the elite field of international criminal justice, it is clear that practitioners engaged in the prosecution of atrocity crimes and those representing the accused of such crimes invest similar yet slightly differentiated forms of expertise. Both groups are highly specialized, and their main capital relates to practical experience with criminal law, in the case of defense counsel supplemented with experience from other legal domains. In activating this expertise, these groups formally represent different interests.

Agents investing practical capital into the prosecution of atrocity crimes formally represent the international criminal courts mandated by states to pursue justice for such crimes. They are the caretakers of a form of prosecution of serious crimes taken over by the state, or in this case several states, to ensure that they are investigated and adjudicated where relevant. As such, they serve as representatives for global society and, through an extended claim, for those wronged by crimes outlawed by international criminal law. Thus, their professional capital becomes almost surreptitiously entangled with the overall mission statement of the field of international criminal justice: ending impunity for atrocity crimes. Their investments embody the use of legal technologies for this, in its own self-perception, progressive purpose, and as such the wider liberal hope of giving international law primacy to structure international politics (Christensen, 2020b). As such, investing practical expertise in international prosecution becomes emblematic of wider hopes of the power and effect of law at a global level, and prosecutors at times become personalized examples of such hopes. This often gives them a strong symbolic platform seen, for instance, when the top prosecutor issues a statement condemning specific situations, an event often followed and commented on by others in the field and at times making headlines also more generally in the public sphere. In other words, international prosecution is not just a practical career, although agents in these positions have mainly practical capital. It is a practical career that carries immense symbolic connotations that also give its elites considerable power beyond directing the casework of the international criminal courts. They are also able to, and to a certain extent expected to, speak for the victims on whose behalf they are prosecuting and ultimately punishing perpetrators.

In contrast, agents who invest practical expertise in defense work do not have the same representative claim. Formally representing those accused of atrocity crimes, the work of the defense attorney is often perceived to go against the punishing mission of international criminal justice, at times to be an irritant to it. Although the role of defense counsel is very important for free and fair legal proceedings, the choice to represent those accused of atrocity crimes is often perceived with some skepticism in the wider field of international criminal justice. For instance, when celebrating the 20th anniversary of the Rome Statute, defense attorneys were often not represented at large public or academic events (Christensen, 2022). This skepticism is linked to the role of defense working against the forms of international punishment around which international criminal justice was organized. In this field, punishment is seen as a positive goal, something that is supported explicitly by a range of stakeholders or is even, at times, taken for granted. In accordance with their role in cases concerning international punishment, defense attorneys focus on their clients' cases as well as their rights after conviction (if convicted) and, in some cases, after having served their sentence. In this context, and arguing against a strong narrative of ending impunity, it can be difficult at times for the legal claims of defense attorneys to gain both formal and informal traction. For instance, defense attorneys recently have been trying to get the attention of international society regarding individuals acquitted or released from their sentence by the International Criminal Tribunal for Rwanda who have been illegally detained in Niger. So far, these efforts have not been successful. Although some defense attorneys take to public channels such as social media and news media to disseminate their perspectives and those of their clients, they do not have the same pre-established networks of supporters that practitioners involved in prosecution can build on. Whereas they hold similar forms of practical capital, their access to influencing international punishment in other ways is limited because their perspectives go against what has become conventional knowledge within the field—that the field of international criminal justice is supposed to deliver punishment for the sake of victims. Using human rights claims to argue for the rights of people acquitted (and convicted) is at best peripheral to such claims and at worst threatens to undermine them by pointing to forms of collateral damage that do not sit well with the mission of this field.

On the other side of the horizontal axis in Figure 7.1 are elite groups engaged in analysis and policy work. These groups often support the overall mission of the field, and as such they are part of the stakeholders pushing for internationalized punishment of atrocity crimes. These groups are also predominantly male and have obtained most of their capital from working in the Global North. Visualized on the left side of the field, the association of academic and NGO capital implies a weak link between these forms of expertise, as represented mainly by the proximity between agents having worked in more than two NGOs and those employed in elite universities. The relative proximity between these elites implies overlaps between their accumulation of capital that are often based on and visible in engagements with research of atrocity crimes justice. Such research takes different forms, including publications in international peer-reviewed journals and in reports published by NGOs. Although these publications are often very different, and there are also sociological distinctions between academic and NGO capital as visible in the field, there are certain overlaps in the expertise of elites who perform research and comment on international criminal justice. Some of these overlaps have been built throughout the careers of people who have invested years of their professional lives in international criminal justice, at times operating at the borders with other fields.

Regarding elites with academic capital, such groups have mainly built their careers around academic institutions where they work and by publishing in academic journals. In other words, there is a clear distinction between academic and practical capital. This is also visible in the representative claim of academia. Whereas practitioners represent particular parties to a legal conflict, academics formally represent the disinterestedness of scholarly inquiry and as such the obtainment of neutral knowledge about law and punishment—a neutrality that can come under pressure if agents are perceived as being too close to other interests. Nonetheless, the value of disinterestedness is visible in academic capital invested toward the publication of knowledge in peer-reviewed journals, where it is quality-assured by the larger scholarly collective. As such, academic investments in international punishment build on larger scholarly claims of contributing disinterested perspectives on the law and its effects, which is evident, for instance, in publications on the retributive, deterrent, and expressive effects of international criminal justice. Scholarly capital can be turned into publicly accessible knowledge that gives its producers a specific role and value in international criminal justice. However, in producing this knowledge, scholars often take specific normative positions. This is visible partly in a broader, and in many cases implicit, support of the project of international punishment of perpetrators of atrocity crimes visible in much legal scholarship, as well as when such scholars support specific legal solutions. Some such support is predicated on the role of the legal scholar as an expert whose perspectives also aim to be of value for the practice of law. Efforts to have such practical impact also show how the supposed disinterest of scholarly production can be weaponized to have practical effects. Prominent scholars are at times placed into positions in which they can have important practical impact—for instance, in the International Law Commission or serving as experts who advise the Prosecutor of the ICC or the defense.

Finally, some agents engaged in NGOs also build part of their capital on research activities, combining it with more political forms of expertise that are visible across the vertical axes in Figure 7.1. With regard to research capital, this is often invested into building evidence of atrocity crimes and supporting prosecutions of them. In this context, and whereas NGO support for international punishment has been vernacularized in the field, there is little self-evident about this support, especially considering the fact that most human rights NGOs were originally organized around skepticism of the state's use of punishment. However, as has been shown by critical scholars (Engle, 2014, 2016), these NGOs, perhaps surprisingly, turned their attention to punishment as a tool for human rights during the 1990s and have become some of the key supporters of institutions such as the ICC (Glasius, 2006; Haddad, 2018; Lohne, 2019). Whereas the power of punishment is still viewed by these organizations as problematic when left in the hands of states, when retooled to be in the service of a community of states, it has become the object of significant investments of capital. These investments of research capital are predicated on NGOs representing victims close to where crimes were committed. A such, NGOs can be seen to represent the wider stakes of victims who may have both converging and conflicting ideas about what kind of justice would serve their interests (Aloyo et al., 2023). This representation is supported by research capacity that at times overlaps with academic expertise, but it is often distinct from academic expertise in its explicit attempt to push for specific solutions, which often, but not always, takes a more discreet form in scholarship. Such pushes are rooted in research on crimes and the rights of victims rather than the (formal) disinterest of research.

## 7.4. CONCLUSION

Punishment, at least formally, gives law power in international relations. International criminal law is based on the promise of holding individuals, including political leaders, responsible for their crimes. This power is interpreted and given direction by the investments of capital from specific professional elites. In distributing punishment and debating its value, often also affecting more public and political debates about its effectiveness, these elites represent particular interests. In this context, it is striking that even across significant social differences between distinct elites, specifically those who prosecute and those who publish on international criminal justice, the support for punishment is prevalent. It is supported by different forms of capital, most significantly practical legal expertise as deployed through large international institutions created by collectives of states, by civil society organizations and academics that often have significant research capacities. These groups represent or claim to represent important interests, including those of the international community, at least as represented by the states that participate in specific courts, as well as those of victims. These ideological interests are embedded in prosecution, NGOs, and academics and thus supported by a variety of different capital investments that often push for punishment as a social and political good. These concurring patterns of representation and capital investment create a strong support for international punishment of atrocity crimes that overrides other claims and ideals. This demonstrates how punitive norms at the international level are embedded in a broad coalition of elites who, from different perspectives and representing different interests, push for punishment. The dominance of this support is embedded in elites across the horizontal axis in Figure 7.1 that accounts for most of the difference in accumulated capital of the elite for international criminal justice. This broad coalition allows for the investment of multiple different forms of expertise toward the goal of shoring up and making effective international prosecution of atrocity crimes, but it can also marginalize other perspectives that might challenge the conventional knowledge of the field.

Whereas this broad coalition of elites in support of atrocity punishment represents or claims to represent both international society and victims at the international stage, the makeup of these elites shows that they are in fact dominated by a narrow group of agents. In other words, while nominally the studied elites represent interests linked to global peace and security as well as the rights of victims throughout the world, at a more sociological level, they are primarily representatives of a very narrow group of well-educated, male professionals, most of whom were trained in and have most of their ties to the Global North. The elite, however, also has members that hail from other places in the world, but they often also have close connections to institutions in the Global North. The fact that a narrow elite seems to dominate international criminal justice has potential consequences for the ways in which punishment are imagined and discussed in this field. Although the data on which this chapter is based do not provide direct information on this issue, the dominance of specific perceptions of punishment might drive the ideals and practices in this social space. This would require further research, but such ideas seem to be related to, and possibly even help buttress, particular visions of a liberal internationalism in which the legal systems of the Global North are often naturalized as role models. This can affect both the ways in which punishment is understood, interpreted, and implemented, including most controversially, where its gaze and technologies are targeted, and the perceived legitimacy of the project of international criminal justice. Such perceptions are organized around international criminal law as a "go-getter" technology in the sense that it directs punishment at the other—often located in the Global South. In contrast to national criminal law domains that are focused on punishing transgressions that occur inside of the sociality of the state itself, the fusing of criminal law with international and human rights norms has created a field that actively has to find crime and criminals in settings that it is itself removed from—patterns of otherness that can also be seen in the focus of hybrid courts and referrals to the ICC. Written into the DNA of the studied elite, there is a risk that the broad ideological coalition among a narrow elite supporting international punishment will reproduce and deepen divides between practices and perceptions developed in or dominated by the Global North and the needs and ideals of victims, often women, and other groups in the Global South.

## REFERENCES

Aloyo, E., Dancy, G., & Dutton, Y. (2023). Retributive or reparative justice? Explaining post-conflict preferences in Kenya. *Journal of Peace Research*, 60(2), 258–273.

Alter, K. J. (2014). *The new terrain of international law: Courts, politics, rights*. Princeton University Press.

Bantekas, I., & Mylonaki, E. (2014). *Criminological approaches to international criminal law*. Cambridge University Press.

Batesmith, A. (2021). International prosecutors as cause lawyers. *Journal of International Criminal Justice*, 19(4), 803–830.

Beets, S. D. (2005). Understanding the demand-side issues of international corruption. *Journal of Business Ethics*, 57(1), 65–81.

Boltanski, L. (2009). *De la critique: Précis de sociologie de l'émancipation* (NRF Essais). Gallimard.

Boltanski, L. (2012). *Enigmes et complots: Une enquête à propos d'enquêtes* (NRF Essais). Gallimard.

Bourdieu, P. (1984). *Homo academicus* (Collection "Le Sens Commun"). Editions de Minuit.

Bourdieu, P. (1986). La Force Du Droit. *Actes de la Recherche en Sciences Sociales, 64*, 3–19.

Bourdieu, P. (1989). *La Noblesse D'état* (Le Sens Commun). Éditions de Minuit.

Bourdieu, P., & Wacquant, L. (1992). *An invitation to reflexive sociology*. University of Chicago Press.

Bringedal Houge, A. (2019). Narrative expressivism: A criminological approach to the expressive function of international criminal justice. *Criminology & Criminal Justice, 19*(3), 277–293.

Burgis-Kasthala, M. (2016). Scholarship as dialogue? TWAIL and the politics of methodology. *Journal of International Criminal Justice, 14*(4), 921–937.

Burgis-Kasthala, M. (2019). Entrepreneurial justice: Syria, the Commission for International Justice and Accountability and the renewal of international criminal justice. *European Journal of International Law, 30*(4), 1165–1185.

Cakmak, C. (2006). Coalition building and the NGO Coalition for the International Criminal Court as an actor of global politics. *Sivil Toplum, 4*(13–14), 135–153.

Christensen, M. J. (2015a). The emerging sociology of international criminal courts: Between global restructurings and scientific innovations. *Current Sociology, 63*(6), 825–849.

Christensen, M. J. (2015b). From symbolic surge to closing courts: The transformation of international criminal justice and its professional practices. *International Journal of Law, Crime and Justice, 43*(4), 609–625.

Christensen, M. J. (2016). Preaching, practicing and publishing international criminal justice: Academic Expertise and the development of an international field of law. *International Criminal Law Review, 17*(2), 239–258.

Christensen, M. J. (2018). International prosecution and national bureaucracy: The contest to define international practices within the Danish Prosecution Service. *Law & Social Inquiry, 43*(1), 152–181.

Christensen, M. J. (2019). The judiciary of international criminal law: Double decline and practical turn. *Journal of International Criminal Justice, 17*, 537–555.

Christensen, M. J. (2020a). The creation of an ad hoc elite: And the value of international criminal law expertise on a global market. In K. J. Heller, F. Megret, S. Nouwen, J. Ohlin, & D. Robinson (Eds.), *The Oxford handbook of international criminal law* (pp. 89–105). Oxford University Press.

Christensen, M. J. (2020b). The Perestroika of international criminal law: Soviet reforms and the promise of legal primacy in international governance. *New Criminal Law Review, 23*(2), 236–270.

Christensen, M. J. (2020c). Power, position and professionals in international criminal justice (iCourts Working Paper Series No. 223). SSRN.

Christensen, M. J. (2021). The professional market of international criminal justice: Divisions of labour and patterns of elite reproduction. *Journal of International Criminal Justice, 19*(4), 783–802.

Christensen, M. J. (2022). Celebrating international criminal justice: A sociology of the twentieth anniversary of the International Criminal Court. *London Review of International Law, 9*(3), 351–373.

Christensen, M. J., & Levi, R. (2017). Introduction: An internationalized criminal justice: Paths of law and paths of police. In M. J. Christensen & R. Levi (Eds.), *International practices of criminal law: Social and legal perspectives* (pp. 1–13). Routledge.

Christoph, S. (2012). Collective reparations at the Extraordinary Chambers in the Courts of Cambodia. *International Criminal Law Review, 12*(3), 457–490.

Clarke, K. M. (2019). *Affective justice: The International Criminal Court and the pan-Africanist pushback*. Duke University Press.

Combs, N. A. (2007). *Guilty pleas in international criminal law: Constructing a restorative justice approach*. Stanford University Press.

Cryer, R., Robinson, D., & Vasiliev, S. (2019). *An introduction to international criminal law and procedure*. Cambridge University Press.

Dancy, G. (2018). Searching for deterrence at the International Criminal Court. In J. Nicholson (Ed.), *Strengthening the validity of international criminal tribunals* (pp. 43–73). Brill Nijhoff.

DeGuzman, M. M. (2012). Choosing to prosecute: Expressive selection at the International Criminal Court. *Michigan Journal of International Law, 33*(2), 265–320.

Dezalay, S. (2017). Weakness as routine in the operations of the Intentional Criminal Court. *International Criminal Law Review, 17*(2), 281–301.

Dietrich, J. (2014). The limited prospects of deterrence by the International Criminal Court: Lessons from domestic experience. *International Social Science Review, 88*(3), 1–29.

Dixon, P., & Tenove, C. (2013). International criminal justice as a transnational field: Rules, authority and victims. *International Journal of Transitional Justice, 7*(3), 393–412.

Dixon, P. J. (2016). Reparations, assistance and the experience of justice: Lessons from Colombia and the Democratic Republic of the Congo. *International Journal of Transitional Justice, 10*(1), 88–107.

Dothan, S. (2021). The ICC is not a slice of cheese. *Journal of International Criminal Justice, 19*(4), 877–891.

Dothan, S., Holtermann, J. v. H., & Kjeldgaard-Pedersen, A. (2021). Who is afraid of the International Criminal Court? Deterrence in international criminal justice: Foreword. *Journal of International Criminal Justice, 19*(4), 855–857.

Drumbl, M. A. (2003). Toward a criminology of international crime. *Ohio State Journal on Dispute Resolution, 19*(1), 263–282.

Durham, H. (2012). The role of civil society in creating the International Criminal Court Statute: Ten years on and looking back. *Journal of International Humanitarian Legal Studies, 3*(1), 3–42.

Durkheim, É. (1893). *De La Division Du Travail Social, Étude Sur L'organisation Des Sociétés Supérieures*. Alcan.

Engle, K. (2014). Anti-impunity and the turn to criminal law in human rights. *Cornell Law Review, 100*, 1069–1128.

Engle, K. (2016). A genealogy of the criminal turn in human rights. In D. M. Davis, K. Engle, & Z. Miller (Eds.), *Anti-impunity and the human rights agenda* (pp. 15–67). Cambridge University Press.

Fedorova, M. (2012). *The principle of equality of arms in international criminal proceedings*. Intersentia.

Fichtelberg, A. (2005). Crimes beyond justice? Retributivism and war crimes. *Criminal Justice Ethics*, 24(1), 31–46.

Fisher, K. J. (2020). Messages from the expressive nature of ICC reparations: Complex-victims in complex contexts and the trust fund for victims. *International Criminal Law Review*, 20(2), 318–345.

Foucault, M. (1975). *Surveiller Et Punir*. Gallimard.

Garland, D. (1993). *Punishment and modern society: A study in social theory*. University of Chicago Press.

Garland, D. (2013). Penality and the penal state. *Criminology*, 51(3), 475–517.

Glasius, M. (2006). *The International Criminal Court: A global civil society achievement*. Routledge.

Greenawalt, A. K. (2013). International criminal law for retributivists. *University of Pennsylvania Journal of International Law*, 35, 969–1044.

Haddad, H. N. (2018). *The hidden hands of justice: NGOs, human rights, and international courts*. Cambridge University Press.

Hagan, J. (2003). *Justice in the Balkans: Prosecuting war crimes in the Hague Tribunal*. University of Chicago Press.

Hagan, J., & Levi, R. (2004). Social skill, the Milosevic indictment, and the rebirth of international criminal justice. *European Journal of Criminology*, 1(4), 445–475.

Hagan, J., & Levi, R. (2005). Crimes of war and the force of law. *Social Forces*, 83(4), 1499–1534.

Hagan, J., Levi, R., & Ferrales, G. (2006). Swaying the hand of justice: The internal and external dynamics of regime change at the International Criminal Tribunal for the Former Yugoslavia. *Law & Social Inquiry*, 31(3), 585–616.

Haque, A. A. (2005). Group violence and group vengeance: Toward a retributivist theory of international criminal law. *Buffalo Criminal Law Review*, 9(1), 273–328.

Hobbs, H. (2014). Victim participation in international criminal proceedings: Problems and potential solutions in implementing an effective and vital component of justice. *Texas International Law Journal*, 49(1–3), 1–33.

Hodgson, N. (2020). Exploring the International Criminal Court's deterrent potential: A case study of Australian politics. *Journal of International Criminal Justice*, 19(4), 913–936.

Holá, B., Smeulers, A., & Bijleveld, C. (2011). International sentencing facts and figures: Sentencing practice at the ICTY and ICTR. *Journal of International Criminal Justice*, 9(2), 411–439.

Holá, B., & Van WIjk, J. (2014). Life after conviction at international criminal tribunals: An empirical overview. *Journal of International Criminal Justice*, 12(1), 109–132.

Holtermann, J. v. H. (2010). A "slice of cheese"—A deterrence-based argument for the International Criminal Court. *Human Rights Review*, 11(3), 289–315.

Holtermann, J. v. H. (2021). In defence of a metaphor: A reply to Shai Dothan's critique of applying the Swiss cheese model on deterrence to the International Criminal Court. *Journal of International Criminal Justice*, 19(4), 893–912.

Jo, H., & Simmons, B. (2016). Can the International Criminal Court deter atrocity? *International Organization, 70*(3), 443–475.

Koleva, P. M., & Vigh, H. (2021). Critical stasis and disruptive performances: ICJ and the Anwar R trial in Koblenz. *Theoretical Criminology, 25*(3), 437–453.

Kreß, C. (2014). *Towards a truly universal invisible college of international criminal lawyers* [Occasional paper]. Torkel Opsahl Academic EPublisher.

Lebaron, F. (2009). How Bourdieu "quantified" Bourdieu: The geometric modelling of data. In K. Robson & C. Sanders (Eds.), *Quantifying theory: Pierre Bourdieu* (pp. 11–29). Springer.

Le Roux, B. (2010). *Multiple correspondence analysis*. SAGE.

Levi, R., Hagan, J., & Dezalay, S. (2016). International courts in atypical political environments. The interplay of prosecutorial strategy, evidence, and court authority in international criminal law. *Law and Contemporary Problems, 79*(1), 289–314.

Lohne, K. (2018). Penal humanitarianism beyond the nation state: An analysis of international criminal justice. *Theoretical Criminology, 24*(2), 145–162.

Lohne, K. (2019). *Advocates of humanity: Human rights NGOs and international criminal justice*. Oxford University Press.

Luban, D. (2013). After the honeymoon. *Journal of International Criminal Justice, 11*(3), 505–515.

Manley, S. (2016). Referencing patterns at the International Criminal Court. *European Journal of International Law, 27*(1), 191–214.

Mégret, F. (2020). The anti-deterrence hypothesis: What if international criminal justice encouraged crime? *Journal of International Criminal Justice, 19*(4), 859–876.

Mennecke, M. (2007). Punishing genocidaires: A deterrent effect or not? *Human Rights Review, 8*(4), 319–339.

Moffett, L. (2015). Meaningful and effective? Considering victims' interests through participation at the International Criminal Court. *Criminal Law Forum, 26*(2), 255–289.

Negri, S. (2005). The principle of equality of arms and the evolving law of international criminal procedure. *International Criminal Law Review, 5*(4), 513–571.

Nickson, R. (2016). Participation as restoration: The current limits of restorative justice for victim participants in international criminal trials. In K. Clamp (Ed.), *Restorative justice in transitional settings* (pp. 95–114). Routledge.

Palmer, N. (2020). International criminal law and border control: The expressive role of the deportation and extradition of genocide suspects to Rwanda. *Leiden Journal of International Law, 33*(3), 789–807.

Parmentier, S. (2011). The missing link: Criminological perspectives on transitional justice and international crimes. In M. Bosworth & C. Boyle (Eds.), *What is criminology?* (pp. 380–392). Oxford University Press.

Pena, M., & Carayon, G. (2013). Is the ICC making the most of victim participation? *International Journal of Transitional Justice, 7*(3), 518–535.

Popovski, V. (2000). The International Criminal Court: A synthesis of retributive and restorative justice. *International Relations, 15*(3), 1–10.

Powderly, J. (2020). *Judges and the making of international criminal law*. Brill.

Roberts, P., & McMillan, N. (2003). For criminology in international criminal justice. *Journal of International Criminal Justice, 1*(2), 315–338.

Rothe, D. L., & Friedrichs, D. O. (2006). The state of the criminology of crimes of the state. *Social Justice, 33*(1), 147–161.

Sander, B. (2019a). The expressive limits of international criminal justice: Victim trauma and local culture in the iron cage of the law. *International Criminal Law Review, 19*(6), 1014–1045.

Sander, B. (2019b). The expressive turn of international criminal justice: A field in search of meaning. *Leiden Journal of International Law, 32*(4), 1–22.

Schachter, O. (1977). Invisible college of international lawyers. *Northwestern University School of Law Review, 72*, 217–226.

Sloane, R. D. (2017). The expressive capacity of international punishment: The limits of the national law analogy and the potential of international criminal law. In M. Bohlander (Ed.), *Globalization of criminal justice* (pp. 315–370). Routledge.

Smeulers, A., & Haveman, R. (2008). *Supranational criminology: Towards a criminology of international crimes*. Intersentia.

Smeulers, A., Hola, B., & Van Den Berg, T. (2013). Sixty-five years of international criminal justice: The facts and figures. *International Criminal Law Review, 13*(1), 7–41.

Smeulers, A., Weerdesteijn, M., & Holá, B. (2015). The selection of situations by the ICC: An empirically based evaluation of the OTP's performance. *International Criminal Law Review, 15*(1), 1–39.

Smeulers, A., Weerdesteijn, M., & Holá, B. (2019). *Perpetrators of international crimes*. Oxford University Press.

Sperfeldt, C. (2013). The role of Cambodian civil society in the victim participation scheme of the Extraordinary Chambers in the Courts of Cambodia. In T. Bonacker & C. Safferling (Eds.), *Victims of international crimes: An interdisciplinary discourse* (pp. 345–372). Asser Press.

Sperfeldt, C. (2017). The trial against Hissène Habré: Networked justice and reparations at the Extraordinary African Chambers. *International Journal of Human Rights, 21*(9), 1243–1260.

Sperfeldt, C. (2022). *Practices of reparations in international criminal justice*. Cambridge University Press.

Stahn, C. (2020). *Justice as message: Expressivist foundations of international criminal justice*. Oxford University Press.

Stappert, N. (2018). A new influence of legal scholars? The use of academic writings at international criminal courts and tribunals. *Leiden Journal of International Law, 31*(4), 1–18.

Travis, H. (2015). Reparations for mass atrocities as a path to peace: After Kiobel V. Royal Dutch Petroleum Co., can victims seek relief at the International Criminal Court? *Brooklyn Journal of International Law, 40*(2), 547–617.

van Sliedregt, E. (2021). One rule for them: Selectivity in international criminal law. *Leiden Journal of International Law, 34*(2), 283–290.

van Wijk, J., & Holá, B. (2017). Acquittals in international criminal justice: Pyrrhic victories? *Leiden Journal of International Law, 30*(1), 241–262.

Weber, M. (2007). Politics as a vocation. In H. H. Gerth & C. W. Mills (Eds.), *From Max Weber: Essays in sociology* (pp. 77–128). Routledge.

Wheeler, C. (2016). No longer just a victim: The impact of victim participation on trial proceedings at the International Criminal Court. *International Criminal Law Review, 16*(3), 525–546.

Whiting, A. (2021). Could the crime of aggression undermine deterrence? *Journal of International Criminal Justice, 19*(4), 1017–1026.

# 8

# International Sanctions and Contested Normative Authority

ELIN HELLQUIST

Does it matter for international politics who the sender of a sanction is? Three main types of actors impose sanctions in present-day international politics: the United Nations (UN; multilateral sanctions), states or coalitions of states against a third country (unilateral sanctions), and regional organizations against their members (regional sanctions). Accordingly, when an international norm is violated, there are often three contenders that may react with punitive measures. There is, indeed, a significant overlap between sanctions from different senders in crises throughout the world (Brzoska, 2015; Charron & Portela, 2015, 2016; Von Borzyskowski & Portela, 2016, p. 8). All three types of actors contribute to the unprecedented prevalence of sanctions, which shapes international relations from the micro level of individual exchanges all the way up to the macro level of international normative order.

The sanctions literature has not paid systematic attention to what the evolving composition of actors in the sanctions landscape says about international relations at large. This is surprising because sanctions—as institutionalized punitive practices closely tied to international norms—offer an empirical opportunity to observe competing attempts to exercise normative authority in the international system. As Wagner et al. state

Elin Hellquist, *International Sanctions and Contested Normative Authority* In: *Punishment in International Society*. Edited by: Wolfgang Wagner, Linet R. Durmuşoğlu, Barbora Holá, Ronald Kroeze, Jan-Willem van Prooijen, and Wouter Werner, Oxford University Press. © Oxford University Press 2024. DOI: 10.1093/oso/9780197693483.003.0008 in Chapter 1 in this volume, "punitive practices are highly revealing of a society's social fabric, normative order, and power structure."

In response to the just mentioned research gap, this chapter outlines the contours of a relational understanding of sanctions. This approach pinpoints how sanctions characteristically revolve around social processes of exclusion and inclusion, of distance and proximity. The argument goes that because the punishment of sanctions consists in altering the "normal" terms of interaction between sender and target, it matters who the sender is and what type of prior relationship it has to the target. The first part of the chapter presents this argument.

The second part of the chapter expands on this reasoning by exploring how the basis of authority differs between the different senders of sanctions in contemporary international relations. The UN appeals to the universal legitimacy of international law, but the de facto great power bias of the UN Security Council (UNSC) undermines the UN's claim to act on behalf of the world community. Unilateral senders take on a self-assigned role as guardians of international norms, but their sanctions suffer from a prima facie legitimacy deficit because they are out-group measures. By contrast, regional organizations build their sanctions on the premise of membership, thereby potentially relaxing the association of sanctions with external interference.

## 8.1. A RELATIONAL UNDERSTANDING OF SANCTIONS

The international politics of sanctions are a multilevel battle over normative substance (what is good/bad, who merits punishment) and procedure (who should decide, who should lead). The instrument—as old as international relations themselves—is nowadays an umbrella for measures oscillating between traditional collective punishment and semi-legalized individual responsibility. Different senders have access to a similar portfolio of concrete measures that—by law or convention—fall under the label of "sanctions." Sanctions cut relational privileges, halt cultural exchanges, freeze assets, restrict travel, and selectively or comprehensively ban trade with certain goods or services.

Across political trends and specific measures, sanctions consistently constitute a public rupture with "customary" or "normal" interactions in reaction to an alleged wrongdoing (Baldwin, 1985; Hufbauer et al., 1990, p. 2). The alternation of normality conveys a communicative act of condemnation: The sender signals that its limits of toleration have been crossed (Adler-Nissen, 2014, pp. 170–171; Hoffmann, 1967; Lindsay, 1986, p. 166; Rawls, 1993). Also in a very concrete sense, there is a before and after a sanctions decision: The target becomes excluded from political contexts it previously had access to. The exclusion is sometimes physical: Country representatives are physically hindered from entering meetings (BBC, 2016), or targets of sanctions are banned from entering the territory of the sender.

Precisely because sanctions alter the normal terms of interactions, they are also illuminative of the normal state of international affairs. If it were normal for senders of sanctions not to trade, not to engage in political dialogue, not to receive visitors on their territory, not to accept foreign investment, etc., it would consequently not be able to impose sanctions in these domains (Baldwin, 1999, p. 101). In a highly interdependent world, thus, there are plenty of occasions to impose sanctions. At the same time, the expansion of sanctions modifies, step-by-step, this very conception of normal (Beaucillon, 2021a). The normalization of punitive practices may fortify rather than resolve normative difference, unless they prove effective in changing the target's behavior.

For the reasons just discussed, social alteration is crucial for understanding both how sanctions operate at the case level and how they shape the macro level of international relations. This implies that a conception of sanctions that does not ponder the relationship the sender has to the target will be distorted. Much sanctions scholarship has privileged power as the relational premise underpinning sanctions (e.g., Drezner, 2000; Levitsky & Way, 2010; Martin, 1994; Morgan & Schwebach, 1997). The reasoning goes that powerful states have material leverage to inflict costs on the target and are able to take on high costs themselves.

That "sanctions and power are very closely related" (Piddocke, 1968, p. 280), with power asymmetry working in favor of the sender, is clear from comparing the constellations of actors involved in sanctions. However, that power determines who becomes a sender of sanctions or not does not mean that sanctions reach their intended effects by means of power. Rather, the history of sanctions suggests that material power mostly fails to systematically produce effective or legitimate sanctions. Repeated occurrences of highly harmful but ineffective sanctions indicate that for targets to change, the punishment itself is insufficient. That "sanctions cannot achieve their end without the consent of the person against whom they are applied" has long been acknowledged for interpersonal social sanctions (Piddocke, 1968, p. 269). The same can be said for international sanctions: The targets need to be *involved* for the desired change to happen.[1]

The conditions for involvement to "work" rely not just on material power or on trade flows (Hufbauer et al., 1990, p. 99; Whang, 2010). As discussed in the following section, the three main groups of senders—the UN, (coalitions of) states, and regional organizations—operate on highly different relational premises and—by extension—possess different potential means of involving the target.[2]

## 8.2. A CROWDED PLAYFIELD

By the end of the 1990s, the so-called sanctions decade (Cortright et al., 2000), sanctions were profoundly delegitimized as "weapons of mass destruction" (O'Connell, 2002, p. 63), associated with the devastating humanitarian consequences of comprehensive embargoes against Iraq and Haiti, among other cases. Sanctions were thereafter reinvented in the form of targeted or "smart" sanctions punishing individuals responsible for wrongdoings rather than placing entire societies "under siege" (expression from Jones, 2015). Yet, the old logic of aiming beyond responsible

---

[1]. The crucial exception is directly constraining sanctions, which seek to deprive the target of whatever resource it needs to sustain its norm violation (see Giumelli, 2011).

[2]. On the link between legitimate authority and punishment, see Nossal (1989).

offenders (in social psychology, known as displaced or vicarious punishment; see Chapter 2, this volume) soon made its way back, as third parties (in the context of this chapter, unilateral sanctioners) imposed measures against crucial economic sectors in, for instance, Iran, Syria, and Russia.

Yet, there have long been divergent views on whether sanctions, by their very nature, amount to punishment or not. According to David Baldwin (1971), negative sanctions are "actual or threatened punishments" to be distinguished from positive sanctions, which are "actual or promised rewards" (p. 23). In another classic contribution, Nossal (1989) elaborated a view on punishment as the omnipresent purpose of sanctions, which "by its very nature, always 'works'" (p. 315). Other authors reject that sanctions are a type of punishment. Cortright et al. (2000, p. 16), for instance, propose that sanctions are best understood as pieces in a wider bargaining game, where the infliction of hardship is disciplinary measure of sorts, aimed to bring the target to the negotiation table. Rose (2005, p. 472) speaks of a "bargaining model" of sanctions in which persuasion is attempted through a combined "carrot-and-stick strategy," wherein the target is also rewarded for partial compliance. He contrasts the bargaining model with a "punitive model," which contains solely negative measures that are eased only when the target complies fully.

Policymakers themselves are often inclined to stress that their sanctions are *not* punitive but, rather, aim at changing the target. This echoes what Wagner and Werner (2018) have found with regard to military force, whose "punitivity has been silenced in justifications of the use of force but not disappeared" (p. 324; see also Chapter 1, this volume). Just as for military force, a punitive "undercurrent" (Wagner & Werner, 2018, passim) persists in discourse on sanctions. Even as explicitly punitive language is avoided, justifications of sanctions center on the severity of the crime and on how to ensure the target is indeed harmed (Hellquist, 2012). As discussed by Nossal (1989), explicitly linking harm to a norm violation is—by definition—a type of punishment (see also Chapter 2, this volume).

Thus, a characteristic combination of symbolic disapproval and material harm lies at the heart of sanctions' nature (for a similar argument, see Hofer, 2021, p. 198). In this capacity, sanctions are widely understood as litmus tests of which side an actor is on when it comes to violations of international norms. This "moral economy of symbolic politics" (Hurd, 2005, p. 523) confirms and alters the positions of different actors in the international system (Bull, 1977, pp. 10–11). The target's breach of a cherished norm becomes an explicit counterpoint to the sender's allegiance to the same norm. As "a public expression of the community's moral disapproval of the act" (Nossal, 1989, p. 306), sanctions are an institutionalized way for the sender to display that it is different from—ultimately better than—the target. This message is not only aimed at the target but also may send "a signal of strength, power, and the existence of a 'moral compass'" to the own constituency (see Chapter 2, this volume).

Punishment in the form of sanctions not only transforms relationships between senders and targets but also has potential implications for any actor with a point of contact to either of these (for a comprehensive discussion of extraterritorial sanctions, see Beaucillon, 2021b). In the increasingly crowded playfield of sanctions, the space for neutrality has shrunk. Bystanders are made partisan through the United States' insistence on extraterritorial loyalty to sanctions (Lowe, 1997; Lowenfeld, 1996) or through the European Union's (EU) policy to ask neighbors to commit to its already finalized sanctions decisions (Hellquist, 2016). Targets likewise have strategies for engaging third countries. They often set up counter-campaigns, seeking to convince other countries that sanctions are ungrounded, illegitimate, or illegal. These regularized practices further highlight how sanctions are first and foremost a social game, where both senders and targets seek to involve third parties.

### 8.2.1. UN Sanctions

As the designated normative authority in international society, the UN is in theory uniquely placed to exercise normative judgment over its 193 members. Ideally, UN sanctions would contribute to establishing a genuinely universal set of norms that promote peaceful international relations. However, indications are that the UN in practice does not offer the necessary "directness of association" (Padelford, 1954) for UN sanctions to be broadly recognized as measures by the international community for the international community.

In the establishment of the UN Charter, the legality of sanctions was deliberatively closely tied to the Security Council, which was "given significant power to impose on member States obligations to impose non-forcible measures against miscreant member States by virtue of Article 41 of the Chapter" (the UN General Assembly [UNGA] can recommend sanctions) (White & Abass, 2006, p. 510). The result was "a system of centralized 'sanctions' based on notions of hierarchy and governance" supposed to coexist with a "self-help system of non-forcible measures deriving from an earlier period of international relations" (p. 518). Hence, in the family of different nonforcible coercive measures (countermeasures, retorsion, and reprisal) described in international law, only UNSC measures are defined as lawful "sanctions," which "raise no issue under the non-intervention principle" (Jamnejad & Wood, 2009, p. 69).

Despite "apparent virtues in terms of legitimacy and universality" (Doxey, 2000, p. 1), UN sanctions are contested. The UN's prima facie legitimacy advantage is questioned, as the world organization is "criticized for failing to effectively coordinate appropriate responses to many of the world's most pressing global security threats or breaches of international norms" (Moret, 2021, p. 19). Another issue is that perceptions of UN sanctions largely hinge on perceptions of the Security Council, which has full powers in the field of sanctions. Any imposition of sanctions that is to be binding on UN member states needs to be approved by at least 9 out of 15 members of the Council, including all permanent members. In addition, most UNSC decisions are already prepared by the permanent 5 in closed and informal meetings. The actual Council meetings are "a pro forma affair," which the president "almost invariably" opens noting that "the Security Council is meeting in accordance with the understanding reached in its prior consultations" (Hurd, 2002, p. 43).

According to Hoffmann (1967), the "nature" of sanctions requires them to be "organised at an international level," which "almost presupposes an organisation capable of mobilizing the 'world community'" (p. 144). Yet, the UNSC was deliberately designed to ensure great power control over normative discipline in international affairs. Due to the veto, the five permanent members have always been outside of the scope of UN sanctions (see Doxey, 1996, p. 1). The great power bias, together with a lack of transparency and resistance to reform the UNSC, mismatches with the "myth of collectivity" that UN legitimacy revolves around (Hurd, 2002, p. 48). One implication is that UN sanctions, despite being nominally in-group measures, risk being understood as de facto out-group measures.

Binder and Heupel (2015) have shown that the Security Council suffers from a legitimacy deficit in the opinion of UN member states. They find that 75% of all statements about the UNSC at the UNGA between 1991 and 2012 make negative legitimacy judgments. Complaints about lacking procedural legitimacy are the major concern across countries, but "nondemocracies are systematically more critical of the Council's alleged transgression of its legal mandate than are democracies" (p. 246). The opposite critique is also well known—that is, that the UNSC, due to the veto power and great power structure, fails to live up to its mandate under international law. The expansion of non-UN-mandated sanctions illustrates well that a powerful minority of the world's countries do not consider UNSC action sufficient.

Unilateral/autonomous measures are often the direct consequence of the UN's non-action. The EU permanent members of the Security Council usually try the UN route before turning to autonomous sanctions. However, it is also common for unilateral senders such as the EU to add on their own measures to existing UN regimes. According to Charron and Portela (2016), "the UNSC constitutes an 'enabling' condition allowing the EU to decide on extra measures," providing a " 'threshold' in terms of legitimacy" (pp. 114–115). Hence, the EU's autonomous sanctions policy is not a principled rejection of UN authority but, rather, a pragmatic reply to its passivity in handling international crises in line with the EU's preferences. In recent years, the EU has topped up the UN's sanctions cases with at least as many cases of its own.

Targets of UN sanctions engage in more or less ambitious campaigns to have measures lifted. Ian Hurd analyzed Libya's anti-sanctions diplomacy in detail and found "an active strategy to delegitimize the sanctions among the key audience of third-party states" (Hurd, 2002, p. 46). Libya did not challenge the UN's authority but, rather, "publicly championed liberal internationalism" (Hurd, 2005, p. 496) and criticized sanctions for "being at odds with the professed values of the international community" (Hurd, 2002, p. 47). When the fellow members of the Organization of African Unity (OAU) collectively left UN sanctions against Libya (Organization of African Unity, 1998), it was the starting point for the creation of the African Union (AU) (Hellquist, 2015; Sands & Klein, 2009; Takeyh, 2001). Impressed by this expression of African brotherhood, Muammar Ghaddafi initiated and financed the new organization (Schneider, 1998; Sturman, 2003). Hence, the Libyan anti-sanctions campaign indirectly led to the birth of a regional sanctions mechanism as African regionalism was transformed from the OAU into the AU.

### 8.2.2. Unilateral Sanctions

Non-UN actors—whether individual states or coalitions of states— frequently employ punitive measures in a "collective" or "general" interest, without having been aggressed (Alland, 2002; White & Abass, 2006, p. 526). In relational terms, these measures correspond to third-party punishment (see Chapter 2, this volume); that is, they are imposed without the sender being the direct victim of the norm violation. Unilateral sanctions are typically carried out in defense of the violated norm itself rather than to rehabilitate specific victims. The sanctions confirm that the norm that has been violated is alive to the sender, as argued by Panke and Petersohn (2012, p. 721), and e contrario, the absence of punishment, can be seen as "the necessary condition for norm disappearance" (see also Piddocke, 1968).

At the interpersonal level, third-party sanctions have sometimes been associated with altruism or "genuine concern for justice" (see Chapter 2, this volume). However, in international society, measures imposed without UN authorization lack "additional status—legitimation" and run the risk of being labeled illegal (Doxey, 1980b, p. 485). Ultimately, the absence of explicit legality boils down to fundamental conceptions of sovereignty, which international law only partially modifies. As argued by Wagner et al. in Chapter 1 in this volume, "that a sovereign would be judged and punished by a peer" goes against the modern state system's "core principle of sovereign equality."

Nonetheless, in practice, much of international relations revolves around the selective distribution and withdrawal of relational privileges. According to Lowenfeld (2001, p. 96; cited in White & Abass, 2006, p. 522), in the absence of explicit legality, a habitual power of practice has been established: "Sanctions have become sufficiently common—and often better than the alternatives—to have become tolerated (not to say accepted) as a tool of foreign relations."

Furthermore, states (or coalitions of states) are under no obligation to engage to the same extent with all other states. The existence of selective trade agreements and visa unions throughout the world testifies to this point. More than two decades ago, David Baldwin (1999) noted that it is impossible to "do nothing" in reaction to norm violations: "What is usually implied by such phrases is that a country should do what it would have done had the problem at hand not arisen" (p. 100). To uphold normal relations even after a severe crime has been committed is not a neutral stance but, rather, one that may directly enable the crime to continue. Similarly, Samuel Nili (2016) has argued that to avoid complicity with norm violations, no special justification is required for a state to reduce or cease (economic) interactions.

This perspective features in justifications of sanctions against Russia following its full-scale invasion of Ukraine in February 2022. Whereas it is unclear whether sanctions influence political decision-making in Russia (Congressional Research Service, 2022), the punitive measures can be understood as an attempt to avoid complicity with a brutal norm violation by cutting contributions to the war economy. In addition, the sanctions against Russia have reawakened the old debate over whether a population can have a derived responsibility for norm violations (e.g., Mounk, 2022; Neier, 2022). In the case of antiwar sanctions against Russia, the scale and severity of the crime—the invasion and associated norm violations—appear to have created acceptance for sanctions as a type of retributive punishment that is "strongly associated with anger about the offense" (on retribution, see Chapter 2, this volume).

Opinions on unilateral foreign policy sanctions are a normative watershed in international politics. Permanent members of the UNSC are divided on whether their sanctions are a "floor" or a "roof" for action (Biersteker & Moret, 2015, p. 70). Whereas the United States, the United Kingdom, and France view the UNSC sanctions policy as a "floor" on which others may build, Russia and China argue that UNSC sanctions set the "legitimate limit" (Biersteker & Moret, 2015). Emerging powers Brazil, India, Indonesia, and Turkey all lean toward the latter interpretation, giving an indication that disagreements on the topic of sanctions are likely to remain. Criticism of non-UN-mandated sanctions has been central to the BRICS' (Brazil, Russia, India, China, and South Africa) attempt to formulate an alternative vision for international order (e.g. BRICS, 2014, para. 27).

As the use of unilateral/autonomous measures has increased, a counter-campaign within the UN system has formed. Since 2015, there has even been a (controversial) UN "Special Rapporteur on the negative impact of the unilateral coercive measures on the enjoyment of human rights": Algerian diplomat Idriss Jazaïry until 2020, succeeded by Belarusian lawyer Alena Douhan. On a yearly basis since 1997, UNGA resolutions have condemned "unilateral coercive measures," framing the critique strongly in terms of sovereignty and human rights, with a special emphasis on negative effects for women, children, and other vulnerable groups (see, e.g., United Nations General Assembly, 1997, 2022). In this context, EU CFSP sanctions (restrictive measures) are seen as unilateral measures, and the EU is counted among the most active senders (Office of the High Commissioner for Human Rights, 2017; United Nations Human Rights Council, 2015).[3] The EU is the only regional organization

---

3. The Targeted Sanctions Consortium (2016) at the Graduate Institute in Geneva categorizes not only regional organization sanctions against members but also EU foreign policy sanctions as regional sanctions. EU sanctions are regional in the sense that the sender coalition is a

that uses autonomous/unilateral sanctions regularly. By contrast, the EU has preferred measures other than its internal sanctions provision—suspension under article 7 TEU—when reacting to norm-violating members (Hellquist, 2019). Other regional organizations do not normally use sanctions against third countries when there is no clear regional dimension to the issue at hand.[4] The exception to this rule is that several regional organizations were involved in anti-apartheid sanctions against South Africa.

The voting patterns at the UNGA and UNHRC reveal that the pro-unilateral/autonomous sanctions camp is a coalition of the Western world and allies. At the Human Rights Council, as well as in the General Assembly, this group is a minority facing a majority of non-Western and/or developing states, with targets of sanctions being particularly vocal. That targets complain about sanctions being illegal or harmful to human rights (e.g., Permanent Mission of the Syrian Arab Republic, 2014) can easily be dismissed as distasteful, in view of their own records in this regard. Nonetheless, the patterns of contestation within the "international community" are there and matter for our understanding of what sanctions do and do not do to international relations.

### 8.2.3. Regional Sanctions

The arrival of regional sanctions after the end of the Cold War fundamentally transformed the relationship between regional organizations and

---

regional organization with members geographically located in the same region. However, the issues addressed by EU sanctions have rarely been of a "regional" character, and the entire policy is justified in erga omnes terms—that is, as a matter of defending universal values.

4. The Arab League's more than half-century-long boycott of Israel and its spin-off sanctions against the United States and the Netherlands (1973–1974), as well as against Canada (1979), are examples of an isolated use of foreign policy sanctions around an issue of extraordinary regional concern. The conflict with Israel also gave rise to sanctions against a member. Following the Camp David peace agreement, Egypt was suspended from the League (1979–1989) and placed under economic sanctions (1978–1983).

their members. Whereas regional cooperation had traditionally aimed at shielding members from external interference, organizations started to specify conditions for active involvement in what had been considered domestic affairs (Coe, 2019; Hellquist & Palestini, 2021). At the same time, most countries in regional organizations that are nowadays active senders of sanctions against members remain critical of unilateral sanctions, and sometimes they have their own painful experiences of being targets. Thus, their rethinking of sanctions builds exclusively on the relational premise of membership.

If the UN has a unique claim to universal multilateralism, regional organizations appeal to a regional multilateralism applicable within the community. As suggested previously, the basic relationship underpinning regional sanctions is membership in an organization with a defined normative authority over regional affairs. The title of Jon Pevehouse's 2002 *American Journal of Political Science* article, "With a Little Help from My Friends?" pinpoints that "regional IOs [international organizations] are not an outside entity" (Pevehouse, 2002, p. 611). In a piece from 1964, Harvard legal scholar Louis Sohn likewise touched upon the comparative advantage of regional actors in imposing membership sanctions, arguing that "international regional organizations are more likely to be concerned with the like-mindedness of their members than are international organizations global in scope" (Sohn, 1964, p. 1416). Thus, in contrast to the two other types of senders, regional sanctions are pronouncedly in-group measures. This has at least four noteworthy implications.

First, as members of regional organizations, "governments are both rule-makers and enforcers" (Closa & Palestini, 2015, p. 1; see also Doxey, 1980a, p. 139). This means that the shadow of the future permeates regional sanctions policies: The roles may swap one day. Therefore, in-group sanctions tend to be limited to norms that the members have a clear shared interest to defend. The often, by implication if not by direct intent, regime-preserving anti-coup sanctions of the African Union are a case in point.

Second, the sanctions of regional organizations approximate contractual punishment because members have voluntarily committed to a set of rules with certain declared consequences.[5] "A firm legal position" (Negm, 2021, p. 235)—that is, a sufficiently precise sanctions mandate agreed beforehand—offers recourse from "wild justice" revenge (Chapter 2, this volume; see Jacoby, 1983). Sanctions always contain a degree of political interpretation, but a doctrine directed at strictly defined situations of norm violations will minimize this problem and provide for foreseeability.

Third, if members are like-minded enough to perceive of the region as a relevant normative community, and of the regional organization as a legitimate authority to act on behalf of the community, the highly detrimental association of sanctions to "external interference" could be softened. The institutionalization of a regional sanctions mandate already signals a principled recognition of regional authority in situations that have traditionally been confined to national sovereignty. To fully endorse normative authority beyond the nation-state is certainly another, much more demanding, matter. At the same time, precisely the human experience of building nation-states, often with complex horizontal and vertical divisions of responsibilities, shows that it is possible to reach an advanced level of acceptance and even trust between citizens and state as well as between different levels of political organization.

Fourth, regional organizations acting against members have a pronounced interest to keep the sanctions episode brief. The AU, the world's leading sender of regional sanctions, deliberatively combines sanctions (baseline measure: suspension of membership) with positive engagement in order to quickly resolve the crisis giving rise to sanctions (Hellquist, 2021, 2022). This is in line with social psychology research, which has found that "offenders from a social group to which the punisher does *not* belong (an 'out-group') are punished more harshly than offenders who belong to the same social group as the offender ('in-group')" (see Chapter 2, this volume). In short, ceteris paribus regional sanctions resonate with ideas of restorative justice, which constructively engages with—rather than strictly isolates—the target (see Chapter 2, this volume).

---

5. UN sanctions and unilateral measures both refer to countries' obligations under international law, but especially for unilateral sanctions the absence of an explicit contractual connection between sender and target caters to accusations that measures are illegal.

It is clearly unpractical for regional organizations to have members that do not take full part in regional affairs. After all, as noted by Laurence Whitehead (2021), states in a region "are fated by geography to continue operating alongside each other" (p. 552). In addition to this practical concern, most regional organizations have an idea of what their full group of members should look like. Exclusion needs to be temporary to not break with a holistic conception of the region where geographically linked countries are destined to belong together. As stated by a top official at the AU, the idea of sanctions is to place countries in the "sick room" and then "bring them back" (Addis Ababa, personal communication, December 7, 2010). Indeed, AU sanctions are on average resolved much more quickly than the EU's foreign policy measures (Hellquist, 2022, p. 109).

## 8.3. CONCLUSION

> A study of social sanctions is therefore ipso facto a study of social relationships.
> —Piddocke (1968, p. 269)

Unlike much scholarship on sanctions, this chapter has been occupied neither with the technical aspects of the measures themselves nor with their measurable impact on targets. Instead, the chapter has introduced a relational approach to sanctions, starting from the well-established observation that sanctions—in all their diversity—characteristically modify some aspect of "normal" relations between the sender and the target. The increasingly crowded landscape of international sanctioning is a social environment in which contestation over different actors' authority to punish alleged norm violators thrives. Friction and cooperation emerge nonrandomly in this social playfield. Criticism of unilateral sanctions—often based on sovereignty, ethical, or legal arguments—is a long-standing pillar in the foreign policies of a majority of the world's states. For the (coalitions of) states that impose unilateral sanctions on third countries, punitive measures represent credible rejection of behavior deemed intolerable.

However, as this chapter has shown, it would be a shortcut to reduce the debate on sanctions to a pro and contra camp. Rather, different senders of sanctions appeal to different punitive logics, which are based on which type of relational bond they have to the target. In addition, the use of sanctions in a certain punitive logic may prompt other actors (countries and organizations) to join or reject their sanctions. Regional organizations have entered this multi-actor game with new cards in their hands, appealing to a notion of in-group normative discipline that sharply contrasts with the out-group perspective of unilateral—or even UN—sanctions. The emergence of resolution-oriented versions of punishment at the regional level is still in its infancy and faces considerable obstacles. To be accepted as a normative authority in a world of sovereign states is an uphill endeavor for any regional organization and especially as concerns sensitive domains of domestic governance. However, the hill is likely even steeper for conventional out-group sanctions. In view of the urgency to find strategies that go beyond posturing to actually protect and promote desirable norms, it is worthwhile to consider closely the theoretical promise of in-group sanctions. Ultimately, if regional organizations would mature in this regard (it is, admittedly, a big "if"), the habitual exercise of normative discipline at the regional level could redraw the normative world order as we know it.

## References

Adler-Nissen, R. (2014). Stigma management in international relations: Transgressive identities, norms and order in international society. *International Organisation*, 68(1), 143–176.

Alland, D. (2002). Countermeasures of general interest. *European Journal of International Law*, 13(5), 1221–1239.

Baldwin, D. A. (1971). The power of positive sanctions. *World Politics*, 24(1), 19–38.

Baldwin, D. A. (1985). *Economic statecraft*. Princeton University Press.

Baldwin, D. A. (1999). The sanctions debate and the logic of choice. *International Security*, 24(3), 80–107.

BBC. (2016, December 15). *Venezuela Mercosur: Battle of rooms at Latin American summit*. http://www.bbc.com/news/world-latin-america-38328489

Beaucillon, C. (2021a). An introduction to unilateral and extraterritorial sanctions: Definitions, state of practice and contemporary challenges. In C. Beaucillon (Ed.), *Research handbook on unilateral and extraterritorial sanctions* (pp. 1–17). Elgar.

Beaucillon, C. (Ed.). (2021b). *Research handbook on unilateral and extraterritorial sanctions*. Elgar.

Biersteker, T., & Moret, E. (2015). Rising powers and reform of the practices of international security institutions. In J. Gaskarth (Ed.), *Rising powers, global governance and global ethics* (pp. 57–73). Routledge.

Binder, M., & Heupel, M. (2015). The legitimacy of the UN Security Council: Evidence from recent General Assembly debates. *International Studies Quarterly*, 59(2), 238–250.

BRICS (2014). "Fortaleza Declaration." http://www.brics.utoronto.ca/docs/140715-leaders.html

Brzoska, M. (2015). International sanctions before and beyond UN sanctions. *International Affairs*, 91(6), 1339–1349.

Bull, H. (1977). *The anarchical society: A study of order in world politics*. Macmillan.

Charron, A., & Portela, C. (2015). The UN, regional sanctions and Africa. *International Affairs*, 91(6), 1369–1385.

Charron, A., & Portela, C. (2016). The relationship between United Nations sanctions and regional sanctions regimes. In T. J. Biersteker, S. E. Eckert, & M. Tourinho (Eds.), *Targeted sanctions: The impacts and effectiveness of United Nations action* (pp. 101–118). Cambridge University Press.

Closa, C., & Palestini, S. (2015). *Between democratic protection and self-defense: The case of UNASUR and Venezuela* (Robert Schuman Centre for Advanced Studies research paper No. RSCAS 2015/93). SSRN.

Coe, B., N. (2019). *Sovereignty in the South: Intrusive regionalism in Africa, Latin America, and Southeast Asia*. Cambridge University Press.

Congressional Research Service. (2022). *Russia's war on Ukraine: The economic impact of sanctions*. https://crsreports.congress.gov/product/pdf/IF/IF12092

Cortright, D., Lopez, G. A., Conroy, R. W., Dashti-Gibson, J., Wagler, J., Malone, D. M., & Axworthy, L. (2000). *The sanctions decade: Assessing UN strategies in the 1990s* (Vol. 1). Rienner.

Doxey, M. (1980a). *Economic sanctions and international enforcement*. Springer.

Doxey, M. (1980b). Economic sanctions: Benefits and costs. The World Today, 36(12), 484–489.

Doxey, M. (1996). *International sanctions in contemporary perspective* (2nd ed.). Macmillan.

Doxey, M. (2000). United Nations sanctions: Lessons of experience. *Diplomacy and Statecraft*, 11(1), 1–18.

Drezner, D. W. (2000). Bargaining, enforcement, and multilateral sanctions: When is cooperation counterproductive. *International Organisation*, 54(1), 73–102.

Hellquist, E. (2012). *Creating "the self" by outlawing "the other": EU foreign policy sanctions and the quest for credibility* [PhD thesis]. European University Institute.

Hellquist, E. (2015). Interpreting sanctions in Africa and Southeast Asia. *International Relations*, 29(3), 319–333.

Hellquist, E. (2016). Either with us or against us? Third-country alignment with EU sanctions against Russia/Ukraine. *Cambridge Review of International Affairs*, 29(3), 997–1021.

Hellquist, E. (2019). Ostracism and the EU's contradictory approach to sanctions at home and abroad. *Contemporary Politics*, 25(4), 393–418.

Hellquist, E. (2021). Regional sanctions as peer review: The African Union against Egypt (2013) and Sudan (2019). *International Political Science Review*, 42(4), 451–468.

Hellquist, E. (2022). The African Union in a world of sanctions. In A. Charron & C. Portela (Eds.), *Multilateral sanctions revisited: Lessons learned from Margaret Doxey* (pp. 99–115). McGill-Queen's University Press.

Hellquist, E., & Palestini, S. (2021). Regional sanctions and the struggle for democracy: Introduction to the special issue. *International Political Science Review*, 42(4), 437–450.

Hofer, A. (2021). Unilateral sanctions as a challenge to the law of state responsibility. In C. Beaucillon (Ed.), *Research handbook on unilateral and extraterritorial sanctions* (pp. 186–203). Elgar.

Hoffmann, F. (1967). The functions of economic sanctions: A comparative analysis. *Journal of Peace Research*, 4(2), 140–159.

Hufbauer, G. C., Schott, J. J., & Elliott, K. A. (1990). *Economic sanctions reconsidered: History and current policy* (2nd ed.). Institute of International Economics.

Hurd, I. (2002). Legitimacy, power, and the symbolic life of the UN Security Council. *Global Governance*, 8(1), 35–51.

Hurd, I. (2005). The strategic use of liberal internationalism: Libya and the UN sanctions, 1992–2003. *International Organisation*, 59(3), 495–526.

Jacoby, S. (1983). *Wild justice: The evolution of revenge*. Harper.

Jamnejad, M., & Wood, M. (2009). The principle of non-intervention. *Leiden Journal of International Law*, 22, 345–381.

Jones, L. (2015). *Societies under siege*. Oxford University Press.

Levitsky, S., & Way, L. A. (2010). *Competitive authoritarianism: Hybrid regimes after the Cold War*. Cambridge University Press.

Lindsay, J. M. (1986). Trade sanctions as policy instruments: A re-examination. *International Studies Quarterly*, 30(2), 153–173.

Lowe, V. (1997). US extraterritorial jurisdiction: The Helms–Burton and D'amato Acts. *International and Comparative Law Quarterly*, 46(2), 378–390.

Lowenfeld, A. F. (1996). Congress and Cuba: The Helms–Burton Act. *American Journal of International Law*, 90(3), 419–434.

Lowenfeld, A. F. (2001). Unilateral versus collective sanctions: An American's perception. In M. G. Rubio & H. Hadj-Sahraoui (Eds.), *United Nations sanctions and international law* (pp. 95–103). Brill Nijhoff.

Martin, L. L. (1994). *Coercive cooperation: Explaining multilateral economic sanctions*. Princeton University Press.

Moret, E. (2021). Unilateral and extraterritorial sanctions in crisis: Implications of their rising use and misuse in contemporary world politics. In C. Beaucillon (Ed.), *Research handbook on unilateral and extraterritorial sanctions* (pp. 19–36). Elgar.

Morgan, T. C., & Schwebach, V. L. (1997). Fools suffer gladly: The use of economic sanctions in international crises. *International Studies Quarterly*, 41(1), 27–50.

Mounk, Y. (2022, April 3). We are not at war with the Russian people. *The Washington Post*.

Negm, N. (2021). The sanctions regime of the African Union in response to unconstitutional changes of government. In I. Johnstone & S. Ratner (Eds.), *Talking international law: Legal argumentation outside the courtroom* (pp. 218-236). Oxford University Press.

Neier, A. (2022, March 29). Russians' collective responsibility for Putin's war. *Project Syndicate*.

Nili, S. (2016). Rethinking economic "sanctions." *International Studies Review, 18*(4), 635-654.

Nossal, K. R. (1989). International sanctions as international punishment. *International Organization, 43*(2), 301-322.

O'Connell, M. E. (2002). Debating the law of sanctions. *European Journal of International Law, 13*(1), 63-79.

Office of the High Commissioner for Human Rights. (2017). *Special Rapporteur on the negative impact of the unilateral coercive measures on the enjoyment of human rights*. http://www.ohchr.org/EN/Issues/UCM/Pages/SRCoerciveMeasures.aspx

Organization of African Unity. (1998, June 8-10). *The crisis between the Great Socialist People's Libyan Arab Jamahiriya and the United States of America and the United Kingdom*.

Padelford, N. J. (1954). Regional organization and the United Nations. *International Organization, 8*(2), 208-216.

Panke, D. D., & Petersohn, U. (2012). Why international norms disappear sometimes. *European Journal of International Law, 18*(4), 719-742.

Permanent Mission of the Syrian Arab Republic. (2014, October 7). *Response to the questionnaire on "human rights and unilateral coercive measures"* (No. 264).

Pevehouse, J. C. (2002). With a little help from my friends? Regional organizations and the consolidation of democracy. *American Journal of Political Science, 46*(3), 611-626.

Piddocke, S. (1968). Social sanctions. *Anthropologica, 10*(2), 261-285.

Rawls, J. (1993). The law of peoples. *Critical Inquiry, 20*(1), 36-68.

Rose, E. A. (2005). From a punitive to a bargaining model of sanctions: Lessons from Iraq. *International Studies Quarterly, 49*(3), 459-479.

Sands, P., & Klein, P. (2009). *Bowett's law of international institutions* (6th ed.). Thomas Reuters.

Schneider, H. (1998, October 4). Libya's Gadhafi says his future is African; Pan-Arab unity is no longer the goal. *The Washington Post*.

Sohn, L. B. (1964). Expulsion or forced withdrawal from an international organization. *Harvard Law Review, 77*(8), 1381-1425.

Sturman, K. (2003). The rise of Libya as a regional player. *African Security Review, 12*(2), 109-112.

Takeyh, R. (2001). The rogue who came in from the cold. *Foreign Affairs, 80*(3), 62-72.

United Nations General Assembly. (1997, March 13). *Human rights and unilateral coercive measures* (A/RES/51/103. 12 December 1996, Distr.: General).

United Nations General Assembly. (2022, January 7). *Human rights and unilateral coercive measures* (A/RES/76/161. 16 December 2021, Distr.: General).

United Nations Human Rights Council. (2015). *10 February, 28th Session. Research-based progress report of the Human Rights Council Advisory Committee containing recommendations on mechanisms to assess the negative impact of unilateral coercive measures on the enjoyment of human rights and to promote accountability*. Accessed November 19, 2022, from http://daccess-ods.un.org/access.nsf/Get?Open&DS=A/HRC/28/74&Lang=E

Von Borzyskowski, I., & Portela, C. (2016). *Piling on: The rise of sanctions cooperation between regional organizations, the United States, and the EU* (KFG working paper No. 70). Freie Universität Berlin.

Wagner, W., & Werner, W. (2018). War and punitivity under anarchy. *European Journal of International Security*, 3(3), 310–325.

Whang, T. (2010). Structural estimation of economic sanctions: From initiation to outcomes. *Journal of Peace Research*, 47(5), 561–573.

White, N., & Abass, A. (2006). Countermeasures and sanctions. In M. D. Evans (Ed.), *International law* (2n ed., pp. 509–532). Oxford University Press.

Whitehead, L. (2021). Regional organizations and democratic conditionality: Family resemblances and shaming. *International Political Science Review*, 42(4), 546–560.

# 9
# Deciphering International Punishments

*A Perspective from the Global South*

SIDDHARTH MALLAVARAPU

## 9.1. INTRODUCTION

My initial point of departure in this chapter is to concur with what the editors of this volume claim in Chapter 1, namely that "international punishment [is] an established practice in international politics." This is borne out with ample evidence across several registers in the lived histories of the Global South. Here, I offer a broader canvas or normative framework that seeks to undergird any serious effort to situate international punishment in the light of this backdrop. I understand punishment to mean "a negative sanction intentionally applied to someone perceived to have violated a law, rule, norm, or expectation" (Vidmar & Miller, 1980, p. 568). Punishment involves stigmatization, and when it is international in character, there is much more in play than is visible to the naked eye. Fundamental questions need to be posed in relation to who is stigmatizing whom, under what political conditions, and with what effect? There are no one-size-fits-all answers here, but there is a meta-context against which many of these questions can be better contextualized. It is precisely this endeavor that makes it attractive for me to think about the provenance, nature, and outcomes set in place by the theory and practice of international punishment.

There are at least three inviting registers from which to think about punishment from the perspective of the Global South. While I heuristically classify them here as literary, legal, and political registers, the truth is that these are not hermetically sealed compartments but, rather, much more fluid conceptions that allow for active intermixing. Literary insights are not devoid of political character and legal insights depending on the telling. At their best, they tend to have both a literary and political side to them. Likewise, the political often has a literary side to it and is entangled in legalities of one kind or another. However, for the purposes of systematization and neater focus, I intend sifting through illustrations in each of these domains and potentially to encourage further critical scholarship in this vein.

In literary terms, the first illustrative text that does the opening for me in terms of my intellectual project here is *The Nutmeg's Curse* by Amitav Ghosh (2021). Although Ghosh is a well-known novelist, he is also something of an exemplar with regard to his nonfiction genre. While making no tall claims in offering us social science insights, in effect Ghosh gives us a state-of-the-art lesson on colonial histories, "racial capitalism," and a picture of imperial formations and resource extraction dynamics in a concrete empirical context—that is, the role of the Dutch in Banda Islands, Indonesia. He raises first-order questions relating to "military and geopolitical enmeshments" and the "inequities of power," both critical to offering serious purchase into the nature of international punishments. This relates both to their etiology and the perspective of those at the receiving end of this deep relational asymmetry predominantly in the Global South.

In the same register, I also turn to the work of Lisa Lowe and Kris Manjapra on "Comparative Global Humanities After Man" (2019). Both of them innovatively problematize our Eurocentric conception of the human figure which we often take as our gold standard with regard to thinking about international punishment. More significantly, they advance a meaningful plea to break out of both "colonial and Cold War epistemologies" when it comes to reimagining the human figure (Lowe & Manjapra, 2019, pp. 26–27). Of particular salience here is the international suffering visited on those trapped in frameworks often co-constitutively constructed by both the colonizer and the colonized (Nandy, 2009).

In addition to the literary register, I tap into critical scholarship in international law that offers valuable insights with regard to thinking of international punishment from the vantage point of the Global South. Here, I lean more heavily on Third World Approaches to International Law (TWAIL scholarship) as a conscious choice given its attention to imperial continuities and deep dive into concrete arenas of law and policy. My focus here is on a continuum—international humanitarian law, human rights law, and international criminal justice frameworks (Gaeta, 2014; Nowak, 2014; Reynolds & Xavier, 2016; Schabas, 2014). None of these are stand-alone, but it is vital to see the possibilities each of these domains opens up as well as each domain's limits—offset by old-style geopolitics, political economy imperatives, and ambitious but flawed initiatives in global governance.

International law offers us a full typology of international punishments—the catalog extends from corporal and capital punishment to crimes against humanity to war crimes. Is law an ally of the good (and whose good) or is it complicit in forging excesses (vis-à-vis whom) are questions we may need to confront in this context. While attentive to North–South power asymmetries, premised on the existing scholarship, I ask what the limits of mainstream positivism in international law are with regard to mainstream narratives on international criminal justice. Furthermore, I ask what political projects are often camouflaged in legal sophistry rendering law in these circumstances anything but "benign" and "neutral" (Mutua, 2000).

Finally, I reside in the crevice of the political. What is it to suggest that histories matter or political economy matters when it comes to questions such as international punishment? If politics is the art of the possible, it makes international punishment tangible and real. It also, it is hoped, offers us a way out of the traditional impasse of "victor's justice' and opens a conversation of the limits of law and the "apology/utopia" tension that lies at the heart of emancipatory projects in law (Koskenniemi, 2006). Can the Global South demand its share of recompense premised on the treatment meted out to its peoples by the dominant major powers in history? Illustratively, why are the voices for reparations mounting a sustained attack on the need for recompense today? What explains the official unwillingness to even study the question of reparations to African Americans in the materially wealthiest nation of the world—that is, the United States (Coates, 2014)? I conclude the chapter by again feeling invited by the editors claim of "a rehabilitative penal philosophy" to briefly ruminate over its possible content especially from the perspective of the Global South (see Chapter 1, this volume). Ultimately, what does the term "international responsibility" look like today, and what obligations does it impose across the board? If the chapter provides hunches and some pathways to probe these questions further with rigor and clarity, I shall consider my task accomplished.

## 9.2. LITERARY INSIGHTS

To begin with, why should we care about nutmegs and their colonial extraction by the Dutch in Banda Islands, 17th-century Indonesia? Ghosh (2021) suggests that

> if we put aside the myth-making of modernity, in which humans are triumphantly free of material degradation on the planet and acknowledge the reality of our ever-increasing servitude to the products of the Earth, then the story of the Bandanese no longer seems so distant from our present predicament. To the contrary, the continuity between the two are so pressing and powerful that it could be even said that the fate of the Banda Islands might be read as a template for the present, if only we knew how to tell the story. (p. 19)

Ghosh is no stranger to good storytelling and is persuasive on diverse counts.

This is a story of several tropes that are often constitutive though invisibilized in conventional accounts of international punishment. I shall proceed through an inventory of categories that I have distilled from Ghosh's (2021) account to eventually suggest that none of these have exhausted their potential to explain much of what is ongoing in the contemporary worlds we inhabit. The broader effort in Ghosh's narrative is to posit a connection between colonial predation and climate change. Such a framing is prescient especially if we consider climate change an umbrella term today that captures an ensemble of punishments being meted out particularly to more vulnerable countries in the Global South. However, I do not intend to digress. Let us take stock of the inventory.

The first usage that is perhaps worth mulling over is the term "colonial mindsets." Ghosh (2021) asks, "How must it feel to find yourself face-to-face with someone who has made it clear that he has the power to bring your world to an end, and has every intention of doing so?" (p. 6). The question encapsulates the essence of the colonial mentality that greeted several continents (Latin America, Africa, and Asia) and countries located in the Global South. Emer de Vattel, an 18th-century jurist, suggested that "nations are justified in uniting together as a body with the object of punishing, and even exterminating such savage peoples" (as cited in Ghosh, 2021, p. 26). This is the first idiom of international punishment that proclaims a "standard of civilization" and justifies a modality of rule in the language of punishment (Anghie, 2007). What we now know is not just theoretical but real—the brutal massacre of the Bandanese in 1621 in Indonesia. Ghosh's contribution here is not a work of fiction but, rather, a work of nonfiction. What is worse is the amnesia that follows. He reminds us that "the slaughter of thousands of Bandanese men, women, and children vanished from memory" (p. 44). As Ghosh demonstrates, the "evisceration" was not merely physical. It was an attempt to eliminate the entire lifeworlds of the Banadanese people—their relation to their land, their cultural inheritances, and, most significantly, their meaning-making.

This brings us to our next "trope—"racial capitalism" that is not just a placeholder but also a grim reminder of the actual workings of an economic system that is deeply hierarchical and predatory. Although there are "varieties of capitalism," racial capitalism remains an enduring trope in the history of capitalism (Hall & Soskice, 2001; Leong, 2013). What several scholars have made evident is "that colonial conquest, slavery and race were essential to the emergence of capitalism as a system" (Ghosh, 2021, p. 117). As Ghosh succinctly records,

> In short, capitalism was never endogenous to the West: Europe's colonial conquests and the mass enslavements of Amerindians and Africans were essential to its formation. Nor was it based mainly on free labour—not even in the nineteenth and twentieth centuries, where many of the raw materials required by Western factories were produced by non-White workers under conditions of coercion, if not outright slavery. In the final analysis, it was the military and geopolitical dominance of the Western empires that made it possible for small minorities to exercise power over vast multitudes of people: over their bodies, their labour, their beliefs and not (least) their environments. (p. 119)

These concerns are not a thing of the past. They have a palpable way of manifesting in our enduring present.

To bring these developments up to speed in relation to the Black Lives Matter movement, Ghosh (2021) argues that "whatever the Black Lives Matter movement may or may not achieve, it has already succeeded in making manifest the insistent vitality of the past" (p. 192). This brings me back to the other terms in the Ghoshian inventory that merit reflection in the light of our interests in international punishments from a Global South provenance. A dimension worth flagging here is not unfamiliar to any student of world politics. It refers to the "military and global enmeshments" that remain an important piece of the puzzle when it comes to deciphering why and how complex motivations continue to inform apparently benign humanitarian endeavors. These are often laced with the "inequities of power," reek of a "liberal paternalism" that is unmistakable in its imprints, and effect predatory resource extraction through the machinations of the "global hierarchies of power." This is another variant of the resource curse argument. Nutmeg, which should have been a boon in the Banda Islands, turned out to be a "curse" because it manifest Dutch imperial desire and wreaked havoc on the Bandanese people (Ross, 2015, pp. 239–259). The matter does not end there. Settler colonialism persists today, and its attendant biopolitics have skewed human–nonhuman interactions.

Neatly reinforcing this normative drift is the claim Lowe and Manjapra (2019) make in relation to the figure of the human in our histories. They argue that "the history of modernity and of modern disciplinary knowledge formations are in this sense, a history of modern European forms monopolizing the definition of the human and placing other variations at a distance from the human" (p. 24). As a response to this distortion, they "propose an *analytic of relation* or a mode of study that attends to the contradictory and tensile entanglements that are the conditions for different modes of social organization in the larger time of the global" (p. 26).

Focused on the Caribbean "plantation complex," Lowe and Manjapra (2019) capture stark continuities in the present moment. They note that

> plantations are sites that disclose relationality, are not consigned to the past, but are distributed interstitially throughout the tissues of our present: in informal economies, sweatshops, slums, Indigenous hinterlands, zomies, prisons, extractive land-scapes, human trafficking networks, detention sites, refugee camps, occupied homelands, curfewed enclaves, and migrant worker tenements. (p. 32)

The Global South continues to receive its share of international punishments. In the Lowe and Manjapra idiom, this is referred to as "the new Souths of our times" (p. 32). They rather tellingly conclude that "we might even imagine our contemporary world as a global plantation archipelago" (p. 32). It is worthwhile asking in this context what structures perpetuate this reality and who are the protagonists and critics of this complex assemblage bleeding and blending into our present.

## 9.3. LEGAL INSIGHTS

While thinking about the global history of international punishments, it is fair to ask, "Where was international law in all of this? And equally importantly, where wasn't it?" (Thomas, 2016, p. 898). One approach squarely alluding to the Global South is referred to as Third World Approaches to International Law or TWAIL. Drawing on the work of a range of scholars from this tradition (see, e.g., Anand, 2004; Anghie, 2007; Chimni, 2006; Gathii, 2011; Nesiah, 2016; Okafor, 2005), I have sought to encapsulate some key concerns of TWAIL here. These include, first, the notion that the world is not a clean slate. TWAILers agree that imperial and colonial continuities persist in the contemporary world. Second, the prior justificatory rationales for colonial modes of rule persist—these include both "trade" and the "civilizing mission." Third, schisms of race, gender, caste, and class structure international life. Unproblematized universality is a problem. Fourth, uneven development is widespread, and this has to do with the broader historical structuring of the international system. Fifth, TWAILers emphasize the need to think about the forms that opposition could assume to prevailing dominant structures. There is an inclination to pursue counterhegemonic discourses and possibilities. Sixth, contemporary international law reveals the continued validity of TWAIL concerns. For instance, it is difficult to believe that the Responsibility to Protect can be studied at all absent the broader history of interventionism by major powers in the international system (Mallavarapu, 2015). Seventh, TWAILers contest the high "moral ground" occupied by the Global North. They problematizes various elements of "liberal paternalism." Eighth, TWAILers seek to expose the double standards in the observance of international law. The use of drones is a good example of these double standards. Ninth, TWAILers distinguish between ruling elites and the people. Lived experiences of people in the Third World matter as distinct from the Third World state. Finally, TWAILers are opposed to nihilism. Many TWAILers would not be uncomfortable with the idea that global justice needs to be engaged thoroughly as also the potential for transforming international law to accomplish a more egalitarian world. Of course, the key question would be what kind of global justice and pertinently how genuinely inclusive is the frame.

How can the TWAIL framework help us decipher international punishments? Going by the underlying philosophy of TWAIL, there are at least three moves that are important to make. First, there is a need to historicize the question of international punishment. My turn to colonialism in the previous section is in sync with this approach. Second, it is important to establish historical continuities to our present age. These are amply evident in the arguments advanced by both Ghosh (2021) and Lowe and Manjapra (2019) with regard to resource imperialism and the extension of the plantation complex metaphor to explain our present global circumstance, especially from the perspective of the Global South. Third, it is vital to think about a constructive way forward in the spirit of the editors' plea for "a rehabilitative penal philosophy." I seek to give all these dimensions some further thought here.

Okafor's scholarship offers us a good point of departure to revisit the question of international suffering more than two decades following the September 11, 2001 (9/11), terrorist attack framing. Writing originally in 2005, 4 years after 9/11, Okafor argues that "it is through the subtle displacement of third-world suffering from internationalist consciousness that the construction of this 'post-9/11' world as a significantly new world order has been made possible" (p. 173). Locating TWAIL within a larger tradition of "critical internationalism," Okafor observes,

> Informed by their deep attentiveness to the fact that "universality" and "common humanity" claims have long facilitated and justified Europe's colonial subjugation and continuing exploitation of much of the Third World, TWAIL scholars are wary of glib assertions of universality that tend to elide or mask underlying politics of domination. (p. 179)

Suspicious of the newness of 9/11, Okafor contends that

the structure of the newness argument has been made in support of the imperial style international law reforms that have been urged by the United States and some of its allies bears an unnerving resemblance to the structures of the kinds of newness claims that European powers deployed in the sixteenth and nineteenth centuries, and even much later, as they sought to legitimize their imperial conquests and exploitations of the Third World. (p. 189)

What is stark here are the conspicuous silences in the discourse on international punishment. For far too long, "many global powers have managed to maintain 'a posture of innocence' throughout long national and international histories of slavery, racism, dispossession, destitution, and exploitation in the Third World" (p. 190).

International criminal justice is not without its own angularities from a TWAIL perspective either. Quite apart from the dual sins of "operational selectivity" stemming from obvious "geopolitical biases," John Reynolds and Sujith Xavier (2016) suggest the need to transcend the question of "unequal enforcement to reconceptualise the forms of violence committed at the design level" (p. 961). International criminal justice has been faulted by Reynolds and Xavier on ideological grounds as well. They observe that "international criminal law ... is aligned with an imperial discourse devoted to imposing 'good governance' techniques and free market ideology" (p. 961). Without being nihilist, they suggest that

if international criminal law is to take seriously its claim to be part of a project of global justice, it must at some point begin to tackle the economic contexts of war, exploitation and scarcity: "to reconsider the boundaries of criminalization," and question for example the legality of sanction regimes, the role of structural adjustment and austerity programs imposed by international financial institutions, the competition between China and Western states for access to resources in third states, or the propriety of reparations for slavery and colonialism. (p. 980)

On a more cautious note, they recommend "the need to continually think about whether non-criminal processes will offer or ultimately offer a better path towards the objectives of deterrence, reparation, truth and reconciliation" (p. 982).

Specifically on the question of poverty, Jason Beckett (2016) persuasively demonstrates in his scholarship that "the wealth of the North produces (and is produced by) the poverty of the South" (p. 990). He elaborates eloquently:

> The "plunder" of the Third World is written into the DNA of international law; it is its raison d'etre. This can be seen in everything from the definitions of statehood and government (and the powers "granted" to governments), to structural adjustment policies, bilateral investment treaties (BITs), international economic law and debt peonage. The basic structure of international law incentivizes the creation of poverty. This flows from a combination of the focus on territoriality; the commitment to effectiveness (rather than legitimacy); the resource and borrowing privileges available to governments; and the rights of governments to buy and sell arms. (p. 990)

He further suggests that the human rights focus obscures deeper structural anomalies in the global political economy (Beckett, 2016, pp. 985–1010).

There are three other facets worth mulling over in terms of the equation of international law and punishment. The first relates to armed conflict and war, the second to the question of criminalization when it comes to transnational migrants, and the third to examine claims to transitional justice in postconflict environments. With regard to the first dimension, David Kennedy (2012) refers to the American penchant for "lawfare" (pp. 158–183). This translates into a willingness to deploy "law as a strategic asset, an instrument of war" (p. 160). Can law in Clausewitzian terms be "the continuation of war by other means?" (p. 161). Simply stated, in this idiom, "law has infiltrated the war machine" (p. 162). From the perspective of the Global South, some of the questions Kennedy raises become particularly salient. He asks,

> When does the privilege to kill replace the prohibition on murder? Where does war begin and end? What counts as "perfidy," "terror" or "torture"? Which civilians are innocent? And when can civilians, innocent or not, be killed, their deaths "collateral" to a legitimate military objective? (p. 165)

These questions assume an urgency in the world we inhabit. The ambivalence surrounding these questions has culminated in a realization that "international law can echo with virtue and stand firmly on the side of peace while pursuing a proliferating and professional engagement with the practice of war" (p. 165).

Global migration flows generate their own version of criminalization. While reflecting on the subject of transnational migration, Chantal Thomas (2016) recognizes the asymmetries between the Global North and the Global South with regard to framing issues around migrants. He observes in this connection that "aggressive criminalization can create perverse consequences that contribute to irregular migration, whether in the form of undocumented labour migration or in the form of refugees and asylum seekers" (p. 894). The role of the global political economy as well as the orchestration of global governance around migration issues generates in his assessment its own skewed trajectory. He ruefully notes that

> it is not the lack of imagination of alternatives to the status quo that has constrained the development of new international legal rules and institutions on migration but the lack of any political imperative. The countries of the global South simply do not harbour enough influence to persuade countries of the global North to make concessions on migration. (p. 913)

Similarly, when it comes to tracking down the "value chains that underpin transitional justice," Vasuki Nesiah (2016) demonstrates in this domain "how hegemonic approaches get normalized, how distributive questions get displaced, and legitimacy performed" (p. 781). While keenly aware of the emancipatory pull of human rights "moral universalism" and its close compact with "the broader architecture of political liberalism," Nesiah seeks to rescue transitional justice from the straightjacketing that human rights discourses impose on it. She is keen to contest this assumption rather than be "assimilated within it," meaning the dominant discourse of liberal human rights. Is a "counter-hegemonic approach to transitional justice" possible and what might that look like? It is in this context that Nesiah gestures to the "claims calling on the United States for reparations of slavery and on the British for reparations of colonialism" (p. 795). Although there has been little progress in both these instances in real material terms, it clearly points to a shifting tide of public sentiment regarding what constitutes global right and what constitutes global wrongdoing. Punishment of one form or another is inevitably embroiled in this discourse. Nesiah eloquently voices a broader sentiment. Her intent is "to explore the yield of the last coinage of subaltern economies to interrogate the dominant currency" (p. 796).

## 9.4. POLITICAL INSIGHTS

Politics is germane to all the issues laid out in this chapter with regard to widening our canvas in terms of thinking about international punishments with a Southern lens. The category of "punishment" speaks to a particular kind of arrangement. These arrangements hinge on widely prevalent normative frameworks at particular junctures of history, economic, and political edifices that enable some possibilities and constrain others and also on legal norms that often service the prevailing international social order with occasional successes in progressively moving the needle of history.

I have relied on the preceding registers in some ways to do the work of politics in this chapter. The first and foremost political insight is that history matters. Whether it is contending with Dutch colonialism as a consequence of the "nutmeg's curse" in the Banda Islands in Indonesia or the recourse to law in order to establish terra nullius claims with the intent of eviscerating the local inhabitants, the strategies of imperial consolidation have never ceased resurfacing. Ghosh's (2021) tethering of the colonial mindset and histories to questions of climate change today speaks to an equation with nature that has gone awfully wrong on a global scale. To reiterate, who is punishing whom and under what political conditions and to what effect are questions that merit closer scrutiny all over again.

The "plantation complex" moment is not over. The belied promise of modernity has extracted a price on all of us (especially in the Global South) and continues to do so. When it comes to resource extractions, when it comes to rendering unsuspecting populations' hostage to biopolitics, when it comes to the sustenance of racial capitalism on an unprecedented scale in myriad forms, and when it comes to pauperizing parts of the world without batting an eyelid while nourishing the war machine, the Global North has much to answer for. Can we not treat each of these as massive international punishments visited upon the Global South? The Global North, much like the Global South, is not a monolith. However, it is co-constitutive of the Global South. Although the Global South has had its share of failures both institutionally and in adapting to the avowed ideal of stateness, it is a conversation that cannot be had absent the historical path dependencies that have hollowed out in some instances and deeply disadvantaged in others the sovereign rights of the post colony to discover its own political genius and form in the manner it deems best. It has incessantly been hobbled either tacitly or explicitly by "military and geopolitical enmeshments" and the pervasive "inequities of power."

A conversation about international punishment cannot be had without invoking a notion of international responsibility. I am not referring to responsibility here in the form of colonial tutelage—mandates and trusteeship systems that international institutions were quick to erect. Nor am I alluding to the responsibility to protect doctrine that I have critiqued elsewhere (Mallavarapu, 2015, pp. 305–322). However, I am thinking of responsibility in terms of collective obligations of international actors to forging a wider ecumene of belonging. Two potential models are offered by Tzvetan Todorov and Ashis Nandy (Blaney & Inayatullah, 1994, pp. 23–51). Is there an international society or is that merely a euphemism for the major powers of the day? Is collective morality, as E. H. Carr (2016) suggested, inescapably tied to the dominant powers of the day? If this is true, does it mean that we are condemned to some version of "victor's justice"? In which case the discourse on punishment is shaped and curated by a select few in the charmed circle of the international distribution of power.

There are no easy answers to these questions. However, my hope is that by posing these questions, we can begin to view international punishment against a much wider canvas of historic propensities and possible futures. We need to think of the many meanings stigma might assume today in a complex world. Whom do we designate as heroes and whom do we condemn as villains? Are structural factors the real villains, or are they always concrete agents who are to blame? Individual culpability has been established in contemporary international law in the much contested domain of international criminal justice. Although I am inclined to applaud the penalization of those who carry out the orders in a brutalized political ecology notwithstanding their claims to political innocence, it does not let us off the hook entirely. We still need to think of imperial complicities and culpabilities in the shaping of the world we inhabit. We need to be able to ask our sovereign leaders difficult questions in distraught times. None of this is likely to be easy.

However, we must not cease thinking of what "a rehabilitative penal philosophy" might look like in the 21st century. This is a question that has attracted some worthwhile attention. Judith Butler's book, *The Force of Non-Violence: An Ethico-Political Bind* (2020) is one such endeavor. However, as the historian Faisal Devji (2020) reminds us, leading figures from the non-West are virtually missing. Devji remarks,

> There are notable absences from Butler's book, which relies on a small number of familiar European authorities instead. The causal manner in which she dismisses those outside this canon can be gauged from the careful way Butler cites [Walter] Benjamin's essay in English as well as the original German, whereas her few mentions of Gandhi are either drawn from a secondary source or a collection of his excerpted works. Martin Luther King Jr., meanwhile is confined

to an epigraph and a footnote. Nelson Mandela, to say nothing of Tolstoy, is altogether ignored. This is not a question of minority representation, as these obscured figures were at the forefront of developing nonviolence as a name as much as a practice.

As a corrective to these occlusions, we will need to draw on a much more diverse inventory to rehabilitate our conceptions of good conduct at the international plane. This is also a plea for opening up to intellectual traditions outside the mainstream and seeking a much wider palette of opinions with regard to thinking about global justice and, more significantly, its relationship with contemporary international law. It is perhaps worth asking what it might mean to decolonize international punishment in the 21st century (Aliverti et al., 2021, pp. 297–316). There are some possibilities worth pursuing here both in theory and practice, but a fuller treatment is warranted elsewhere. I shall confine myself here to claims around reparations and ask what this might offer in terms of another fresh look at rehabilitative possibilities for historical wrongdoers.

## 9.5. REVISITING REPARATION CLAIMS

There are several ways in which we can think about reparations today. To begin with, an acknowledgment of wrongdoing is important. Claire Coleman (2007), an Aboriginal from the Noongar country of Western Australia, argues that it was only as recently as 1992

> with the High Court's Mabo decision, terra nullius, a declaration that some say was never made until it was convenient to enforce it retroactively, was overturned and for the first time Australian law has acknowledged that Aboriginal people lived on this continent before 1788, before 1606 (the first confirmed sighting of the European continent) and, then and now, have ownership rights and connection to land. (p. 3)

She adds,

> Terra nullius was never true in Australia, it was in fact a lie. The courts did not render it untrue by their decision. Rather, they declared it to have always been false, we were not suddenly here, we always have been here. (p. 3)

However, as Coleman reminds us, this is only the beginning.

Olúfẹ́mi O. Táíwò (2022) succinctly captures both different idioms in which reparations can be approached as well as different species of reparations. In terms of the former, reparations could have both "material" and nonmaterial dimensions that they seek to address and assuage. Whereas the material facets often boil down to financial commitments for recompense, the nonmaterial dimensions entail "considerations such as political representation, as well as attempts to consider symbolic injustices, such as monuments and memorials that continue to propagate the ideology of global racism" (p. 9). In terms of the latter dimension, Táíwò suggests that

> for some, reparations are a national project, as in the United States. For others, it is regional or supranational: examples include the Caribbean nations' CARICOM project, reparations projects formed on the African continent, and demands from Indigenous groups who have collaborated across their nations to push for redress of grievances. (p. 9)

Táíwò (2022) advances a case for a "constructive" perspective on reparations which recognizes that a "broader struggle for social justice, is concerned with building the just world to come." (p. 74). The accent here is on distributive justice and the long view as opposed to a more limited "snapshot" view of our recent past (p. 85). In this rendition, "global racial empire, and its history of slavery and colonial domination, will be fully conquered only when their effects on the accumulation of advantages and disadvantages are also conquered" (p. 87). It is the accretion and sedimentation of past privileges stemming from the most predatory forms of political, economic, and social exploitation that continue to manifest as the hidden structural privileges and continued dominance of elites entrenched over time.

To return to Ghosh (2021), climate justice entails an acknowledgment of some forms of recompense, a position that is also affirmed in *Reconsidering Reparations* (Táíwò, 2022, pp. 149–190). However, urging requisite caution in any such framing, Gurminder K. Bhambra and Peter Newell (2022) suggest that

> understanding climate change in the context of colonial histories implies more than the payment for loss and damages experienced today as a result of accumulated emissions. It requires instead a broader recognition of how socially and regionally uneven concentrations of wealth, which have resulted in climate-changing emissions, were created in the first place. It is not simply that climate change follows from the logic of the market, but that the market is embodied in private property relations and that the latter are misunderstood if the colonial appropriation of land is not made central. Colonialism appears to be a metaphor because its continuity is elided. It is the reality that a reparative approach to climate justice reinstates. (p. 6)

Although this needs to be avoided, arguably reparations could potentially be reframed in a manner that allows for these sensibilities to be taken on board meaningfully and translated into more pragmatic and plausible solutions.

A persuasive advocate of the Caribbean reparation cause is Hilary Beckles, the author of *Britain's Black Debt: Reparations for Caribbean Slavery and Native Genocide* (2013). Alluding to the classic scholarship of Eric Williams (1944) on the relationship between capitalism and slavery, Beckles suggests that

> the modern Caribbean reparations movement is a legal, political, and moral response of grassroots organizations and political

networks to the evidence presented by many scholars, but notably in William's seminal study. Since then, there have been many criticisms, refinements and reaffirmations of this work, but its continued capacity to stimulate further research speaks to its essential correctness. (p. 4)

The loss of more than "fifteen million enchained Africans" amounts to "a global tragedy now described universally as the African holocaust" (p. 164).

Culpability is not difficult to establish, although former colonial powers have been slippery and evasive to say the least. Beckles (2013) argues that "the British state must take legal, political and moral ownership of these crimes as the body invested with the collective, continual responsibility for the wealth of nations" (p. 166). This is not the end of the story. Beckles adds that "other European states and institutions have a similar case of reparations to answer. Spain, Portugal, Netherlands, France, Germany, Russia and the Nordic nations were the other principal investors and participants in trafficking and enslavement of Africans" (p. 166). Why should they be let off the hook?

In India, Shashi Tharoor, a member of the Indian Parliament, has argued in his book, *An Era of Darkness: The British Empire in India* (2016), the need to think of the reparations idea symbolically as "atonement." Drawing attention to a 1970 gesture referred to as "Kniefal von Warschau" by Willy Brandt, then Chancellor of Germany, Tharoor noted that the head of State "was recognizing the moral responsibility of the German people" when "he sank to his knees at the Warsaw Ghetto in 1970 to apologize to Polish Jews for the Holocaust." There have been other such gestures of sincere apology, and they affirm a politics of earnest "atonement." What made Brandt's gesture remarkable, Tharoor notes, is that in 1970, "there were hardly any Jews left in Poland, and Brandt, who as a socialist perscecuted by the Nazis, was completely innocent of the crimes for which he was apologizing" (pp. xxii).

We cannot conclude a piece on international punishment without a discussion of its converse freedom. As Ruth Wilson Gilmore (2022) observes,

"Abolition geography starts from the homely premise that freedom is a place" (p. 474). Turning the spotlight inward on the contemporary practices of criminalization within an advanced industrialized state such as the United States may give us some valid hunches on where not to venture and what we may have to critically rethink to erect a more humane architecture of belonging and humanity.

Gilmore (2022) should have the final word here. She writes,

> The processes contributing to both the development and epochal ordinariness of criminalization have been the focus of research, action, advocacy, and other forms of study trying to make sense of experience. A general but not exhaustive summary goes like this: In the United States, the multidecade crisis-riven political economy threw off surpluses that became prison expansion's basic factors: land, people, money-capital, and state capacity. The elements of "the prison fix" neither automatically nor necessarily combined into extensive carceral geographies. Rather, an enormously complicated people, income-, and asset rich political economy made a relatively sudden turn and repurposed actors, redirected the social wage, used public debt, and serially removed thousands and thousands and thousands and thousands and thousands and thousands of modestly educated people from household and communities. (pp. 476–477)

Any "rehabilitative penal philosophy" worth its salt in the 21st century must thoroughly scrutinize this mess—both in the imbrications of the domestic and the global and in the co-constitutive trajectories of the Global North and the Global South. The novelist Bilal Tanweer best captures this zeitgeist in the title of his fictional venture, *The Scatter Here Is Too Great* (2013).

## References

Aliverti, A., Carvalho, H., & Chamberlen, A. (2021). Decolonizing the criminal question. *Punishment & Society*, 23(3), 297–316.

Anand, R. P. (2004). *Studies in international law and history: An Asian perspective*. Springer.

Anghie, A. (2007). *Imperialism, sovereignty, and the making of international law* (Cambridge Studies in International and Comparative Law). Cambridge University Press.

Beckett, J. (2016). Creating poverty. In A. Oford, F. Hoffman, & M. Clark (Eds.), *The Oxford handbook of the theory of international law* (pp. 985–1010). Oxford University Press.

Beckles, H. (2013). *Britain's black debt: Reparations for Caribbean slavery and native genocide*. University of West Indies Press.

Bhambra, G. K., & Newell, P. (2022). More than a metaphor: "Climate colonialism" in perspective. *Global Social Challenges Journal, 1,* 1–9.

Blaney, D., & Inayatullah, N. (1994). Prelude to a conversation of cultures in international society? Todorov and Nandy on the possibility of dialogue. *Alternatives, 19*(1), 23–51.

Butler, J. (2020). *The force of non-violence: An ethico-political bind*. Verso

Carr, E. H. (2016). *The twenty years' crisis*. Palgrave Macmillan.

Chimni, B. S. (2006). Third World approaches to international law: A manifesto. *International Community Review, 8*(3), 3–27.

Coates, T.-N. (2014, June 27). The case for reparations. *The Atlantic*.

Coleman, C. (2007). *Lies, damned lies: A personal exploration of the impact of colonialism*. Ultimo Press.

Devji, F. (2020, July 17). The virtue in violence. Los Angeles Review of Books.

Gaeta, P. A. (2014). War crimes and other international "core" crimes. In A. Clapham & P. Gaeta (Eds.), *The Oxford handbook of international law in armed conflict* (pp. 737–765). Oxford University Press.

Gathii, J. T. (2011). TWAIL: A brief history of its origins, its decentralized network, and a tentative bibliography. *Trade, Law & Development, 3*(1), 26–64.

Ghosh, A. (2021). *The nutmeg's curse: Parables for a planet in crisis*. University of Chicago Press.

Gilmore, R. W. (2022). *Abolition geography: Essays towards liberation*. Verso.

Hall, P., & Soskice, D. (2001). *Varieties of capitalism: The institutional foundations of comparative advantage*. Oxford University Press.

Kennedy, D. (2012). Lawfare and warfare. In J. Crawford & M. Koskenniemi (Eds.), *The Cambridge companion to international law* (pp. 158–183). Cambridge University Press.

Koskenniemi, M. (2006). *From apology to utopia: The structure of international legal argument*. Cambridge University Press.

Leong, N. (2013). Racial capitalism. *Harvard Law Review, 126*(8), 2152–2226.

Lowe, L., & Manjapra, K. (2019). Comparative global humanities after man: Alternatives to the coloniality of knowledge. *Theory, Culture & Society, 36*(5), 23–48.

Mallavarapu, S. (2015). Colonialism and the responsibility to protect. In W. Maley & R. Thakur (Eds.), *Theorizing the responsibility to protect* (pp. 305–322). Cambridge University Press.

Mutua, M. (2000). What is TWAIL? *Proceedings of the ASIL Annual Meeting, 94,* 31–38.

Nandy, A. (2009). *The intimate enemy: Loss and recovery of self under colonialism*. Oxford University Press.

Nesiah, V. (2016). Theories of transnational justice: Cashing in on the blue chips. In A. Orford, F. Hoffman, & M. Clark (Eds.), *The Oxford handbook of the theory of international law* (pp. 779–796). Oxford University Press.

Nowak, M. (2014). Torture and other cruel, inhuman, or degrading treatment or punishment. In A. Clapham & P. Gaeta (Eds.), *The Oxford handbook of international law in armed conflict* (pp. 387–409). Oxford University Press.

Okafor, O. C. (2005). Newness, imperialism and international legal reform in our time: A TWAIL perspective. *Osgood Hall Law Journal, 43*(1–2), 71–191.

Reynolds, J., & Xavier, S. (2016). "The dark corners of the world": TWAIL and international criminal justice. *Journal of International Criminal Justice, 14*(4), 959–983.

Ross, M. L. (2015). What have we learned about the resource curse? *Annual Review of Political Science, 18*, 239–259.

Schabas, W. A. (2014). The right to life. In A. Clapham & P. Gaeta (Eds.), *The Oxford handbook of international law in armed conflict* (pp. 365–386). Oxford University Press.

Táíwò, O. (2022). *Reconsidering reparations.* Oxford University Press.

Tanweer, B. (2013). *The scatter here is too great.* Random House.

Tharoor, S. (2016). *An era of darkness: The British empire in India.* Aleph.

Thomas, C. (2016). Transnational migration, globalization, and governance. In A. Orford, F. Hoffman, & M. Clark (Eds.), *The Oxford handbook of the theory of international law* (pp. 882–919). Oxford University Press.

Vidmar, N., & Miller, D. T. (1980). Social psychological processes underlying attitudes toward legal punishment. *Law and Society Review, 14*(3), 565–602.

Williams, E. (1944). *Capitalism and slavery.* The University of North Carolina Press.

# 10

# Punitivity and Norm-Setting in the History of Colonial and Postcolonial Relations

*The End of the Inter-Governmental Group on Indonesia in 1992*

FARABI FAKIH AND RONALD KROEZE

## 10.1. INTRODUCTION

This chapter analyzes international punishment from a historical perspective, where we study Dutch–Indonesian relations from the period of Dutch colonial rule to the recent past. We focus on Indonesian president Suharto's (1967–1998) decision in 1992 to force the Netherlands to resign as chair of the Inter-Governmental Group on Indonesia (IGGI), a vehicle to organize aid from the West to Indonesia. Suharto's measure was an act of punishment that was a reaction to a half-hearted punitive act from the Dutch government that threatened to end development aid in a response to the "Dili massacre" in East Timor in November 1991—a major human rights violation conducted by the Indonesian military.

Studying Dutch–Indonesian relations through a "punitive lens" highlights the enormous changes in the normative order as well as in the power relations between the two countries. Moreover, our analysis highlights that punitive practices are closely interwoven with questions of status and prestige. During the colonial period, punitive practices were closely linked to alleged challenges to Dutch superiority over its colonial subjects, and they were used to reconfirm the unequal hierarchical relationship between the two entities in an international order dominated by imperial thinking and the "politics of difference" (Burbank and Cooper, 2011). This is in stark contrast to the period around 1992. The forced resignation from the IGGI chair punished a violation by the Dutch government of the postcolonial norm of the equality of sovereign nations. Our study shows that this punitive act also communicated with and to a broader audience of international actors. A punitive lens, therefore, helps identify the norms and values undergirding the international order as well as existing concepts of social justice, structures of power and authority, and the potential for conflict and cooperation—that is, the norms parties (dis)agree on and the legitimate strategies to maintain or change them.

Taking a historical perspective informs us that although punitive acts are of time immemorial, they are seldom recognized as an official means to settle disputes (see Chapter 3, this volume). Second, because of this, punitive acts are often disguised. However, as a third feature, there are periods in history in which punitive acts were used more openly, such as during the era of European colonialism (15th–20th centuries). This was especially the case during the heyday of modern imperialism around 1900, when a specific type of punitive act (namely "punitive expedition") was used to enforce and maintain unequal power relations. Hence, the context of (post)colonial relations is not without relevance. The notion of punitive expedition conjures an asymmetric use of violence that was employed to display the force of empire, which is as such not restricted to the time of European colonialism. In contemporary history, the U.S. invasion of Iraq is frequently viewed as a punitive war (Rose, 2005), interestingly often linked to the doctrine of "shock and awe." Ullman et al. (1996, p. 8) defined it as a doctrine based on the use of overwhelming power, dominant battlefield awareness, and spectacular display of force to paralyze an adversary's perception of the battlefield in order to destroy its will to fight. Our case study of the 1992 event broadens the study of international punishment beyond the use of military force to include coercive diplomacy whose punitive character was very well understood. Moreover, Suharto's strategic actions had similarities to a well-prepared military operation. While punishment operated at a diplomatic level, the objective of effecting enemy behavior through "shock and awe" is clearly apparent in this case, and thus akin to a punitive act.

The political dynamics of colonialism and decolonization are relevant for at least three additional reasons. First, Indonesia was a former colony of the Netherlands until it declared its indepence in August 1945, which was rejected by the Dutch. The violent colonial war (1945–1949) that followed was ended in a Round Table Conference, in which the Netherlands recognized Indonesia's independence in December 1949. Second, IGGI fits into a pattern of efforts since Indonesian independence to develop Indonesia based on modernization schemes that were informed by Western (Dutch and U.S.) examples but served to make Indonesia more economically independent (Fakih, 2014). Third, IGGI was chaired by the Netherlands, the former colonizer of Indonesia. This context provided opportunities to impose foreign norms that could undermine Indonesian sovereignty and that had to be countered by Indonesia. Moreover, this setting offered a breeding ground to accuse the Netherlands of neocolonialism. Hence, in this chapter, we analyze the role of different actors and the public debate the act sparked, from both a Dutch and an Indonesian perspective, in order to establish what the 1992 event can tell us about the role of punishment in postcolonial history. We situate punitive acts in a longer history of the Netherlands–Indonesian relationship and shed light on the role of colonialism. We also emphasize how this specific punitive act served to communicate norms that undergird relations in a postcolonial world.

## 10.2. PUNITIVE EXPEDITIONS IN THE HISTORY OF THE NETHERLANDS–INDONESIAN COLONIAL RELATIONSHIP

Broadly speaking, two dominant historical approaches to punishment can be distinguished. A main part of historical studies on punishment deals with the relationship between a state and its subjects and/or citizens. This line of research has revealed different types of punishment in history: from punishment through violence (corporal punishment) to punishment through fines (money), (legal) sanctions, and other more "sophisticated" means to discipline subjects (Foucault, 2012 [1975]; Geltner, 2014; Morris & Rothman, 1995). The history of punishment between states has also attracted attention, especially from scholars of international law and international relations, with an emphasis on different types of (il)legitimate war and sanctioning (see Chapter 3, this volume).

Punishment in the context of (former) colonial relations has its own history, although there is overlap with the previously mentioned lines as well as with the field of "colonial violence." Hugo Grotius' famous works *On the Law of War and Peace* (Grotius, 2012 [1625]) and *The Freedom of the Seas* (Grotius, 1916 [1609]) were already efforts to define when certain acts of war and punishment were legitimate responses to repair wrongdoing, and when not. He formulated this in a time of global competition between European empires—including the Portuguese and Dutch in Southeast Asia—and their respective trading companies (Hathaway & Shapiro, 2017; van Ittersum, 2010). During the time of Dutch colonialism, punishing internal and external enemies was used in different forms to maintain colonial rule in Indonesia. It could take the form of quick and violent punitive expeditions, but also longer lasting military campaigns to "pacify" a region. Moreover, it included the banishment of political opponents, such as princes or noblemen, who made claims to the throne of a sultanate or kingdom that was allied to the Dutch: They could be banished without trial to South Africa or Sri Lanka. Later in the 19th century, eastern Indonesia became a space of exile when the Dutch sent communists and nationalists to Boven-Digoel on Papua (Schrikker, 2021).

The consequences of the colonial dimension become even clearer when we look at a specific type of punitive acts: punitive expeditions (*strafexpedities*).[1] In the case of the Dutch–Indonesian relationship, the act against the Banda Islands is notorious. In 1621, to finally set the Dutch monopoly on the cultivation and trade of nutmeg, which nutmeg-rich Banda was not willing to accept, the Dutch United East India Company (Vereenigde Oostindische Compagnie [VOC]) occupied the island and killed the majority of the population. The VOC saw this as an act of punishment for violating their monopoly that, according to the Dutch, had been agreed upon in an earlier treaty (Emmer & Gommans, 2012). In the late 19th and early 20th centuries, when the sphere of influence of the Dutch colonial state was extended, punitive expeditions—and *gunboat diplomacy*—were used to take "revenge" on local rulers who did not accept Dutch rule or had committed "treason"—for example, against princes on Java, sultanates on Sumatra (during the Aceh War, 1873–1904), and rulers of Lombok (1894) and Bali (1906) (Van den Doel, 2011).

As a term, punitive expeditions had come into usage in the English language and British empire—the most powerful colonial empire of the 19th century—with regard to efforts to control India's northwest frontier from the late 1860s onwards. Thereafter, it was transferred to and more often applied in other imperial contexts (Ballard, 2017; Ballard & Douglas, 2017). Punitive expeditions were common practice during the period of modern imperialism and the "Scramble for Africa" (1870s–1910s) (Ballard, 2017). Modern imperialism is characterized by European colonial powers that rapidly extended their sphere of influence in existing or new colonized areas. This process itself was informed by the Berlin Conference of 1884–1885 that stipulated "effective" control in order to claim a colony, as well as the search for new markets and resources. The accompanying rise of the discourse of "civilizing missions" to legitimize colonialism suggested that European colonizers brought development to "backward" areas of the world (Van den Doel, 2011). The Dutch equivalent of this process

---

1. Other punitive acts included banishment to remote islands or to Europe, paying fines, and imprisonment based on a flimsy legal position such as the "act of sowing hate."

was the combination of increasing trade liberalization, war and punitive expeditions, together with the "Ethical Policy"—the Dutch civilizing mission in the decades around 1900.

At that time, international law experts argued that "punitive expeditions" were legitimate when the honor or prestige—and thus power—of the (colonizing) state was harmed. This was "the fundamental ground for intervention, with the scale of intervention closely linked to the need to remove the means of doing further harm or to prevent repetition", as Ballard and Douglas (2017) emphasized.[2] In a similar fashion, Pizzo (2012) defined some of the distinctive elements of punitive expeditions as follows: "Punitive expedition" refers to a military operation undertaken to "'punish' an enemy, usually for some sort of perceived insult to the honour or reputation of an imperial power." Henk Wesseling (1981, p. 53), an expert on Dutch and European colonialism, stressed that the euphemistic connotation surrounding "punitive acts"—they were presented as legitimate acts against "terrorism," "banditry," and "piracy"—served these goals, too. Ballard and Douglas (2017) also argued that punitive expeditions were some sort of "rough justice," taking the form of "formal military actions, sanctioned at various levels by an imperial or colonial power, and dispatched across a border of some kind to inflict retribution or impose a lesson on a non-state or a putatively 'uncivilized' enemy." They also stressed that "the label is not applied uniformly, either by contemporaries or subsequently." For example, around 1800, punitive expeditions were used in broader terms and linked to "facility, ease, promptness and speed" as the primary meaning, whereas the military application was "metaphoric." The "decision to apply or withhold it serves to illuminate the moral and political underpinnings of a particular form of colonial violence . . . in response to lawlessness within territories claimed by imperial powers." Equally interesting is their remark that punitive expeditions "pretended to a formal status, governed by certain military and civilian rules and moral codes which reflected the ways in which an imperial or colonial power conceived of its sovereignty and honour." Furthermore, although punitive expeditions chiefly took the

2. They refer to Stowell (1921).

form of a small war or violent raid, contemporary punishers tried to justify them in moral and political terms, referring to norms that ungirded international society of that time (Ballard & Douglas, 2017).

Hence, although often applied in an imperial setting and taking the form of a military action, for the purpose of our analysis, it is important to emphasize that a punitive act was characterized by taking the form of punishing a territory or its rulers for some sort of perceived insult that was connected to international power relations. Moreover, punishers also claimed that their punitive acts were legitimate under specific circumstances: when the norms that ungird international relations were harmed. Finally, punitive acts were supposed to have a learning effect: an important means to make another people (or their leading representatives) "listen," "obey," and "change their mind" (Menger, 2022). In short, punitive expeditions reconfirmed *the colonial core norm of inequality and difference between the various territories of an empire*. The colonizing country had the right to punish other territories within its realm in order to maintain unequal power relations, and the international norms that ungirded them within a context of imperialism.

## 10.3. PUNISHMENT AND NORM-SETTING IN THE NETHERLANDS–INDONESIAN RELATIONSHIP AFTER 1945

In the decades after World War II, empires fell apart. Many former colonies turned into independent countries that became members of the United Nations (UN), an international order based on *the norm of equality between sovereign territories*. World War II had this effect on the Netherlands–Indonesia relationship, too. In 1942, the Dutch colonial army was defeated, and Japanese forces occupied Indonesia. By August 1945, the empire of Japan surrendered, and the Republic of Indonesia was proclaimed by Indonesian nationalist leaders Sukarno and Mohammad Hatta; in response, the Netherlands reclaimed its former colony and sent troops. However, this colonial war could not prevent Indonesian self-determination. Under high pressure from the United States and the UN, the Netherlands had to accept Indonesia's independence, which was formally laid down at the Round Table Conference in December 1949. Thereafter started an uneasy period of reformulating the relationship between both states (Brocades Zaalberg & Luttikhuis, 2020).

During the era of president Sukarno (1945–1966), on the one hand, relations were detached and cool, whereas on the other hand, there were still strong economic, cultural, and personal ties between the two countries. Moreover, while the Netherlands struggled with the end of its empire, Indonesia self-confidently took up its role on the international scene, organizing the first conference of the Non-Aligned Movement in Bandung in 1955, chaired by Sukarno (Giebels, 2001). In 1957, Sukarno nationalized Dutch businesses and forced Dutch citizens to leave Indonesia. This was a form of punishment for the fact that the Dutch were opposed to serious negotiations about surrendering Netherlands New Guinea—a territory that remained a Dutch colony until 1962—to Indonesia, as had been promised in 1949 (Lindblad, 2008).

Internally, Indonesia faced power struggles and economic hardship, while Sukarno was increasingly accused of corruption by his opponents. This culminated in a failed coup against the government in September 1965, followed by a military takeover that was led by general Suharto, who would succeed Sukarno as president in 1967. Suharto was an eminent example of an anti-communist Third World leader and a client of the United States. One of his most important aims was economic recovery, including improving Indonesia's standing in the Western bloc in order to attract foreign investments (Simpson, 2008). By 1967, Indonesia had amassed approximately $2.3 billion in international debt from both the Western and Eastern blocs (Seda, 1989). Much of this aid was short term, and the country was unable to pay for the next tranche of debt repayment. The economy was also hit by hyperinflation (Arndt, 1967). Between March and September 1966, a team of Indonesian experts made intensive visits to Europe, the United States, and Japan in order to inform these countries of Indonesia's plan for a donor forum. In September 1966, Western creditors met in Tokyo to discuss the restructuring of

Indonesian debt, as well as the possibility for Indonesia to obtain new credit (Seda, 1989). In these circumstances, at a 1967 conference organized by the Netherlands, IGGI was founded to coordinate foreign aid to Indonesia (Posthumus, 1999).

At first, as a former colonizer, the Netherlands was reluctant to take the position of chair, but because of Dutch business interests—and especially upon Indonesia's request—it accepted this "prestigious" role (Posthumus, 1999). Indonesian sources have paid considerable attention to the reasons why. First, Indonesia and the Netherlands had only recently revived their diplomatic relations after the abrogation of ties in 1957. The Netherlands was thus seen as being motivated to maintain a good relationship. Second, as a former colonizer, the Netherlands was regarded as having a better understanding of Indonesian conditions and needs. Third, Indonesia under Sukarno had alienated itself from Western nations, and the Netherlands was considered capable of bridging the gap. Last, the Netherlands was, unlike regional economic powerhouse Japan, a minor power far away in Europe. As a result, there would be less motivation from the Netherlands to impose itself, so the Indonesian government believed (Nasution, 1992; Prawiro & Parera, 1998).

IGGI was a rather unique forum: There was no other country-specific aid development vehicle like it. Whereas other debt forums were headed by international organizations (usually the World Bank), the IGGI was headed by the former colonizer. In this case, international organizations such as the World Bank, the International Monetary Fund (IMF), and the Asian Development Bank were only involved as consultants (Seda et al., 1992). IGGI aid was also unique because it continued after the early 1970s, by which time Indonesia's debt crisis was over, since loans had become a primary component in the Indonesian economic development strategy. The function of the forum was to provide soft loans in order to underwrite the government's development budget; in the post-Sukarno period, the policy was to reach a "balanced budget" (Chouwdure & Sugema, 2005). Thus, much of the state deficit was financed through IGGI loans. Between 1970 and 1992, IGGI met 34 times in the Netherlands and provided approximately $45 billion in loans to the Indonesian government (Seda, 1990).

In Indonesia, IGGI was seen by various technocrats as an Indonesian strategic deployment throughout the years but with a danger of the imposition of Western creditors to its economic sovereignty (Seda et al., 1992). Indeed, IGGI served for donor nations to structure Indonesian fiscal, monetary, and international behavior according to Western norms, with this process of norm-setting being stipulated in the late 1960s between Indonesia and donor nations. Furthermore, Indonesia would maintain strict anti-inflationary policy and rationalize its system of debt repayment. Hence, IGGI bonded Indonesia's national development policy to internationalized macroeconomic and fiscal policy (Tan, 1966). IGGI became a tool to communicate other more politicized norms as well. The promotion of human rights and principles of good government in the form of corruption critique, via the use of conditional aid agreements became more common in the Western world as a tool from the 1970s onwards (Cooper, 2010; Van Dam & Van Dis, 2014; Kroeze, 2016).

Changes in the late 1980s redefined the relationships between Indonesia and other countries and became a breeding ground for new tensions. As Indonesia's economy underwent a structural transformation toward industrialization, IGGI loans became essential in upholding the financial solvency of the country during this period (Seda, 1990). Yet, complaints of corruption remained freguent, and the regime, while slowly democratizing by the early 1990s, simultaneously conducted a series of major human rights abuses. Furthermore, the collapse of the Soviet Union and the end of the Cold War (1989–1991) was a major game changer as Indonesia's anti-communist credentials became less relevant. Human rights abuse and corruption no longer needed to be silenced for geopolitical reasons (Johnston, 2005; Kroeze, 2016). At the same time, while several authoritarian regimes with corrupt elites were overthrown in this era, Indonesia remained relatively stable and Suharto became ambitious to take up a new role on the international scene. He set about presenting his polices and governing style as a beacon of economic development and social stability (Elson, 2001). In these circumstances, punitive acts could be useful means for different parties to communicate the new norms of the changing international order.

## 10.4. THE PUNITIVE ACT OF 1992: THE DUTCH PERSPECTIVE

In 1989, Jan Pronk (PvdA, Partij van de Arbeid [Labour Party]) was appointed as the Netherlands' Minister for Development Cooperation in the third cabinet of Prime Minister Ruud Lubbers (CDA, Christelijk Democractisch Appel [Christian democrats]). This was a coalition government, composed of the center-left social democratic PvdA and the center-right Christian democratic CDA. Pronk had been a Minister for Development Cooperation before: He had served in the cabinet of Prime Minister Joop den Uyl (PvdA) from 1973 until 1977, a cabinet with the reputation for being the most progressive in Dutch history (van Baalen & Bos, 2022; Wielenga, 2015). Back then, Pronk certainly had contributed to that image as he had promoted human rights, decolonization, and economic development of Third World countries. Already in 1975, he had formulated a policy memorandum stating that recipient countries should demonstrate the promotion of human rights as at least one of the three criteria for receiving development aid. Moreover, during his academic training, Pronk had been influenced by Jan Tinbergen, a famous Dutch developmental economist and Nobel Prize winner. In addition, also because of his Protestant background, he felt a moral obligation to "repair" the damage that colonialism had brought. Pronk, reflecting on his career in an interview with historians in 2008, stated, "You cannot reverse the colonial past, but you can help cushion the consequences so that the future is not mortgaged" (Van Damme & Smits, 2011, p. 181). However, this did not mean he wavered from setting norms in relations with former colonies—to the contrary, for instance, in the negotiations leading to Surinam's independence in 1975, another former Dutch colony. In the years following, Pronk insisted on strict terms on how 3.5 billion guilders of financial aid would be spent by the Surinamese government. On the other hand, he was also sensitive to personal opinions about him, resulting in what was seen as arbitrary and capricious behavior, as well as interfering in administrative decision-making and diplomatic processes. Especially regarding Indonesia, this was no mere incident. For instance, at the opening of the 1973 IGGI conference, Pronk did not refrain from discussing the worsening human rights situation in Indonesia. In 1975, when he visited Indonesia, he met with dissidents and irritated Suharto by paying a visit to Sukarno's graveyard, much to the disapproval of diplomats and the Dutch Minister of Foreign Affairs Max van der Stoel (PvdA). In 1977, Pronk caused a crisis in the Dutch cabinet when he published a critical evaluation of Indonesian's human rights record. The evaluation was perceived as one-sided because it only examined Indonesia, rather than also reviewing the situations in other countries as well (Malcontent, 1999). Jan de Koning (CDA), who succeeded Pronk as Minister for Development Cooperation in 1977, had "to repair the bursts in the relationship between the Netherlands and Indonesia," as one former high-ranking Dutch official remembered. "Indonesians called Pronk the inspector-general because he was always full of criticism" (Van Damme & Smits, 2011, pp. 205–206). Like De Koning, Eegje Schoo (VVD, Volkspartij voor Vrijheid en Democratie [Liberal Party]), Minister for Development Cooperation between 1982 and 1986, acted differently than Pronk. She once stated, "Collaboration on equal footing and with mutual respect . . . and that does not relate well to threats or rewards. . . . [Moreover, Dutch] development aid money was for Indonesia also peanuts. That's why they could suspend it easily, later on" (cited in Van Damme & Smits, 2011, p. 283).

Therefore, in 1989, after almost 12 years in opposition and with ministers for development cooperation who had held a different approach toward Indonesia, Pronk got a new chance to set the agenda: "I arrived in November 1989 with the idea that I would be able to take up some of the things that I had had on my list since the 1970s." He was highly motivated and, in retrospect, he saw the years from 1989 until 1992 as a period of "euphoria of democracy, human rights, peace, sustainability: Everything was possible and beautiful . . . the visions of that short period were then replaced by globalization, conflicts, civil wars and the like" (cited in Van Damme & Smits, 2011, p. 187). Hence, looking back, 1992 was the end of Pronk's optimism. Moreover, while behind the scenes unease about Suharto's corrupt and oppressive regime had increased in Dutch and international circles by the late 1980s and early 1990s, official policy was different. Former Dutch diplomat P. J. H. Jonkman stated that although "Suharto's regime was not particularly good," Jonkman also belonged to that group of Dutchmen that favored collaboration with Suharto's Indonesia for "historic reasons" and because "you could influence its development, especially also because we chaired IGGI" (cited in Van Damme & Smits, 2011, p. 137). Another high-ranked policy advisor of that era, W. A. Erath, stated in an interview (Van Damme & Smits, 2011),

> It was of course an extraordinary corrupt mess. Indonesia was then well organized, but corruptly organized.... Anyhow, as they were economically successful—they had of course oil and a lot of development funding—Suharto's regime was legitimized. Moreover, he knew how to keep peace in the country. (p. 195)

In general, Dutch officials who worked with Suharto's entourage felt discomfort, as Erath recalled while referring to corruption and human rights: "Whenever I shook hands with Suharto, I always had the strong feeling to wash my hand quickly" (cited in Van Damme & Smits, 2011, p. 207). Nonetheless, they doubted whether it was "professional," "diplomatic," and "effective" for the Netherlands and Indonesia to express these feelings. Pronk in that sense stood out, causing discomfort among fellow Dutchmen. Former Dutch official J. J. A. M. van Gennip remembered (cited in Van Damme & Smits, 2011),

> I had great difficulty with the way in which Jan Pronk treated the Indonesians. Of course, I knew that Suharto embezzled money, but there were also very good forces in Indonesia that contributed a lot to the development of the country. The provocations [by Pronk] had already started in my time, but it became an excoriation when I was gone. (p. 236)

The direct breeding ground for a crisis and punitive acts was the "Dili" or "Santa Cruz" massacre on November 12, 1991, when a public funeral turned into a mass rally for the independence of East Timor, which was in turn violently shut down by Indonesian security forces. International journalists were able to smuggle footage out of the country showing how protesters were molested and killed by these forces. Tensions had already been increasing after the banning of a visit by a group of journalists and the UN Special Rapporteur for Human Rights on Torture (the Dutch international law expert Pieter Kooijmans), which had been planned for October 1991. Moreover, the protest epitomized a much longer conflict between pro-independence movements in East Timor (and their international advocates) and the Indonesian government since former colonizer Portugal had abandoned East Timor in 1975 (Vickers, 2005).

Internationally, human rights organizations as well as citizens and journalists were shocked by this event. Still, officially many governments tried to maintain what was called a *"real politik"* approach to Indonesia, as a long-time Cold War ally and an economic growth market. Subsequently, countries such as the United States and biggest donor Japan remained silent (*De Volkskrant*, November 26, 1991; *NRC Handelsblad*, December 14, 1991). In the Netherlands, on November 14, 1992, the ambassador of Indonesia was summoned to provide an explanation, but the official line was also to first await an Indonesian investigation, as Minister of Foreign Affairs Hans van den Broek (CDA) explained in an official letter to parliament on November 20, 1991, written also on behalf of Pronk.[3] On November 21, 1991, the letter was debated in parliament. Dutch members of parliament (MPs) from opposition parties such as Groenlinks (Green Left party) and progressive liberal party D66 demanded harsh measures, including suspending official development cooperation and urging other countries to do the same. Others, such as MPs from the conservative liberal party VVD, emphasized the importance of an independent investigation, whereas the social democratic party PvdA wanted to put all new aid projects on hold, as well as a planned visit of Dutch MPs to Indonesia. Some Dutch MPs even claimed that Indonesia had no right at

---

3. "Brief van de Minister van Buitenlandse Zaken" ("Letter from the Minister of Foreign Affairs"), November 20, 1991, 22 300 V, No. 20.

all to intervene in East Timor, as the UN had already proclaimed to support East Timor's request for self-rule.[4]

While Minister of Foreign Affairs Van den Broek maintained and justified cabinet's position, Minister Pronk interfered during the November 21, 1991, debate by stating, "From now until further notice, until clear conclusions can be drawn, no new aid will be offered to Indonesia." It was a punitive act against Indonesia. In a normal situation, Pronk continued, this was a decision that could only be taken after an evaluation, but this situation justified a prompt response. He also called for the installment of an independent investigation committee, much to the dislike of Van den Broek, who maintained that an internal Indonesian investigation should first be awaited.[5] In parliament, both CDA and PvdA, the two Dutch parties that supported the cabinet, expressed their support for Pronk's decision, putting much pressure on the cabinet to accept Pronk's interference as the new cabinet position.[6]

While Prime Minister Lubbers and Minister of Foreign Affairs Van den Broek might have been irritated, the Indonesian government was furious. Minister of Foreign Affairs Ali Atalas and President Suharto angrily responded, "Indonesia can very well do without help from Western countries if they [the foreign donors] want to link their development aid to the deaths of mourners at a cemetery in East Timor" (*Nederlands Dagblad*, December 13, 1991). They added, "We will not accept aid if it comes with political conditions.... Other countries have the right to stop giving us aid, but they should not interfere in our affairs" (*De Volkskrant*, December 13, 1991). When in late November 1991 an Indonesian investigation team confirmed the deaths of 19 protesters, local sources and human rights activists were furious, claiming the number was much higher. By late December

---

4. "Handelingen van de Staten-General van de Tweede Kamer" ("Proceedings of the Dutch House of Representatives"), No. 27, November 21, 1991, 1625–1640, see 1625–1627.

5. "Handelingen van de Staten-General van de Tweede Kamer" ("Proceedings of the Dutch House of Representatives"), No. 27, November 21, 1991, 1635.

6. "Handelingen van de Staten-General van de Tweede Kamer" ("Proceedings of the Dutch House of Representatives"), No. 27, November 21, 1991; "Pronk schort hulp aan Indonesië op," *De Volkskrant*, November 22, 1991.

1991, a more extensive investigation committee confirmed 50 deaths and a further 90 people still missing (eventually, 250 deaths would be confirmed), this being the result of an uncontrolled action of the local security forces against demonstrators. Two Indonesian generals were fired, but overall, the government in Jakarta was not to be blamed for anything. International civil rights activists, Indonesian students, and critical voices abroad (*De Volkskrant*, November 23, 1991) and Western journalists—who viewed the event as a "a new test for the New World Order [read: post-Cold War]" (*De Volkskrant*, November 26, 1991)—forced Western governments to reconsider their positions. Australia and Denmark hesitatingly did so while the Dutch government, in the person of Jan Pronk, reconfirmed no new aid would be provided as long as Suharto opposed an independent investigation into what had happened (*De Volkskrant*, December 30, 1991).

This response made Suharto even more furious. In early 1992, he retaliated by completely terminating collaboration with the Dutch in the field of development cooperation; projects were stopped overnight, and exchange students had to leave, too. Now, a recoiling Pronk withdrew his earlier decision to postpone aid, even claiming he had been forced by Dutch parliament to act as he had done, but it was too late (Malcontent, 1999). On March 25, 1992, Indonesian Minister of Economic Affairs Radius Prawiro published an infamous letter on behalf of President Suharto. In this letter, he accused the Dutch government of "using development aid as an instrument to threaten Indonesia." He reminded the Netherlands of its colonial misdeeds, too, and officially announced the termination of development cooperation. Dutch politicians and media considered it an "unusually sharp letter" (*Nederlands Dagblad*, July 25, 1992).

Parliament was surprised, although some MPs recognized that it was a sign of change. For example, MP Beckers of Groenlinks stated the following in parliament on April 2, 1992: "It is unique for a developing country to terminate an aid relationship, but it is not necessarily bad. Since the end of the East–West conflict, we have seen stronger and more confident acts by developing countries."[7] At the same time, during the

---

7. "Handelingen van de Staten-General van de Tweede Kamer" ("Proceedings of the Dutch House of Representatives"), No. 70, April 2, 1992, 4364.

debate, MPs criticized Pronk because of his interview in the Dutch daily *Algemeen Dagblad* a few days earlier. The interview was also translated by the *Jakarta Post* and deeply upset Suharto's government. In the article, Pronk expressed his irritation about the critique of his role, both from MPs and Dutch business organizations and from the Indonesian government. Pronk was especially irritated that he was accused of behavior which resembled that of a past colonizer:

> If people refer to the way the Netherlands behaved during the colonial era, it is not an accusation against me. People know that I have regularly distanced myself from that colonial past. That is why I feel very upset when Indonesia now compares the relationship we suggest, between human rights and development cooperation, with the way the Netherlands acted in the colonial era. That irritates me. I reject it, I don't accept it (*Algemeen Dagblad*, March 28, 1992).

However, what caused most turbulence was his answer to the question, "Do you anticipate a recovery of the aid relationship?" Pronk responded, "No. Maybe with the next political generation, but not before" (*Algemeen Dagblad*, March 28, 1992). The interview put pressure on the political collaboration between social democrats and Christian democrats in the Netherlands, the latter of whom were in favor of maintaining a good relationship with Indonesia at all costs.

In the meeting of ministers, Prime Minister Lubbers criticized Parliament's critique and the level of antagonism between the Christian democratic CDA and the social democratic PvdA, the two parties that supported his cabinet: "The tone of yesterday's debate in the House of Representatives reached the limit of what can be considered a normal working relationship between members of a coalition."[8] Nonetheless, this could not prevent CDA politicians from remaining very critical about Pronk's role. Van den Broek (CDA), the minister of Foreign Affairs, called

---

8. "Notulen van de Ministerraad" ("Minutes of the Meeting of the Council of Ministers"), April 3, 1992, p. 42.

the Indonesian decision "dramatic,"[9] and other Dutch Christian democratic politicians, including spokesman Jaap de Hoop-Scheffer, openly held Pronk responsible for this deterioration of the Dutch–Indonesian relationship.

A diplomatic mission headed by the Christian democratic Minister of Foreign Affairs had to repair the damage. It took place during a visit to Indonesia on July 16–18, 1992. Prime minister Lubbers interrupted his holiday in France during that same time to meet the Indonesian minister Radius Prawiro secretly and, via him, convince Suharto to meet with Van den Broek (*Algemeen Dagblad*, July 29, 1992). Lubbers' willingness as a prime minister to meet an "ordinary" minister, even during his holiday, was seen (and communicated as such) as respecting "Javanese protocol" and a sign of goodwill from the Dutch government (*Nederlands Dagblad*, July 25, 1992). On the other hand, some Dutch commentators were critical at what they viewed as the Dutch "mea culpa-complex" in the relationship with Indonesia, itself a result of the colonial past and the cruelties of the war of independence (1945–1949). During Van den Broek's visit to Indonesia, he was told—as it was leaked to the press—that normal relations would only be resumed when Pronk was removed from office (*Nederlands Dagblad*, July 18, 1992). Nevertheless, Suharto seemed willing to restore the relationship, too. He explained that his decision to terminate development cooperation did not stem from retaliation or resentment but, rather, from a concern about the quality of the relationship between the two countries. "Indonesia was particularly peeved at the way in which Minister Pronk (development cooperation) constantly addressed the human rights situation," as a Dutch newspaper summarized Suharto's position (*Algemeen Dagblad*, July 20, 1992). Postponing development aid in a response to what had happened on East Timor was believed to be an "intimidation tool" by the Indonesians, another Dutch daily noted (*Nederlands Dagblad*, July 20, 1992). Van den Broek, therefore, did not discuss the issue of human rights but focused instead on economic affairs with the intention "to largely

---

9. "Handelingen van de Staten-General van de Tweede Kamer" ("Proceedings of the Dutch House of Representatives"), No. 70, April 2, 1992, 4380.

undo the negative gap that had emerged between the Netherlands and Indonesia over the development relationship. We [the Dutch] have turned the page," Van den Broek publicly concluded (*Algemeen Dagblad*, July 20, 1992). Furthermore, after a meeting with Indonesian ministers, Van den Broek revealed that Pronk had "nothing more to do" with Indonesia anymore (*Nederlands Dagblad*, July 18, 1992). Pronk did not have to step down officially, but he was ordered to leave "Indonesia" to other ministers. Only some PvdA MPs responded critically about Van den Broek's emphasis on economic relations and the fact that Suharto had influenced Dutch politics in an unusual manner. However, they still accepted that it was "too early" to openly discuss what had happened in East Timor, as long as a UN report on what had happened was not published (*Het Parool*, July 20, 1992).

Still, all was not over. At the same time, Suharto was elected chair of the Non-Aligned Movement. In that role, he criticized the West, and the Netherlands in particular, for its role in South Africa's apartheid regime, and he asked for a reform of the UN (*Trouw*, September 2, 1992).

In September 1992, efforts to repair the relationship were taken up again. Looking at Dutch press coverage and parliamentary debates, Suharto was in the lead. When the social democratic Minister of Education Jo Ritzen (PvdA) visited Suharto, he was invited to Suharto's home address already on the first day, which was regarded as a great gesture from Suharto. Suharto stated that he wanted to "forget the past and move on." This could be done by setting up collaborative aid projects, no longer in Indonesia but instead in third-party countries—knowledge based on experience would be provided by Indonesia and money by the Netherlands (*De Volkskrant*, September 22, 1992). When Ritzen returned home, he wrote a report on his findings for cabinet and parliament "from the perspective of renewing cooperation." The overall tone was that of relief that Suharto was prepared to "leave the past behind"; it also emphasized technical and scientific collaboration, and there was an absence of any reference toward human rights, corruption, or the conditionality of aid. Ritzen also highlighted several arrangements between Indonesia and the Netherlands that were laid down in a separate document, beginning with "most important is that cooperation takes place on the basis of equality and common dignity and common interests and will be of mutual benefit."[10]

In the meantime, Indonesia remained irritated about Pronk, although, tellingly, the ambassador of Indonesia in the Netherlands "did not want to mention persons explicitly," as he stated in October 1992. Development cooperation, as it had been organized until 1992, would indeed not return, although this turned out to be a good thing and Dutch commentators echoed Suharto: It showed the two countries were really on equal footing now (*Algemeen Dagblad*, October 7, 1992).

Looking back at December 1992 in an overview article titled "Pronk's Lesson," a Dutch newspaper concluded,

> President Suharto's decision was an expression of national self-respect. Interference from outside is not appreciated, certainly not from the former colonizer. Is it any wonder that Indonesia is struggling with this very thing? Did we [as a colonial power] act so much differently towards Aceh [during the Aceh war 1872–1904] than Indonesia does now in East Timor? . . . We do not admire the Indonesian policy on human rights. But we do respect this expression of self-awareness. The Dutch government can continue to spread its message about the importance of political freedoms, also in Jakarta. But it [the development cooperation] can no longer be used as a threat. (*Nederlands Dagblad*, December 29, 1992)

Because of this affair and some other failures, the term of Minister Pronk was turning into a complete "disaster," as concluded by Paul Hoebink, an academic and expert on development cooperation, in his overview article titled "Minister Pronk Created His Own Disaster Year" (*Het Parool*, December 2, 1992). However, the Dutch government could be relieved. "The storm has passed, the air has cleared somewhat. Indonesia and the Netherlands now have an almost normal working relationship and the

---

10. "Brief van de minister van Onderwijs en Wetenschappen, ( "Letter from the Minister of Education and Sciences"), September 28, 1992, 22 839, No. 1.

talks were conducted in a business-like tone this time," as under-minister Yvonne van Rooy (CDA) stated in December 1992 (*NRC Handelsblad*, December 17, 1992).

Overall, Suharto's punitive act was regarded as a lesson for Pronk and for the Netherlands: In a world order based on the norms of the sovereignty of states, and of the equality of these states in international affairs, the Netherlands had to accept these norms, too. A special historical relationship with Indonesia was no reason for different—that is, unequal—treatment of one another.

## 10.5. INDONESIAN PERSPECTIVE: A WELL-PREPARED PUNITIVE ACT WITH A CLEAR AIM?

Nevertheless, the question remains: In what way was Suharto's act intentional and really had the aim to punish the Netherlands in order to communicate norms? The primary reasons for the cancellation of Dutch aid relations and the abrogation of the IGGI may be found in the reaction of Indonesian leadership, particularly President Suharto. Suharto's insistence on the abrogation of IGGI itself caught some of his technocrats by surprise. As discussed above, many in the Indonesian technocracy viewed IGGI as an Indonesian creation and a strategic means to manage the aid policy of Western governments to Indonesia (Seda, 1992). On first instance, to cancel IGGI as a result of perceived Dutch intransigence would be akin to throwing the baby out with the bath water, as Indonesian technocrats had become attached to IGGI over the years.

However, right from the start, a kind of unease about IGGI had developed, too. We therefore have to go back to the founding years of IGGI. The decision to place the Netherlands as chair of the IGGI was taken by Indonesian policymakers in the late 1960s, with the assumption that the Dutch valued highly the restoration of Dutch–Indonesian relations. Yet, as early as 1973, the appointment of Pronk as Minister for Development Cooperation had raised doubts about the role of the Netherlands. Pronk's insistence on visiting villages and slums and talking to civil society and ordinary Indonesian incensed Jakarta because it reminded Indonesians of the actions of old colonial officers. Yet, the country's relative financial weakness during the 1970s meant that its response had been tepid. Moreover, Pronk's behavior nurtured critical voices in Indonesia. *Tempo*, an important Indonesian magazine that also dared to raise critical questions during Suharto's dictatorship, described Pronk as a new kind of "Dutch officer," an example of a new generation that was free from a colonial hangover (*Tempo*, November 17, 1973). Pronk's actions did give hope to civil society that it would help moderate the government's authoritarian policies, while annoying the government at the same time.

Pronk's second term, which started in 1989, was thus met with mixed responses. The government was suspicious because one of Pronk's first actions was to withhold $27 million of additional aid from Indonesia, following the execution of four of Sukarno's former bodyguards who were implicated in the coup of 1965. *Tempo*, meanwhile, celebrated Pronk's appointment by stating, "his presence bringing fresh air as an example of naivety, informality, sincerity in beliefs and openness and transparency in his dialogues with various groups in Indonesia." *Tempo* appreciated his return to office as a "nostalgia of 1973" (*Tempo*, April 11, 1990).

The conditions in Indonesia in 1991 differed from those in the mid-1970s; the Indonesian economy was undergoing rapid industrialization as a result of a series of deregulations that were conducted in the 1980s. Due to the stronger Indonesian economy, Indonesian policymakers had greater leeway in relation to aid, which became evermore apparent in the IGGI disbursement, as Japan became the most important partner for trade and investment in Indonesia's development. Japan and the Asia Development Bank (an organization led by Japan) provided half of the total $4.7 billion aid to Indonesia in 1991—or approximately $2.4 billion. The World Bank provided $1.6 billion or more than 30% of the loan. The entire aid from European countries provided 7.5% of the total Indonesian budget—a large amount but much smaller than Japanese and World Bank aid. Within the IGGI loan, the Netherlands provided only 1.9% or approximately $90 million (Van den Ham, 1993, p. 531). An Indonesian economist remarked that this was merely a week's worth of Indonesian oil and gas export and thus negligible (*Tempo*, April 11, 1992).

The second change was the ending of the Cold War (1989–1991). This was significant because the strong relationship between Indonesia and its creditors was partially based on Suharto's New Order's anti-communism and could not be used as leverage to ensure aid commitments anymore. Moreover, there were fears that Eastern European countries would suck in all Western aid and that IGGI loans would suffer as a result (Seda, 1990). In October 1991, Indonesian Minister of Finance J. B. Sumarlin attended the World Bank and IMF meeting in Washington, DC, along with government advisor Ali Wardhana and Bank of Indonesia Governor Adrianus Mooy, to obtain assurances from both organizations that they would not reduce aid to Indonesia. This was prompted when the World Bank had earlier shifted technical aid, originally meant for Indonesia, to Eastern European countries (Winarno, 2012, p. 274).

Added to these worrying developments was the increasing usage of political preconditions, including human rights, anti-corruption, and environmental protection, by creditor nations in order to effectuate political liberalization along with economic liberalization. As noted previously, this was used particularly by the Netherlands, not only with regard to the Dili massacre but also in a series of refrain from debt reduction in a response to several cases of human rights abuses, such as the execution of political prisoners, accusations of enforced violence in family planning programs, and environmental issues (Patmono et al., 1998, p. 287). Thus, from the perspective of Indonesian policymakers, there was growing concern that aid was increasingly linked to political sensitivities.

## 10.6. SUHARTO'S "CALCULATED" ACTION TO PUNISH THE NETHERLANDS

The Dili massacre occurred on November 12, 1991 (Tiessen, 1997). The incident damaged Indonesia's image abroad and put pressure on Western nations to use their influence in order to pressure Indonesia to resolve the issue. In late 1991, Pronk declared that the Netherlands would withhold aid if there was no progress in relation to resolving the Dili massacre. More worrying for Indonesian policymakers was that the Dutch action was followed by other nations, such as Canada and Denmark, which also issued similar statements threatening to withhold aid. The issue was serious enough that the 35th IGGI conference was postponed to mid-July 1992, although in the end it would never take place.

According to economist Kwik Kian Gie, one of the major reasons for Suharto's anger toward Pronk was his letter to the Indonesian government threatening to withhold aid until he could inspect East Timor himself—a geographical area that was closed to foreigners by the Indonesian government for security reasons (Kwik, 2018, p. 249). Suharto reacted angrily to what he perceived as a major act against Indonesian sovereignty. In December 1991, after his trip to Africa and South America, Suharto emphasized that aid should not be conditional to political pressure. This statement was reinforced during the ceremonial acceptance of the new Dutch ambassador to Indonesia in February 1992, in which Suharto spoke of Dutch "colonial behaviour" (Baehr, 1997, p. 369). He reiterated that the country would not sacrifice the principles of sovereignty of nations, and that Indonesia "was committed to development, using our own means according to the direction and manner which we see fit" (as cited in Hadad et al., 1992, p. 49).

The decision to abrogate IGGI to punish the Netherlands was made in a series of long meetings between Suharto and his technocrats and ministers since December 12, 1991. Suharto's economic ministers were tasked with calculating the effect of the cancellation of Dutch aid. On March 25, 1992, the team from the national planning agency (Bappenas) sent its text containing the official decision to no longer accept the Dutch chair of IGGI. A copy of this text was sent to the Netherlands, as well as another to Washington, DC. In The Hague, the Indonesian ambassador gave the letter written by Coordinating Minister for Economic Affairs (Menko Ekuin) Radius Prawiro to Prime Minister Ruub Lubbers. The second team gave a letter written by the Finance Minister J. B. Sumarlin to the World Bank Vice President of the East Asia and Pacific Division, with the request of creating a Consultative Group on Indonesia (CGI) headed by the World Bank, in order to replace IGGI (Chudori et al., 1992, pp. 58–59).

After the formal sending of these letters, Suharto's ministers held a press conference. Minister for the State Secretariat Moerdiono said (as cited in Hadad et al., 1992) that

> both nations have expended significant energy to build a relationship on the painful historical ruins of the oppressive and inhuman colonization that was conducted for centuries, and on the uncivilized cruelty conducted by the colonizing army during the war for independence some 50 years ago. (p. 43)

The Indonesian press was surprised by the level of strong words used in the letter; this was uncommon for New Order politicians because they primarily used diplomatic approaches to solve international issues. It harked back more to the manner of President Sukarno and his strong anti-imperialist stance. Answering the press, Radius Prawiro admitted, "Yes, this is understandable. . . . It isn't exactly a love letter" (as cited in Hadad et al., 1992, p. 44).

The abrupt abrogation of IGGI had the likely intended effect of warning and shocking many parties. The level of shock was displayed when *Tempo* interviewed the spokesman for the Canadian foreign ministry for Indonesia, who claimed that he was not able to sleep from worrying that Canada would receive the same treatment as the Netherlands. The Canadian Foreign Minister Barbara McDougall issued orders for the Canadian ambassador to talk to Minister Radius Prawiro about the issue, and Ottawa sent a letter to clarify its position on the matter, too. A similar response was made by the Danish authorities (Hidayat & Irawanto, 1992, p. 65). While the United States embargoed the selling of military weapons to the Indonesian military, civil aid continued in an unchanged manner (Inkiriwang, 2020). Prior to the abrogation of aid, Foreign Minister Ali Alatas had toured European capitals to ensure the continuation of aid in the aftermath of the Dili massacre. More important, Indonesian diplomats obtained assurances from Indonesia's most important creditors (the

Japanese government, the Asian Development Bank, and the World Bank) that they remained committed to providing aid to secure Indonesian development. Moreover, to the relief of the Indonesian government, no other European nations followed the Dutch, and the Japanese even promised to increase aid to make up the loss of Dutch aid. Most nations accepted the explanation of the Indonesian government to install an investigation committee, displaying a lack of international support toward the Netherlands (Baehr, 1997, p. 374). Furthermore, that Pronk himself was reprimanded at the national level and by Dutch businesses, as the Dutch hurriedly made concessions in order to recharge the Netherlands' bilateral relationship with Indonesia, was a sign of change too (Patmono et al., 1998, p. 286).[11] Still, that Pronk explained his reason for withholding Indonesian aid was based on the threat of a no-confidence vote in Parliament angered many Indonesians because it showed to them that Pronk's decision was made purely in relation to Dutch domestic politics (Patmono et al., 1998, p. 227; Seda, 1992). Therefore, although Suharto's punitive act had harmed Indonesia as well—Dutch aid was no longer accepted and IGGI was dissolved—Indonesia had secured that its main donors would not refrain from providing aid.

The response from Indonesian society was overwhelmingly positive. Amien Rais, the head of a major Islamic organization, decried the IGGI as a form of political forced labor (*kerja paksa*), referring to the forced labor policy of the infamous colonial Cultivation System of the mid-19th century, when Javanese people were practically enslaved for the interests of the colonial state. Rais also accused Pronk of acting like a governor general from the colonial era, and Rais celebrated the abrogation of IGGI as a mental breakthrough.[12] The economist Anwar Nasution wrote that the abrogation of IGGI was a victory for Suharto, similar to his military victory against the Dutch during the colonial war for independence (*janur kuning*) of the late 1940s when Suharto was a young officer. Practically

---

11. Pronk was reprimanded by the Dutch business world, according to Radius Prawiro's biography. This was a victory for Indonesia.

12. Suara Karya, *Bantuan IGGI susupi Kerja Paksa Politik*, 31-02-1992.

everyone in the press celebrated Indonesia's strong stance against the Netherlands, with a few articles that fretted about what this cancelation of Dutch aid would mean. This included 650 Indonesian students in the Netherlands, whose education was paid for by the Dutch government, and the various academic projects between Dutch and Indonesian universities, including approximately 250 Dutch experts working in Indonesia, who were all suddenly abrogated (Hadad et al., 1992, pp. 45, 92).

The calculated manner that the Suharto government conducted this punitive operation was a form of diplomatic shock and awe. Similar to colonial punitive expeditions, the act served not just to punish the offender—in this case, the Netherlands—but also to communicate norms—most importantly that states were sovereign and should refrain from interference in national affairs. In that sense, Suharto's punitive act became so successful that the Netherlands—as a minor international player—not only lost its position as chair of IGGI but also had to accept that its historically informed relationship with Indonesia had turned against the country. It was Suharto's Indonesia that set the norms now.

## 10.7. CONCLUSION

By viewing international punishment through historical lenses that include colonial and postcolonial dynamics, one can conclude the following. First, although punitive acts are not a well-researched topic from a historical perspective, in the era of modern imperialism between the late 19th and early 20th centuries, punishment was quite a common policy. This was especially the case in the form of punitive expeditions that served to "teach lessons" and to communicate norms, clearly linking punitive acts to efforts to maintain an imperial order. One very crucial norm in this respect was the inequality between the different territories of an empire, particularly between colonizer and colony. In the postcolonial world and with the "end of empire," however, many former colonies became independent sovereign nations that officially stood on an equal footing with each other; the new norm became equality between states. Punitive acts served this purpose, but international relations between states also became an arena to discuss, challenge, and set a variety of (conflicting) norms. The 1992 case is a good example of this: In response to the Dili massacre, the Netherlands (especially Minister Pronk) tried to punish Indonesia by threatening to terminate aid in order to impose new norms of good governance. However, soon the decision had to be recalled, and it was Suharto who started a punitive act against the Netherlands. It reflected how power relations had dramatically changed. Moreover, countries of relatively little international power such as the Netherlands—despite their imperial legacy or special status as a former colonial power—should also comply with this new context.

Furthermore, Suharto's act of punishment served to set this norm of equality more firmly. Although it appeared as if Suharto responded overnight, in reality it was based on a well-prepared strategy—that is, securing support or absence of interference from other major players in order to create a shock and awe effect, which was crucial for success. Because of this, Suharto's regime could quite easily "overrun" the Dutch position, which was already weakened by a lack of internal consensus. The punitive act against the Netherlands was decisive and swift, and it was followed by overtures to return to a new normal. Indonesia quickly reconstructed a successor of the IGGI with the help of the World Bank, under the new name CGI, and secured its aid—a development that was already prepared in diplomatic meetings behind the scenes. This proved to be a difference with Pronk, who had a long track record of promoting human rights and blaming countries for not complying to this norm. He, however, overlooked securing enough support and responded hastily to a request from parliament to act in response to the Dili massacre.

Moreover, one should not forget that beyond the core norms—equality between states and their internal sovereignties—the whole affair demonstrated how different actors could conduct punitive actions with the intention of challenging a variety of norms. Because war is the extension of politics by other means, as von Clauzewitz reminds us (von Clauzewitz, 1950), this case highlights that punitive expeditions served to achieve long-term political ends, too, instead of being hasty, unprepared, uncontrolled, or emotional responses to some kind of "sudden" explosive wrongdoing. There was a long buildup in the tensions between the Netherlands/Pronk and Indonesia/Suharto. As such, it was an old wish of the Suharto regime to challenge the impact of conditional aid and the influence of Western corruption-critique, political liberalization, and human rights promotion. This was apparent in the various statements of Suharto and foreign minister Ali Alatas (see Baehr, 1997, pp. 371–372). Another insight is that what is considered punishment—and how severe the punishment is—depends on one's own perspective. Punishment is a relational concept (see Chapter 9, this volume). What is a logical and legitimate act for one is a form of severe and unjustified (or even illogical) form of punishment for another. Hence, approaching international punishment from a historical perspective highlights these dynamics.

Finally, this case shows the communicative dimension of international punishment (see Chapter 2, this volume), with the bystander being the intended audience (in this case, both national audiences and foreign states and the wider international community), not just the victim. Pronk and the Dutch generally were convenient targets because their historical colonial transgressions provided the emotional grounds, making Indonesia's punitive actions possible from a position of justice. It also provided the emotional impetus for the Indonesian population to rally behind the government. Punitivity, thus, has a role in maintaining and changing the international normative order, although it is only used sparingly under special conditions and in specific situations.

## ACKNOWLEDGMENTS

We thank the reviewers consulted by Oxford University Press, the editors of this volume, and Dr. Alicia Schrikker for their comments on earlier versions of the chapter. The research on which this chapter is based was carried out as part of the Dutch Research Council (NWO) project "Colonial Normativity—Corruption and difference in colonial and postcolonial histories of empire and nations: the Netherlands-Indonesian relationship (1870s–2010s)".

## References

Arndt, H. W. (1967). Economic disorder and the task ahead. In T. K. Tan (Ed.), *Sukarno's guided Indonesia* (pp. 129–142). Jacaranda Press.

Baehr, P. R. (1997). Problems of aid conditionality: The Netherlands and Indonesia. *Third World Quarterly, 18*(2), 363–376.

Ballard, C. (2017). Swift injustice: The expedition of imperial punishment. *Journal of Colonialism and Colonial History, 18*(1).

Ballard, C., & Douglas, B. (2017). "Rough justice": Punitive expeditions in Oceania. *Journal of Colonialism and Colonial History, 18*(1).

Brocades Zaalberg, T., & Luttikhuis, B. (2020). Extreem Geweld Tijdens Dekolonisatieoorlogen in Vergelijkend Perspectief, 1945–1962. *BMGN: Low Countries Historical Review, 135*(2), 34–51.

Chouwdure, A., & Sugema, I. (2005). How significant and effective has foreign aid to Indonesia been? *ASEAN Economic Bulletin, 22*(1), 186–216.

Chudori, L. S., Djalil, L., Krisna, A. N., & Harymurti, B. (1992, April 4). Jakarta bersorak, Den Haag dingin. In: IGGI, Lembaga Bantuan Asing yang Merenggang Hubungan dengan Belanda. Jilid III (pp. 57–62). Tempo Publishing.

Cooper, F. (2010). Writing the history of development. *Journal of Modern European History, 8*(1), 5–23.

Elson, R. E. (2001). *Suharto: A political biography*. Cambridge University Press.

Emmer, P., & Gommans, J. (2012). *Rijk Aan De Rand Van De Wereld*. Prometheus.

Fakih, F. (2014). The rise of the managerial state of Indonesia: Institutional transition during the early independence period, 1950-1965 [Doctoral dissertation]. Leiden University.

Foucault, M. (2012[1975]). *Discipline and punish: the birth of the prison*. Random House US.

Geltner, G. (2014). *Flogging others: Corporal punishment and cultural identity from antiquity to the present*. Amsterdam University Press.

Giebels, L. (2001). *Soekarno President: Een Biographie, 1950–1970*. Prometheus.

Grotius, H. (1916 [1609]). Freedom of the Seas or the Right Which Belongs to the Dutch to Take Part in the East Indian Trade. Oxford University Press. Consulted via HeinOnline.

Grotius, H. (2012 [1625]). Hugo Grotius. On the law of war and peace. NY Cambridge University Press. Edited and annotated by Stephen C. Neff.

Hadad, T., Djalil, L., Krisna, A. N., & Jufri, F. (1992, April 4). IGGI Bubar, Binnenhofpun terkejut. In IGGI, Lembaga Bantuan Asing yang Merenggang Hubungan dengan Belanda (pp. 39–56). Tempo Publishing.

Hathaway, O. A., & Shapiro, S. J. (2017). *The internationalists: How a radical plan to outlaw war remade the world*. Simon & Schuster.

Hidayat, Y., & Irawanto, D. S. (1992, April 4). Belanda bukan posisi kunci. In IGGI, Lembaga Bantuan Asing yang Merenggang Hubungan dengan Belanda (pp. 63–77). Tempo Publishing.

Inkiriwang, F. W. (2020). The dynamic of the US–Indonesia defence relations: The "IMET ban" period. *Australian Journal of International Affairs, 74*(4), 377–393.

Johnston, M. (2005). *Syndromes of corruption: Wealth, power, and democracy*. Cambridge University Press.

Kroeze, R. (2016). The rediscovery of corruption in Western Democracy. In J. Mendilow & I. Peleg (Eds.), *Corruption and government legitimacy. A twenty-first century perspective* (pp. 22–40). Lexington Books.

Kwik, K. G. (2018). *Menelusuri Zaman: Memoir Dan Catatan* Kritis. Gramedia.

Lindblad, J. T. (2008) *Bridges to New Business: The Economic Decolonization of Indonesia*. Leiden: KITLV Press.

Malcontent, P. A. M. (1999). De Schaduwminister Van Buitenlandse Zaken: Ontwikkelingshulp Als Politiek Instrument. In J. A. Nekkers & P. A. M. Malcontent (Eds.), *De Geschiedenis Van Vijftig Jaar Nederlandse Ontwikkelingssamenwerking, 1949–1999* (pp. 217–237). SDU Uitgevers.

Menger, T. (2022). "Press the thumb onto the eye": Moral effect, extreme violence, and the transimperial notions of British, German, and Dutch colonial warfare, Ca. 1890–1914. *Itinerario, 46*(1), 84–108.

Morris, N., & Rothman, D. J. (1995). *The Oxford history of the prison: The practices of punishment in Western society*. Oxford University Press.

Nasution, A. (1992, April 23–24). Pembubaran IGGI: Janur Kuning Bagi Suharto. Kompas.

Patmono, S. K., Sumarto, S., & Kobong, T. (1998). *Radius Prawiro*: Kiprah, Peran Dan Pemikiran. Pustaka Utama Grafiti.

Pizzo, D. (2012). Punitive expeditions. In G. Martel (Ed.), *The Encyclopedia of War* (Vol. 4, pp. 1780–1784). Malden Mass.

Posthumus, G. A. (1999). Een Ideale Vorm Van Hulp. In J. A. Nekkers & P. A. M. Malcontent (Eds.), *De Geschiedenis Van Vijftig Jaar Nederlandse Ontwikkelingssamenwerking, 1949–1999* (pp. 145–162). SDU Uitgevers.

Prawiro, R., & Parera, F. M. (1998). *Pergulatan Indonesia Membangun Ekonomi: Pragmatisme Dalam Aksi*. Elex Media Komputindo.

Rose, E. A. (2005). From a punitive to a bargaining model of sanctions: Lessons from Iraq. *International Studies Quarterly, 49*(3), 459–479.

Schrikker, A. (2021). *De Vlinders Van Boven-Digoel*. Prometheus.

Seda, F. (1989, June, 19). Simfoni Tanpa Henti. Kompas.

Seda, F. (1990, June 19). Sampai Kapan Iggi Diperlukan. Suara Pembaruan.

Seda, F. (1992, January 27). Tidak Dengan Sendirinya Iggi Harus Dibubarkan. Kompas.

Seda, F., Dhakidae, D., Bertens, K., & Parera, F. M. (1992). *Simfoni Tanpa Henti: Ekonomi Politik Masyarakat Baru Indonesia*. Yayasan Atma Jaya and PT Gramedia Widiasarana.

Simpson, B. R. (2008). *Economists with guns: Authoritarian development and US–Indonesian relations, 1960–1968*. Stanford University Press.

Stowell, E. C. (1921). *Intervention in international law*. Byrne.

Tan, T. K. (1966). Indonesia's guided economy and its implementation, 1959-1965. *Australian Quarterly*, *38*(2), 9-28.

Tiessen, A. (1997). Images and human rights. *Visual Anthropology*, *9*(3-4), 325-328.

Ullman, H. K., Wade, J. P., Edney, L. A., Franks, F. M., Horner, C. A., Howe, J. T., & Brendley, K. (1996). *Shock and awe: Achieving rapid dominance*. National Defense University.

van Baalen, C., & Bos, A. (2022). *Grote idealen, smalle marges: Een parlementaire geschiedenis van de lange jaren zeventig 1971-1982*. Boom.

Van Dam, P., & Van Dis, W. (2014). Beyond the merchant and the clergyman: Assessing moral claims about development cooperation. *Third World Quarterly*, *35*(9), 1636-1655.

Van Damme, L. J., & Smits, M. G. M. (2009). *Voor De Ontwikkeling Van De Derde Wereld: Politici en ambtenaren over de Nederlandse ontwikkelingssamenwerking, 1949-1989*. Boom.

Van den Doel, W. (2011). *Zo ver de wereld strekt: De geschiedenis van Nederland overzee vanaf 1800*. Prometheus.

Van den Ham, A. P. (1993). Development cooperation and human rights: Indonesian-Dutch aid controversy. *Asian Survey*, *33*(5), 531-539.

van Ittersum, M. J. (2010). The long goodbye: Hugo Grotius' justification of Dutch expansion overseas, 1615-1645. *History of European Ideas*, *36*(4), 386-411.

von Clauzewitz, Carl (1950). *On War. Volume 1*. Jazzybee Verlag.

Vickers, A. (2005). *A history of modern Indonesia*. Cambridge University Press.

Wesseling, H. L. (1981). Colonial wars and armed peace, 1870-1914: A reconnaissance. *Itinerario*, *5*(2), 53-73.

Wielenga, F. (2015). *A history of the Netherlands: From the sixteenth century to the present day*. Bloomsbury.

Winarno, B. (2012). Jb Sumarlin: Cabe Yang Lahir Di Sawah. *Kompas*.

# INDEX

*For the benefit of digital users, indexed terms that span two pages (e.g., 52–53) may, on occasion, appear on only one of those pages.*

African Union (AU), 11–14, 134, 174–75, 179
aid, 12, 67–68, 76–78, 82–83, 87–91, 209, 215–31
air strike, 28, 66
arbitration, 12, 47, 55, 59, 69–70
armed force, 4, 48, 52, 54–55, 62–66, 101–2
arms embargo, 63–64
Articles on State Responsibility, 61, 68
Asia Development Bank, 230–31
atrocity crimes, 11–15, 141–60
authorization, 38, 70–71, 99–101, 175–76

citizen support, 99, 100–1
civil war, 63, 66, 220–21
coercive power, 99–100, 108–10
Cold War, 4–14, 128–29, 141–42, 178–79, 188–89, 217, 222–24, 231
collective security, 9–10, 59–61, 62–64
colonial violence, 212, 214–15
colonialism, 12, 192–93, 195, 196, 198–200, 204, 210–12, 214–15, 219–20
communism, 212, 216–17, 218, 231
compensation
　compensation (general) 45–46, 47, 51, 52, 53, 55, 56, 66–67, 68–70, 71
　financial compensation, 33
　UN Compensation Commissions, 69n.16
　*See also* reparations

compliance, 67, 110, 131–32, 171
conservative, 52, 106–7, 222–23
contestation, 120, 132–34, 178, 181
corruption, 50, 216–17, 218, 220–21, 227–28, 231, 236–37
cosmopolitan penalty, 11, 89, 141–42
countermeasures, 39, 66–69, 173
crimes against humanity (CAH), 4n.1, 75–76, 85n.34, 142–43, 189
criminology, 11, 73–74, 75, 77, 93–94, 125
culture of honour, 29–31, 37

damages
　money damages, 59
　punitive damages, 69–71
democratization, 80–81, 91–92
development cooperation, 219–30
Dili massacre, 209, 223–24, 231–32, 233–34, 235–36
diplomacy, 174–75, 210–11, 213–14
domestic politics, 94–95, 130–31, 233–34

enforcement action, 57, 62
entitativity, 22–23, 34–35, 112
equality
　sovereign equality, 2–3, 130–31, 175–76
European Court of Human Rights, 70
European Union (EU), 76–77, 118–19, 172

fairness, 3, 31–32, 102–12, 133
foreign fighters, 10, 75, 78–88, 85n.34, 90–91, 93–94

genocide, 4n.1, 47, 75–76, 85n.34, 142–43, 204
gender-based violence, 81, 85–86
Global North, 9–15, 141–44, 149–50, 152–53, 156, 159–60, 194–95, 198, 200, 206
Global South, 12, 13–14, 159–60, 187–88, 189–99, 200, 206
governance
 global governance, 189, 198
 good governance, 196, 235–36
 penal governance, 76–77, 88–89
grievances, 87–88, 203
guarantee provision, 60
guilt, 4–6, 46, 48, 49, 58, 61–62, 126, 142–43

human rights
 human rights abuses, 218, 231
 human rights violations, 7, 12, 61–62, 90–91, 210
humanitarian intervention, 3, 6, 9–10, 61–62, 65–66, 129

immigration. *See* migration
imperialism, 47–54, 188, 189, 210–11, 213–15, 233, 235–36
impunity, 79–88, 142–43, 154–56
incapacitation, 24, 125–26
independence, 211, 215–16, 219–29, 233, 234–35
in-group, 11–12, 26, 29, 34, 168, 173–74, 182
Inter-American Court of Human Rights, 70
Inter-Governmental Group on Indonesia (IGGI), 209–37
international community, 4–6, 44–45, 89, 99, 101–2, 126–27, 158–59, 172–75, 237
international courts, 13–15, 47, 102–7, 111–12, 151
international crimes, 4n.1, 5n.6, 75–76, 83–84, 85n.34, 88–95, 99–100, 142–43, 144–52. *See also* crimes against humanity; genocide; war crimes
International Criminal Court (ICC), 4n.1, 75–77, 78–82, 84–88, 86n.37, 89, 104–5, 145–46, 156–58, 159–60
International Criminal Tribunal for the former Yugoslavia (ICTY), 4–6, 5n.3
international institutions, 104–5, 111, 118, 158–59, 200–1
International Law Commission, 61, 156–57
international order, 7, 9–10, 14–15, 80–81, 83–84, 92–95, 119–20, 177, 210, 215–16, 218
international peace, 4–6, 62, 80–81
international prosecution, 142–43, 154–55, 158–59
international sanctioning, 134, 181
International, Impartial and Independent Mechanism, 86–87
Iranian Revolutionary Corps Guards, 131
Iraq, 6, 8–9, 22–23, 27–28, 36, 62–63, 64, 82, 87–88, 100, 109, 115, 170–71, 210–11

Japan, 5n.2, 100–1, 215–18, 222–23, 230–31, 233–34
judicial action, 59
jurisdiction, 4–6, 47, 50, 59, 65–66, 84–88, 86n.36, 99–100, 142–43, 151
just war, 9–10, 47–49, 51–52, 53, 55
justice
 global justice, 76–77, 89, 194–99, 202
 reparative justice, 86
 restorative justice, 1–2, 9, 11–12, 13–14, 17–19, 36–37, 134, 180
 social justice, 203–4, 210
 transitional justice, 33, 37, 198–99

lawbreaking, 49, 54, 60–61
League of Nations, 57, 59–60, 62
legal entitlement, 48, 52
legal wrongdoing, 54, 62–63, 71
legitimacy, 11–12, 33, 77–78, 99–100, 101–2, 103, 112, 133, 159–60, 168, 173–74, 198–99
liberalization, 213–14, 231, 236–37

## INDEX

Libya, 63, 64–65, 174–75

mandate, 62–63, 84–85, 100–2, 107, 154–55, 174, 177, 179–80, 200–1
media, 111–12, 149–50, 155–56, 224
migration, 90–91, 153–54, 198
military action, 8, 101–2, 214–15
morality, 19, 58, 94–95, 201
moral authority, 10, 92, 93–94
moral condemnation, 24–27, 32
moral outrage, 21, 24, 27–28

neocolonialism, 104–5, 211. *See also* colonialism; post-colonialism
non-governmental organization (NGO), 7–8, 76–77, 89, 90–91, 142–58
non-state actors, 2, 7–8, 64, 82, 90, 214–15
norms
 international norms, 2, 4, 8, 9–14, 109–10, 112, 132–34, 167–68, 171–72, 173, 215
 normative authority, 126–27, 167–68, 172–73, 179, 180, 182
Nuremberg trials, 5n.2, 33

Organization of African Unity (OAU), 174–75
out-group, 22, 26, 29, 33–37, 168, 173–74, 180, 182

peace operations
 peace-building, 80–81, 91–92
 peacekeeping, 62–63
penal humanitarianism, 10, 90–92, 93–94
penality
 cosmopolitan penality, 11, 89, 141–42
 transnational penalty (*see* transnational penal power)
Permanent Court of International Justice, 57
policy
 feminist foreign policy, 85–86
 foreign policy, 74–93, 101–2, 132, 177, 180
postcolonialism, 12, 210, 211, 235–36

power relations, 7–8, 12, 145–46, 210–11, 215, 235–36
procedural justice, 3, 37, 103, 109–10
proportionality, 24, 53–54, 65–66, 67, 68
public support, 18–19, 22–23, 33, 104–5, 112
punishment
 capital punishment, 18–19, 189
 corporal punishment, 189, 212
 global punishment, 143–45
 individualization of punishment, 11, 12, 14–15, 129, 130–31
 internationalized punishment, 141–42, 144–45, 156
 interpersonal punishment, 18–19, 20, 35, 36–37, 101–2, 103, 105–6
 intragroup punishment, 18–19
punitive expeditions, 212–15, 235–37

remedy, 9–10, 50, 122
reparations, 12, 13, 14, 33, 80–81, 142–43, 146–47, 189–90, 196, 198–99, 202–6
resolution, 85–86, 100–1, 115, 177–78, 182
restitution, 31–32, 59, 80–81
retaliation, 18, 19–20, 23, 29, 49, 103, 226–27
revenge, 6, 9, 18, 19–20, 22–23, 26–27, 31, 100, 103, 104, 111, 179–80, 213
rules-based order, 84–85, 88
Russia, 2, 8, 70, 71, 92, 121, 123–24, 126, 132, 170–71, 176–77, 205

sanctions
 autonomous sanctions, 174, 178
 coercive sanctions, 125 (*see also* coercive power)
 economic sanctions, 3–4, 11, 60, 62, 103, 118–19, 178
 multilateral sanctions, 167
 regional sanctions, 11–12, 127–28, 167, 174–75, 178–81, 180
 unilateral sanctions, 167
scapegoating, 22–23, 34
securitization, 74–75, 88, 90–91
self-help, 3, 13–14, 15, 49–50, 52, 59, 60–61, 64–66, 104, 108–9, 173

sexual violence, 81, 85–86. *See also* gender-based violence
sociology, 10, 11, 73–74, 75–79, 88–89, 90–91, 93–95, 128, 144–45, 148–49
South African Truth and Reconciliation Commission, 33
sovereignty, 130–31, 175–76, 177–78, 180, 181, 211, 214–15, 218, 229, 232

terrorism, 47, 82–83, 152–53, 214–15
the war on terror, 18–19, 34–35
Third World Approaches in International Law (TWAIL), 189, 194–95, 196
transnational penal power, 10, 76–77, 88–89
Treaty of Versailles, 57–58, 63n.10
Trust Fund for Victims, 80–81, 86
truth commissions, 33, 37

United Nations Charter, 61–62, 66–67, 67n.14, 70n.21, 80, 173
United Nations General Assembly (UNGA), 51, 61, 80–81, 173, 174, 177–78

United Nations Security Council (UNSC), 10–12, 13–14, 60–61, 62–64, 65, 66, 82–83, 84–85, 99–112, 114–15, 168, 172–75
United Nations (UN), 4, 11–12, 14, 30–31, 86n.36, 118, 128–29, 167, 215–16
United States, 1–2, 8–9, 17–18, 22–23, 26–29, 30, 35, 64–66, 70–71, 92, 105–6, 120–28, 134, 172, 177, 180, 196, 198–99, 202–6, 215–18, 222–23, 233–34
utilitarianism, 24, 27–28, 45–46, 47, 52, 53, 56, 63–64, 65–69, 71

Vereenigde Oostindische Compagnie (VOC), 213
vicarious retribution, 21, 27–29, 36

war crimes, 4n.1, 8, 75–76, 83n.24, 86–87, 142–43, 189
weapons of mass destruction (WMD), 121, 126, 170–71
World Bank, 217, 230–31, 232–34, 236